Re-Imagining the Museum

Beyond the Mausoleum

Andrea Witcomb

Routledge
Taylor & Francis Group

LONDON AND NEW YORK

First published 2003
by Routledge
11 New Fetter Lane, London EC4P 4EE

Simultaneously published in the US and Canada
by Routledge
29 West 35th Street, New York, NY 10001

Routledge is an imprint of the Taylor & Francis Group

Typeset in Sabon by
Florence Production Ltd, Stoodleigh, Devon
Printed and bound in Great Britain by
TJ International Ltd, Padstow, Cornwall

British Library Cataloguing in Publication Data
A catalogue record for this book is available from the British Library

Library of Congress Cataloging in Publication Data
Witcomb, Andrea, 1965–
Re-imagining the museum : beyond the mausoleum / Andrea Witcomb.
p. cm. – (Museum meanings)
Includes bibliographical references (p.) and index.
1. Museums – Philosophy. 2. Museums – United States – History. 3. Museums –
Great Britain – History. 4. Museums – Australia – History. 5. Museum exhibits –
Historiography. 6. Museum techniques – Historiography. 7. Cultural policy –
History. 8. Mass media and culture – History. 9. Popular culture – History.
I. Title. II. Series.
AM7 .W585 2003
069–dc21   2002026933

ISBN 0–415–22098–X (hbk)
ISBN 0–415–22099–8 (pbk)

R_e I_ma_gi_ni_g the M_us_eu_m

Re-Imagi... ...reta-
tions of r... ...ange
of case st... ...es to
thinking

In recent ...de of
address. ...nds,
represent ...ptive
to the int... ...oken
with the ...jects
both pos... ...with
popular ...ging
clearly to ...and
popular ...omb
traces thi ...veen
museums ...ook
analyses ...ums
in moder ...s of
contempo

Interdisci... ...rary
commenta... ...The
case studi ...am-
ples in pa ...rac-
tices, pres ...p.

Andrea W...comb was a curator at the Australian National Maritime Museum
and at the National Museum of Australia. She is currently a senior lecturer at
the Research Institute for Cultural Heritage at Curtin University of Technology
in Perth.

Museum Meanings

Series editors
Eilean Hooper-Greenhill
Flora Kaplan

The museum has been constructed as a symbol in Western society since the Renaissance. This symbol is both complex and multi-layered, acting as a sign for domination and liberation, learning and leisure. As sites for exposition, through their collections, displays and buildings, museums mediate many of society's basic values. But these mediations are subject to contestation, and the museum can also be seen as a site for cultural politics. In post-colonial societies, museums have changed radically, reinventing themselves under pressure from many forces, which include new roles and functions for museums, economic rationalism and moves towards greater democratic access.

Museum Meanings analyses and explores the relationships between museums and their publics. 'Museums' are understood very broadly, to include art galleries, historic sites and historic houses. 'Relationships with publics' is also understood very broadly, including interactions with artefacts, exhibitions and architecture, which may be analysed from a range of theoretical perspectives. These include material culture studies, mass communication and media studies, learning theories and cultural studies. The analysis of the relationship of the museum to its publics shifts the emphasis from the museum as text, to studies grounded in the relationships of bodies and sites, identities and communities.

Also in this series:

Colonialism and the Object
Empire, Material Culture and the Museum
Edited by Tim Barringer and Tom Flynn

Learning in the Museum
George E. Hein

Museum, Media, Message
Edited by Eilean Hooper-Greenhill

Museums and the Interpretation of Visual Culture
Eilean Hooper-Greenhill

Museums, Society, Inequality
Edited by Richard Sandell

Contents

Figures

Acknowledgements

When written over a series of years, whenever there is space between teaching, administrative and family responsibilities, books tend to be indebted to a number of people and institutions. This book began its life as a doctoral dissertation and so my first thanks must go to the Australian National Maritime Museum who gave me my first job as a museum curator and the inspiration to write about museums. A number of people in that institution made it possible for me to research the archives of the Museum – Frances Prentice, Jeffrey Mellefont, Mary-Louise Williams and Merv Ryan. I thank you all.

More recently, Curtin University of Technology has provided me with both an intellectual home in the form of the Research Institute for Cultural Heritage and material support through various research grants and some teaching relief. An Early Career Curtin University Research grant enabled me to extend my doctoral work through a study of the Western Australian Maritime Museum. The results of that project can be found in Chapters 2 and 3 of this book. The project itself could not have come off without the full support of the Museum. Andrew Reeves and Graeme Henderson made it possible in their role as directors for the project to go ahead. While all the staff were supportive I would like to give particular thanks to Jeremy Green who graciously allowed me to attend the staff meetings of the Maritime Archaeology Department for an entire year during some of the most difficult moments of that Department's history. I would also like to thank Mike McCarthy, Sally May and Myra Stanbury for their interest in the project and their willingness to share their discussion papers with me. My many conversations with Mike McCarthy were particularly stimulating. I also wish to thank all the staff who gave their time to attend a focus group discussion. While many of you may not agree with my interpretation of a difficult period in the museum's history, I do sincerely thank you for allowing me into your lives during this time. I also want to thank Jacqui Sherriff who was my research assistant for this project.

My Head of School, Professor David Dolan, assisted me by providing some teaching relief in the second half of 2000. Professor Tom Stannage, the Dean of Humanities, who shares my enthusiasm for museums, took the time to make valuable comments on Chapter 3. The Office of the Division of Humanities has also provided very valuable support by granting me a small seeding grant.

I used this to enlist the help of Jan Kelly in transforming my manuscript into the required Routledge format. Her help in this area was invaluable as it gave me what little time I had to concentrate on the actual content of the book. Thank you Jan.

I would also like to say thank you to a number of people who have encouraged me to continue to think and write about museums over the years – Tony Bennett, Jennifer Craik, Gay Hawkins, Barbara Kirschenblatt-Gimblett and Howard McNaughton from within the academy, Ian McShane, Verena Mauldon, Mat Trinca and Ann Brake from the museum world. Special thanks must go to Eilean Hooper-Greenhill who provided me with the opportunity to turn the PhD into a book and has always provided excellent editorial advice along the way. Thank you for your constant support and intellectual stimulation as well as for the opportunity to present Chapter 4 as a seminar to staff and postgraduate students in the Museum Studies programme at Leicester University. The stimulation I received there was of immense help. I would also like to thank the blind reviewers of my book proposal for their very helpful comments and the editors at Routledge – Vicky Peters, Julene Barnes, Polly Osborn and lastly Catherine Bousfield. Both Julene and Polly have been particularly patient in waiting for this book.

Some of the case studies presented here have been published in other contexts and appear here substantially modified. I would, however, like to acknowledge their earlier incarnation. Parts of Chapter 2 have appeared in the *Proceedings of the Museums Australia 1995 National Conference: Communicating Cultures*, Libby Quinn and Lynn Seear (eds), Museums Australia, Brisbane: 124–128 (Witcomb 1997b), and in the *Indian Ocean Week 1997 Proceedings*, edited by Graeme Henderson, Western Australian Maritime Museum, Fremantle (Witcomb 1998b). The discussion of my experiences while a museum consultant in Queensland, in Chapter 4, appeared in an earlier version as part of an article written with Verena Mauldon for *Culture and Policy*, vol. 7(1): 75–84, 1996 (Witcomb and Verena 1996); Chapter 5 has appeared in a number of earlier versions in *Public History Review*, 1993, vol. 2: 135–143 (Witcomb 1993), *Information Flows*, *CQU Working Papers in Cultural Studies*, 1995, Central Queensland University: 35–44 (Witcomb 1995), as part of the Conference Proceedings for *Museums and the Web 97: Selected Papers*, David Bearman and Jennifer Trant (eds), Archives & Museum Informatics, Pittsburgh: 143–150 (Witcomb 1997c) and in *Media Information Australia* incorporating *Culture and Policy*, No. 89, November 1998: 21–33 (Witcomb 1998a); the case study on the Australian National Maritime Museum in Chapter 6 appeared in *Social Semiotics*, 1994, vol. 4/1–2: 239–262 (Witcomb 1994).

And finally I wish to thank my best friend and partner Mark Gibson. Thanks Mark for all those discussions, suggestions for readings, your photographic skills, your careful and patient editing and above all for your faith in me. This book is dedicated to you and our children – Robin and Hannah.

Introduction

The last ten years or so have seen a heated debate between those who argue that museums need to change and those who defend its traditional practices. Often, this debate has been sparked by the development of a number of new and refurbished museums around the Western world. In Australia, where I wrote this book, it has been evident over the opening of the refurbished Museum of Victoria in Melbourne in late 2000 and the opening of the new National Museum of Australia in Canberra in March 2001. Often aggressive in tone, the debate has raised issues on the nature of historical interpretation and questioned the clear orientation of these museums towards market forces, their use of multimedia and attempts to engage with popular culture. Here I want to relate only one such exchange in order to set the scene for this book.

In mid-2001, *The Australian* newspaper staged a public exchange between Dawn Casey and Tim Flannery, directors of the National Museum of Australia and the Museum of South Australia respectively. The debate began with a report quoting Tim Flannery (in DiGirolamo 2001) on the emergence of the 'super museum' – marked by the use of multimedia and other populist strategies for attracting new audiences. For Flannery, their emergence threatened the traditional responsibility of museums to undertake serious research on their collections. It also undermined the museums' distinctiveness from other cultural institutions and the entertainment industry: 'Australia has spent $500 million in the past year on state-of-the-art, multimedia museums in Canberra and Melbourne that try to compete with amusement parks at the expense of research and artefacts' (in DiGirolamo 2001). The 'super museum' was clearly, for Flannery, an opposite of the kind of museum he himself directs. The Museum of South Australia holds one of the largest and most comprehensive collections of indigenous Australian material culture and bases its identity on scholarly research and traditional exhibitions.

Dawn Casey wrote a stinging reply in which she suggested that Flannery's view was the sort of view that held museums back:

> Flannery seems to prefer the old-style museum which invites people to admire serried ranks of boomerangs, rocks or stuffed birds. That's fine; there is plenty of room for diversity in museum practice and no single best

way. However, we find contemporary audiences are fairly sophisticated media consumers and less likely to value a museum that clings to a historic role as a repository of curious objects amassed by nineteenth-century specimen collectors.

(Casey 2001: 15)

The implication was that Flannery was a dinosaur, out of touch with contemporary audiences, their needs and their cultural preferences. Casey went on to defend the use of multimedia, claiming that all exhibitions at the National Museum of Australia were based on serious interdisciplinary research and began from the assumption that objects required interpretation in order to be made intelligible to visitors. She finished by suggesting that it was the new social history museums that were relevant to contemporary issues and concerns.

The exchange reflects the general tenor of many contemporary discussions on museums drawing on a familiar series of oppositions between traditionalists and renovators, objects and multimedia, objects and ideas, education and edutainment. Depending on which set of values and practices a museum chooses it is then characterized as either elitist or popular, hierarchical or democratic, old and musty or new and exciting, irrelevant or relevant to contemporary concerns.

My position is this book is at odds with both sides of the debate. I agree with Casey that museums need to work towards increasing the diversity of their audiences and the range of programmes they offer but I also think there is something in the arguments of those who, like Flannery, wish to maintain more traditional perspectives. The characterization of present developments as a welcome break from past practices prevents a more complex understanding of the issues currently faced by museums. A tit for tat exchange cannot do anything other than simplify very complex issues. For me, the exchange between Casey and Flannery would have been more interesting and helpful if it had addressed some of the questions implicitly embedded in Flannery's complaint. Such questions might include: How do changing research practices and expectations affect the role of the curator as an expert? What is the impact of the increasing expectation that curators should be first and foremost good communicators? How is the 'public' nature of museums affected by the new economic contexts within which museums have to operate? Is it true that it is only through the use of multimedia that museums can become interactive and more democratic? Do objects always need to be placed within an abstract narrative for people to relate to them? And do current developments mark as significant a departure from past practices as both their defenders and attackers seem to think?

These then are some of the questions that lie behind this book. But as well as attempting to deal with them, I am also interested in exploring the reasons behind the polarization of current debates. A possible explanation lies in the nature of available critical traditions on museums, which, until very recently, represented museums as bad objects. This perspective is particularly notable in the avant-garde tradition and those schooled in theories of Marxism and ideology critique. In these traditions, the museum is an institution caught in its nineteenth-century origins, unable to escape its conservative political meanings.

The response of museum professionals to these critiques is often affected by a sense of injustice that their efforts to move museum practices towards more dialogic and democratic ways are not more recognized. One strategy in emphasizing that change has occurred, is to describe the current moment as one of momentous change, as a rupture with the past. Not surprisingly, however, those who respect and treasure traditional museum practices respond to this in a defensive manner, feeling themselves embattled not only by critical discourse but by members of their own profession. The possibility that the history of museums, and consequently their meanings, may not be limited to the perspectives offered by these critiques is not envisaged. The result is that change always needs to be interpreted as radical change and therefore as a battle with those who defend traditional values.

This book, then, is an attempt to grapple both with the nature of contemporary debate on museums and to seek possible explanations for it. In the process, it is also an attempt to engage with actual museum practices. My starting point is a recognition that the issues behind all of these debates are far more complex than most discussions have allowed. I therefore wish to complicate our received understandings of the museum, both in professional discussions and in academic critiques of museums and their practices. My strategies for doing this are threefold. The first is to find, where relevant and possible, a prehistory for the concerns currently under discussion. In this I am indebted to the work of others who have gone into the museum archive. Sometimes I share their interpretation of the material they found there, in others I give it a new interpretation. My concern here is not to negate the value of attempts to place museums in the history of empire and the development of capitalism but to point to the existence of a parallel but contradictory set of meanings.

My second strategy is to ground my discussion of contemporary issues through specific examples wherever possible. I have used my own curatorial experiences as well as analysing the practice of others. A third distinctive strategy is to use these discussions to speak back to the critical literature on museums. Rather than applying one theoretical approach throughout the book, I engage with a limited but important number of commentators in an effort to get at the complexity of the issues and the arguments. This means that while I use contemporary theoretical perspectives, I am concerned to use my case studies to speak back to the more theoretical debates around museums and their practices rather than using theory in a more top down approach privileging theory over practice.

A principal theme throughout is the relationship between museums and their audiences. As a number of key museum commentators have said, this is one of the most pressing issues facing museums today (Bennett 1998a, Clifford 1997, GLLAM 2000, Hooper-Greenhill 1997, 2000, Karp *et al.* 1992). Central to any understanding of how museums forge external relations are two questions: how are meanings made and what do we understand by the concept of 'community'?

3

I explore these two questions by tracing their discursive and practical effect through a number of case studies. These range from established debates around actual attempts to make space for different communities within museums to a range of other discussion sites in which the same issues manifest themselves. These include: museum policy discourses; discussions surrounding the introduction of multimedia into the museum space, especially the notion of 'interactivity'; arguments about the need for curators to become 'facilitators' rather than 'experts'; and the location of museums within leisure and tourist spaces. Where possible, I have sought to establish what might be called a historical lineage for all of these discussions.

A second major theme is the fraught terrain of the commercialization of museums and its impact on their public role. Under this single issue, I engage with the emergence of a discourse in which tourism is seen as a central rationale for the existence of museums, debates around what are often perceived as opposing forces between education and entertainment and the role of museums in urban redevelopments. I argue that all of these discussions are forcing a questioning of two traditional beliefs. The first is that the contemporary public museum may no longer always conceive of their audience as a citizenry and therefore understand their role as primarily one of education. The second is that the contemporary museum is finding it increasingly difficult to define itself in terms of more traditional understandings of research.

A related but distinct set of questions revolves around the introduction of interactive multimedia as a means to make the museum less elitist and more democratic. I am interested in analysing discussions around the increasing 'mediatization' of the museum, arguing that we need a more complex understanding of the ways in which a dialogic relationship between museums and their audiences can be achieved. At the same time, however, I am also concerned to analyse the effects of the discourse around technology as I believe that language is one of the means to effect change in the cultural orientation of institutions.

The structure of the book

The book itself is organized into six chapters. Chapter 1 sets the development of contemporary museums within urban renewal programmes within a longer history of relationships between leisure, tourism, urbanity and museums. I use this history to develop an argument about the need to reassess the dominant understanding of museums as institutions that always reinforce existing power relations. Chapter 2 extends this argument into the present through an analysis of two recent Australian examples – the Australian National Maritime Museum in Darling Harbour, Sydney, and the new Western Australian Maritime Museum in Fremantle's Victoria Quay. Both of these museums have been focal points in the conversion of industrial spaces into tourism and leisure precincts. I am interested here in the discursive and practical effects of treating museums as cornerstones of economic development, in the association between a tourist orientation and openness to popular culture and in the integration of museums into leisure spaces. I argue that one of the most important effects of these developments is a questioning of our received understanding of the museum as, above all, an institution with a mission to educate or reform society.

Taken together, these two chapters suggest the need to recognize important parallels between contemporary and nineteenth-century exhibitionary culture around the function of popular culture. The argument is conducted at a theoretical level through an engagement with the work of Tony Bennett (1988c, 1990, 1995, 1998a) who has consistently argued that museums need to be understood as institutions whose principal educational role is one of civic reform. In developing his arguments, Bennett appeals to the work of Michel Foucault, blending his interest in forms of institutional discipline with his later writings on governmentality. Contrary to Bennett, I argue that the museum has not always been associated with forms of rationality or the exercise of power. The aim is not to argue that such associations are misplaced but to suggest that they need to be understood alongside contradictory forces such as those of popular culture. An openness to the ways in which museums have also had to respond to forces outside of their control calls for an understanding of how museums have always had to engage in dialogue with their audiences.

In conducting the argument through a dialogue between past and present, I hope to avoid an interpretation of the current moment as a radical break from the past. Thus, while I recognize differences, I am also concerned to establish continuities. For example, while I recognize that nineteenth-century museums did articulate their role as one of civic reform, I argue that contemporary museums find it increasingly difficult to do so, despite their continued faith in such a mission. At the same time, I am concerned to demonstrate the links between present day developments and earlier exhibitionary sites such as international fairs and department stores. Such sites, I argue, were highly influential on the way nineteenth-century museums developed and offer another means to question Bennett's rather totalizing claim that public museums represent the eventual governmentalization of all aspects of culture.

In Chapter 3 I extend the discussion by questioning the assuredness with which we tend to equate these developments with the parallel loss of a research culture within museums. While agreeing that something is indeed happening to a tradition of scholarly research within museums, I attribute these changes to a far more complex set of circumstances than simply the commercial pressure of a new tourist economy. My position here is different from those involved in the Heritage debate of the 1980s and early 1990s. In this debate, changes to the heritage industry – which includes museums – are the result of commercial pressures. The debate is between those who interpret these pressures as having a negative affect on professional values and traditions and those who welcome them as a means of rethinking the relationship to audiences. Having established in the first chapter that the nineteenth-century museum was a site in which rationalizing processes coexisted with more 'irrational' tendencies in popular culture, I suggest that we are now returning to that central tension. Only this time, it is the populist side which is predominant, forcing museums to communicate their work to as wide an audience as possible, using a variety of strategies that are not part of the traditional research tool kit. In developing this argument I make use of John Hartley's (1992) argument that the process of modernity has in large part been about the rise of the 'smiling professions' – those professions that both represent and construct the public using populist strategies. I use his arguments to help explain a process of intense change in the curatorial culture of the Western Australian Maritime Museum posed by the development of a new branch in a different location and with a completely different focus. My analysis is conducted through the use of archival material as well as through a focus group discussion conducted with the staff of the Museum.

Chapter 4 focuses in on the relationship between museums and communities through two case studies. The first analyses an exhibition I curated in the community access gallery of the Fremantle History Museum (a branch of the Western Australian Museum). The second looks at the practical effects of a museum policy from a State Ministry with the aim of professionalizing community museums in order to achieve the wider objective of cultural representation. I use these case studies both to support and critique Tony Bennett's (1995, 1998a) argument that museums are not involved in the business of representing communities but of actually constructing them. I do so through a critique of his engagement with James Clifford's (1997) work on museums, especially his interest in fostering the museum as a 'contact zone' between communities. The chapter offers another way of engaging with Bennett's Foucaldian interpretation of museums and extends the critique developed in Chapter 1.

In Chapter 5 I turn my attention to the way in which a focus on relations between museums and their audiences has affected discourses around electronic technologies. Here I argue that these technologies have been framed by a rhetoric of democratization made possible by the challenge to a positivist epistemology offered by the virtual characteristics of the electronic medium. The argument is an extension of the view that the introduction of electronic media technologies displaces the museum as a 'treasure house' as the institution becomes more concerned with information. From the point of view of information, so this argument goes, objects are important not because of their materiality but because they are an archive of information which can then be stored, reproduced and made available for a variety of purposes. This focus on information means that objects are now frequently placed alongside other sources of information such as photographs, film and oral testimony. The effect is a more open, polysemic exhibition practice – a practice that challenges the traditional curatorial authority to offer an exclusive interpretation of the significance of objects based on an intensive study of their material characteristics.

While the view that museums are information centres clearly has its basis in the emergence of debates around the notion of the 'information society' (Castells 1989, 1996, McLuhan 1967, Poster 1990), I will be following the discussion mainly through the work of George MacDonald who, in his capacity as the former Director of the Canadian Museum of Civilization and more recently of the Victorian Museum in Australia, represents one of the most articulate museum spokespersons for these views. I will also draw on examples from the Australian National Maritime Museum and the World Wide Web. I agree with MacDonald in seeing a democratic potential in the use of new technologies. I differ, however, in arguing that this potential has precursors in nineteenth-century relations between museums and the media industry and is not as radical as it is often made out to be.

Finally, in Chapter 6 I turn my attention to the much-discussed issue of inter-activity in the museum. Here I suggest continuities between the introduction of multimedia into museums and an older discussion around interactives. I also attempt to shift the focus from interactives as material things to *interactivity* as a desired mode of display. As well as providing an overview of the history of the term 'interactivity' in relation to museums, this chapter will analyse three different museums as examples of different approaches to interactivity. I develop my own classification for these different approaches, calling them 'technological' interactivity, 'spatial' interactivity and 'dialogic' interactivity. The overall argument is that museums need to move beyond an identification of interactivity with contemporary media and a stereotype of older museums as static and unexciting. In the process, I also develop a corrective to the more positive interpretation provided in Chapter 4 around the introduction of multi-media into the space of the museum. I argue that such introductions do not necessarily effect a more democratic, open relationship between the museum and its audiences; in some cases, the effect is quite the opposite.

The first case study explores the use of interactive technologies at the Museum of Tolerance in Los Angeles, arguing that a 'technological' approach to inter-activity limits the museum's ability to move away from the traditional, author-itative museum narrative. I argue that interactives at this museum are used within a didactic model of communication, limiting visitor opportunities to engage with the theme of intolerance and prejudice at a social level. The draw-back of this approach to interactivity is a lack of historical understanding.

The second case study uses Eric Michaels' (1987) notion of 'self-inscription' as a resource to explore a 'spatial' approach to interactivity. I use 'self-inscription' to explore the breakdown of authoritative linear display designs and the emer-gence of narrative structures which have more in common with television serials in their thematic approach to story telling. This discussion will be illustrated through a critique of a visitor study report done at the Australian National Maritime Museum and will refer to various displays at this museum.

In the final case study, I look at the Museum of Sydney to explore a third approach to interactivity in museums. I have called this approach dialogic inter-activity, in recognition of the efforts of this Museum's first director – Peter Emmett – to work with a notion of museums as a space for dialogue. While the attempt is not entirely successful, I will argue that a dialogic approach to inter-activity holds the most promise for understanding interactivity in a museum context and the uses to which it might be put.

Contributions to the literature on museums

In using a case study approach to develop my arguments, I am concerned to add to the growing number of accounts of contemporary museum practices. When I began the book as a dissertation in the early 1990s such accounts were few and far between. In retrospect, the 'new museology' (Vergo 1989) had hardly begun. There was no tradition that encouraged curators and other museum staff to critically analyse their practice and communicate such analysis in the wider public sphere. Nor was there a long tradition of inviting academics into the museum to curate exhibitions. When scholars began to comment on museums, the reaction from the profession was at first one of mistrust. Now, however, there are a growing number of commentators on museums who write from well theorized positions but also from practical experience. Many of these can be found in edited collections (Barringer and Flynn 1998, Hooper-Greenhill 1997, Karp and Lavine 1991, Karp *et al.* 1992, Pointon 1994, Sherman and Rogoff 1994). I hope this book can add to that literature and most particularly to the attempts to document contemporary practices and develop a more complex sense of the history of museums.

Such an enterprise should be welcomed rather than feared by museum professionals. While still critical, it offers an opportunity to re-imagine the museum's past as well as its future from a more sympathetic perspective. This might be seen as a corrective to the dominant tendency in academic writing on museums. This tendency was set in the eighteenth century by figures such as Quatremere de Quincy. According to Daniel Sherman (1994) de Quincy was the first to articulate the idea that the museum was a mausoleum in its effect on the meaning of objects. Writing at the time of the Napoleonic conquest of Europe, de Quincy witnessed the arrival in Paris of countless artworks from all over Europe as war loot.[1] Most were placed in the Louvre. In distress at this practice, de Quincy argued that objects only have meaning when they remain *in situ*. The only good museum was an open air one where things remained in their place as in Rome. The hoarding of treasures in the Louvre was, by contrast, almost an act of cultural vandalism.

The idea that museums kill objects continued to receive critical attention and is arguably still current today, especially amongst the avant-garde. In a tradition which encompasses nineteenth-century critics such as Friedrich Nietzsche and Paul Valéry, Futurists such as Antonio Marinetti, artists in the Dada and Surrealist movements and Marxists like Theodor Adorno, it continues today in the critiques of figures like Jean Baudrillard (1983), Donald Crimp (1995), Eugene Donato (1979), Rosalind Krauss (1990) and Llellyn Negrin (1993). This tradition is marked by a tendency to take the art museum as emblematic of all museums, defining it as antithetical to the principles of modernity. For those in the avant-garde, the museum is backward looking, essentially a static institution. Bound by tradition and inherently conservative, the museum cannot help but represent the values and interests of the dominant elite. In the view of the avant-garde, the museum could never be a site for representing or participating in change. In describing the museum as a mausoleum, this intellectual tradition places museums outside of wider social, cultural and economic contexts. In its most radical form, some of its proponents even call for its destruction.

The argument became especially prominent in the period after World War One in the aftermath of the Russian Revolution. As Andreas Huyssen (1995) reminds us, the avant-garde called in this period 'for the elimination of the past, by practicing the semiological destruction of all traditional forms of represen-tation, and by advocating a dictatorship of the future . . .' (Huyssen 1995: 18). What is more surprising perhaps is that these ideas continued to receive the support of intellectuals until very recently. As Huyssen points out, amongst those who wrote about museums in the 1980s, few have 'argued that we need to rethink (and not just out of a desire to deconstruct) the museum beyond the binary parameters of avant-garde versus tradition, museum versus modernity (or postmodernity), transgression versus co-option, left cultural politics versus neoconservatism' (Huyssen 1995: 18). Critics of museums have been

> surprisingly homogeneous in their attack on ossification, reification and cultural hegemony even if the focus of the attack may be quite different now from what it once was: then the museum as bastion of high culture, now, very differently, as the new kingpin of the culture industry.
>
> (Huyssen 1995: 18)

Little relief can be found in the major alternative line of writing on museums. Informed by theoretical developments since the 1960s, this tradition argues, in contrast to avant-garde, that museums are *emblematic* of modernity. In this case, however, modernity itself is judged in negative terms. It is associated with capitalism or class interests (Bennett 1988a, Bourdieu and Darbel 1991, Horne 1984, West 1988), with imperialism and colonialism (Ames 1992, Bal 1992, Haraway 1985) and the harmful representation of women (Duncan 1995, Glazer and Zenetou 1994, Porter 1988).

It has become common to counter this sociological critique by pointing to the ways in which museums have changed. For Andreas Huyssen, for example, this critique 'does not seem to be quite pertinent any longer for the current museum scene which has buried the museum as temple for the muses in order to resurrect it as a hybrid space somewhere between public fair and department store' (Huyssen 1995: 15). I would go further, however, and argue that such a view was never quite right. There was never a moment when the museum conformed entirely to the critique. This much is evident in more recent work which extends the perspective of ideology critique by being interested in more nuanced accounts of the museum's involvement in the process of modernity (Barringer and Flynn 1998, Clifford 1997, Coombes 1994, MacDonald and Fyfe 1996). My contribution is to offer another way to aid the development of what Hooper-Greenhill (2000) calls the 'post-museum'. This is to argue for the equally important attempt to recover what positive moments there are in museum histories. For there is a sense in which many, though not all, of these analyses tend to shackle the museum to its negative past in ways that make it very difficult to get away either from a deterministic form of argument in which the museum will always stand as a symbol for domination or alternatively, arguments which call for radical change as the only way to escape the encumbrance of the past.

In providing this alternative the book is also an attempt to engage with the way in which 'cultural studies' has theorized the museum. For in the main, a cultural studies' approach to thinking about museums has tended to make it very difficult to use museums as a site from which to theorize change. In viewing the museum as a static institution, caught within nineteenth-century values and disciplinary methodologies, cultural studies has largely been unable to use museums as a resource for the exploration of its own theoretical assumptions and frameworks. Rather than providing a challenge, museums, as currently viewed within cultural studies, only serve to reinforce prejudices.

McKenzie Wark (1992) for example, suggests that museums are a 'residual' cultural institution and are not, therefore, relevant to contemporary concerns. Wark is interested in questions of mediation and argues that it is contemporary, emerging, technologies such as video, multimedia and computer games, which should be receiving our critical attention. But in so doing, he replays the familiar trope of the museum as a mausoleum. While sympathetic to Wark's interest in new media, I wish to argue that a more careful, specific reading of museums allows an interest in emerging cultural forms and questions of mediation to be linked with museums. The articulation of more established, 'residual' cultural institutions such as museums to new electronic technologies, the media, tourism and economic contexts inevitably changes their meanings. Museums are one more site in which questions of mediation can usefully be pursued. My added concern, as already indicated, is also to historicize this mediation, and to avoid an interpretation which sets these developments as a radical break from the past. To this extent, I am also querying Wark's assumption (amongst many other similar commentators) that what we are witnessing around today's media culture represents a totally new development.

Nevertheless, the continuity of the museum with such contexts, particularly the media, means that cultural studies provides an appropriate set of resources to interpret these new developments. Cultural studies' transdisciplinary approach to the study of cultural sites (texts) and practices means that it offers an imaginative approach which dares to cross between a number of seemingly unrelated sites. It is the field which seems to have most to say about the media, tourism, corporate interests and images in relation to society, culture, and the economy. In examining the relationship between media, education and government, a relationship which neatly encapsulates many of the coordinates of the public museum, cultural studies seems to me an ideal base from which to explore both the historical and the contemporary museum. It offers a methodology for studying the museum in ways that link it to the world, rather than separating it from it.

Despite Wark's view of museums, his description of cultural studies' mode of operation is an apt one for the way in which I approach the study of museums. In his description,

> [c]ultural studies started with the event – the event of Thatcherism. It
> worked back through the vectors which form the contours of its powers,
> and very pragmatically picked the eyes out of a whole range of specialized
> knowledges which might help create a practical knowledge organized
> around the horizon of the event.
>
> (Wark 1994: ix)

To follow the line of the vectors is, for Wark, to respect the integrity and speci-
ficity of the media event. My interest is in museums rather than in a media
event, but Wark's principle still holds. My analysis must respect the integrity of
the various case studies I have chosen. In following the vectors of these examples I too make pragmatic choices about theory. Both the theoretical approaches
and the documentary material I use are chosen for their strategic usefulness
in understanding the contemporary museum rather than for their role in
buttressing any one theoretical approach.

In this respect this book is an attempt to move away from two major approaches
to thinking about and analysing museums, one based on semiotic approaches to
'reading' displays and the other on an appropriation of Foucault's work on discourse and governmentality.

Let me turn first to the semiotic approach. As others have commented, in semiotic approaches museums and their displays are treated as a text from which
meanings can simply be read, assumed to be fixed and then criticized. As
Sharon Macdonald points out:

> The model does not allow for the investigation of whether indeed there is
> such a neat fit between production, text and consumption. It supposes
> both too clear-cut a conscious manipulation by those involved in creating
> exhibitions and too passive and unitary a public; and it ignores the often
> competing agendas involved in exhibition-making, the 'messiness' of the
> process itself, and the interpretative agency of visitors.
>
> (Macdonald 1996: 5)

For me, in its worst forms, this approach assumes that there is a single political
valence to museums and that this is uniformly bad. The approach can be encapsulated by two sentences from one of this tradition's most articulate spokespersons when summarizing the effect of the Museum of American Natural
History:

> The American Museum of Natural History is monumental not only in its
> architecture and design but also in its size, scope, and content. This monu-
> mental quality suggests in and of itself the primary meaning of the
> museum inherited from its history: comprehensive collecting as a form of
> domination.
>
> (Bal 1992: 560)

To counteract this type of reading in the book I take into account questions of
institutional process, of political, economic and technological contexts as well
as the impact of a media culture which insists on the polysemy of meaning.

Wherever possible I draw on archival materials and on wider discussions in an effort to develop a more complex analysis which goes beyond the confines of the text itself. My concern is to get away from an interpretation of museums which shackles them to a narrative of original sin in order to emphasize their complexity and even their contradictoriness.

My differences with Foucaldian approaches may be more surprising. As a number of authors has demonstrated (Bennett 1995, 1998a, Hooper-Greenhill 1992, Sherman and Rogoff 1994), they have the potential to open up more complex and institutionally sensitive perspectives. I argue, however, that they are also limited by framing the representational and discursive practices of museums solely within governmental or disciplinary imperatives. These make it very difficult to move away from an understanding of the museum as an author-itarian institution. While not denying these imperatives, I point to examples of museum practices and institutional contexts that either stand outside of them or which force an engagement between governmental and other types of contexts.

The effort here is to support an understanding of museums as 'contact zones' (Clifford 1997) in which dialogue occurs. Such an understanding allows us to see how museums can sometimes work *against* a legacy of imperialism, patri-archal values, assumptions based on high culture and a privileging of institu-tional knowledge. If museums are to have a valuable role in the construction and representation of culture in the future such instances need to be docu-mented, commented upon and encouraged. One of the book's aims is thus to balance the attack on museums and show how cultural theory can also be used to support and encourage emerging museum practices. This is important if fruitful dialogue is to occur between museum professionals and cultural critics.

In establishing lines of continuity between the museum and other spaces – particularly the media, popular culture and tourism – I have also made it possible for museum professionals to establish a wider context for the changes which are currently taking place. This could be used to move away from discourses of paranoia establishing instead parallel experiences with a number of other cultural industries. The transdisciplinary approach offered by cultural studies also establishes professional bridges between museum workers and media workers, policy makers, cultural critics, historians and urban planners. In *Re-Imagining the Museum* I attempt to build bridges and initiate discussions between museum workers and other cultural workers, including cultural critics. This is in order to consider not only new articulations between nationhood and global flows, new relations between the corporate and popular, and new under-standing of commerce and culture but also how these relations may also connect with earlier moments in the history of museums.

1

Unmasking a different museum: museums and cultural criticism

[M]useums are experiencing a crisis of identity as they compete with other attractions within a tourism economy that privileges experience, immediacy, and what the industry calls adventure.

(Kirschenblatt-Gimblett 1998: 7)

Banners and billboards on museum fronts indicate how close the museum has moved to the world of spectacle, of the popular fair and mass entertainment.

(Huyssen 1995: 21)

Recent years have seen a tremendous growth in the number and status of museums around the world. Much discussion of this growth tends to associate it with a departure from the traditional associations of museums. Both critics and supporters of recent changes see a collapse of a distinction between culture and commerce and discern a new role for museums within a post-industrial, postmodern society. Pointing in particular to the relationship between museums and tourism, the media and new social-political contexts, commentators invoke alternatively a sense of crisis or of opportunity around the idea that museums have fundamentally changed.

The range of new museum developments discussed in these commentaries is extremely varied, extending through new art museums such as Bilbao's Guggenheim to new national museums like the National Museum of Australia, the reinvention of old museums through innovative extensions such as the Louvre to the complete refurbishment and provision of new buildings such as the new Getty or New Zealand's Te Papa. The analysis remains similar irrespective of the disciplinary base of the museum. Developments are seen as challenging traditional associations of museums with high culture, governmental programmes, scholarly research, auratic and authoritative displays (for examples of such discussions see Clifford 1997, Coombes 1992, Duclos 1994, Hooper-Greenhill 1994, 1995, Huyssen 1995, Karp *et al.* 1992, Kirschenblatt-Gimblett 1998, Miles and Zavala 1994, Montaner 1995, Newhouse 1998). The effect of the changes is widely seen to break the association of museums with mausoleums, with removal from everyday life. As Andreas Huyssen puts it, 'The museum's role as site of an elitist conservation, a bastion of tradition and high culture gave way to the museum as mass medium, as a site of spectacular mise-en-scène and operatic exuberance' (Huyssen 1995: 14).

The idea of a radical break from past practices as a positive phenomenon can be partly explained as a reaction against a previous, and perhaps still dominant, emphasis in critical writing on museums. Much of this writing has been concerned with the origins of the public museum in the eighteenth and nine-teenth centuries and the way these have shaped its ongoing role. The museum is mostly seen as inculcating bourgeois civic values that served the needs of the emerging nation-state and the dominant interests within it. The focus is almost exclusively on the way in which museums establish and maintain power rela-tions between centres of empire and colonial peripheries (Bal 1992, Dias 1998, Durrans 1988, Riegel 1996, Teslow 1998), between the bourgeoisie and the working class (Bennett 1988a, 1998b, Taylor 1994, West 1988), between men and women (Duncan 1995, Porter 1988, 1990, 1996), and between the public and private spheres (Porter 1988, 1990).

The focus on questions of power is perhaps strongest within 'textualist' read-ings of the museum, particularly those like semiotics which rely on structuralist theories of language. An example is Mieke Bal's article 'Telling, showing, showing off' which is concerned with describing the American Museum of Natural History as an exercise in the deployment of representation as domina-tion. For Bal, displays are 'a sign system working in the realm between the visual and the verbal, and between information and persuasion, as it produces the viewer's knowledge' (Bal 1992: 561). Thus, for Bal, 'the repressed story is the story of the representational practice exercised in this museum, the story of the changing but still vital complicity between domination and knowledge, possession and display, stereotyping and realism, and between exhibition and the repression of history' (Bal 1992: 588). Working with binary oppositions, Bal builds a picture of the Museum of American Natural History in which the power of the curator to control their audiences' reading of an exhibit is never questioned. Meanings are fixed and by extension so are the power relations between the museum and its audiences.

A slightly softer textualist approach is provided by Carol Duncan in her analysis of art museums. She focuses on demonstrating how 'art museums offer up values and beliefs about social, sexual and political identity in the form of vivid and direct experience' (Duncan 1995: 2). For Duncan, these offerings are made through the medium of ideology. This is conveyed through the use of the museum as a ritual space – a use that is as prevalent today as in the nineteenth century. For example, the Louvre Museum in Paris and the National Gallery in London were 'concerned mainly with the transformation of the European princely gallery into the public art museum – a transformation that served the ideological needs of emerging bourgeois nation-states by providing them with a new kind of civic ritual' (2). Contemporary museums of modern art continue to serve an ideological function. In their case, it is the construction of a 'gendered ritual space that ultimately accords with the consumerist culture outside' (2). This ideological function of the museum, Duncan argues, means that museums 'are therefore excellent fields in which to study the intersection of power and the history of cultural forms' (6).

For Duncan, art museums are especially important sites for the study of the operation of power because they base their claims for truth on 'the status of objective knowledge'. Thus, for her,

> to control a museum means precisely to control the representation of a community and its highest values and truths. It is also the power to define the relative standing of individuals within that community. Those who are best prepared to perform its ritual – those who are most able to respond to its various cues – are also those whose identities (social, sexual, racial, etc.) the museum ritual most fully confirms.
>
> (Duncan 1995: 8)

The concern with power is also there with Foucaldian approaches that focus on the museum as a discursive space rather than as a text. While Foucaldian analyses have the benefit of situating museums within institutional and social contexts, their focus on questions of power relations continues to represent museums as stable sites for the operation of dominant interests. For example, in their introduction to *Museum Culture: Histories, Discourses, Spectacles*, Daniel Sherman and Irit Rogoff place their Foucaldian approach to museums within a range of critical analyses whose aim is to 'unmask the structures, rituals, and procedures by which the relations between objects, bodies of know-ledge, and processes of ideological persuasion are enacted' (Sherman and Rogoff 1994: ix–x). The assumption is that the operation of power within the museum space always has negative impacts on society. For Sherman and Rogoff this impact is one which the museum is at pains to hide. For them, the history of the museum as a site for the expression of dominant ideologies is not only shared by all museums. It is a history that museums consciously strive to hide. Hence the project of the book is to 'unmask' these strategies and name them.

A more unusual Foucaldian approach is that of Tony Bennett who provides a partial lead in the direction I wish to follow. While Bennett, like most other critics, is concerned with describing relations of power, he is concerned to develop an understanding of power that does not perceive it as a destructive force. He is thus quite critical of the very traditions Sherman and Rogoff invoke as the basis for their work. These are the same traditions that inform the work of cultural studies. There is, Bennett argues, a need to get away

> from some of the better known clarion-calls of cultural studies; the call to a politics of resistance, for example; the commitment to organising an alliance of popular forces in opposition to the state; or the strategy of forming affective alliances around changing cultural nodal points.
>
> (1998a: 61)

The Foucault that Bennett invokes is a different one from that of Sherman and Rogoff. Rather than focusing on the early Foucault, Bennett appeals to Foucault's later work on governmentality.[1] In a landmark essay 'The political rationality of the museum' (Bennett 1990), Foucaldian themes are brought

15

directly to bear against the simple oppositional politics of many Marxist approaches to museum critique. The difficulty with representing museums as 'instruments of ruling-class hegemony', he argues, is that they tend to characterize museums as 'amenable to a general form of cultural politics – one which, in criticizing those hegemonic ideological articulations governing the thematics of museum displays, seeks to forge new articulations capable of organizing a counter-hegemony'. 'The difficulty with such formulations', he goes on, 'is that they take scant account of the distinctive field of political relations constituted by the museum's specific institutional properties' (Bennett 1995: 91).

Unlike the critics discussed above, Bennett does not position his critique as external and in opposition to the interests of museums. Instead, he argues that calls for museum reform are not external and in opposition to the museum but programmed by the very 'rationality' of the museum itself. Good examples are the demands constantly made on the museum to be more accessible and democratic in its representational strategies. Drawing on Foucault's concept of 'political rationality' (Foucault 1977), Bennett argues that the tension between the democratic rhetoric governing the conception of public museums as vehicles for popular education and their actual functioning as instruments for the reform of public manners leads to a public rights demand that museums should be equally open and accessible to all. Similarly, in claiming to tell the story of Man, the space of representation brought into being by the public museum embodies a principle of universality against which it will always be possible to hold a particular display inadequate. In other words, the calls for greater access and equity in representation are themselves a *product* of the tension between the rhetoric which sustains the notion of a public museum and its actual practice of representing the dominant class, race or gender.

The emergence of this public democratic rhetoric in the nineteenth century, for Bennett, relied on a new understanding of the museum's visitors. The notion of the 'general public' came into being at the same time as the development of the museum as a public institution. In theory at least, there was free access to the population at large. For the first time, the general public was addressed as a subject with interests in the museum. Bennett argues that 'the museum – addressing the people as a public, as citizens – aimed to inveigle the general populace into complicity with power by placing them on this side of a power which it represented to it as its own' (Bennett 1990: 42). The museum therefore, was a civic institution that played an important role in the contract between the citizen and the state. The citizens gave up their right to control their own representation in order to have it returned by the state in a way which was perceived as benefiting the entire community.

The argument represents Bennett's first move in developing an understanding of cultural politics as an effect of government rather than as the outcome of 'resistance' to forms of oppression. In other work (1994, 1998b) Bennett adds to these insights by arguing that the new concept of the museum visitor as a member of the public was made relevant by another development – the bureaucratization of culture. In this process, culture was made a socially useful discourse for the project of civic reform. Museums, according to Bennett, were one of the institutions that produced culture as a tool for managing a public in need of moral regulation.

This argument can be taken as the extreme point of heightened consciousness about the nineteenth-century museum, as Bennett exposes the rules of the institution, providing a framework within which to understand museological critique itself. It is an understanding that he applies to contemporary museums, arguing that they continue to function as institutions for civic reform, even if the specific aims of such reform are now couched within a rhetoric of cultural diversity rather than public morals.

In terms of the aims of this book, Bennett's arguments are helpful because of his differences from both those who posit a radical break thesis and those who continue to interpret the museum within the traditions of Marxism and ideology critique. His more positive interpretation of the effects of power opens up a space in which to rethink power relations. It also opens up a less destructive relationship between critics and museum professionals by opening up the range of possible interpretations on the function of museums.

There are, however, some limitations to Bennett's account. The first of these limitations is that museum visitors can only be understood as citizens. The museum space is seen as oriented exclusively towards the construction of a national (or imperial) community. The relationship can only be a political one. There is no recognition of the way in which museums can relate to a variety of communities, understood not in terms of opposition but in terms of cross-cultural forms of communication. The second limitation is that the social function of museums can only be considered in terms of governmentality to the exclusion of other relations such as popular culture, consumerism and the pursuit of pleasure. The effect of this is to obscure two other histories of the museum – a history of popular pleasure spaces and a history of economic interests in the museum. Yet, these histories may be of more relevance to the present day concerns of museums and their attempt to find a place for themselves within a post-industrial economy – an argument developed in the following chapter. Third, Bennett limits his interpretation of the sphere of governmentality to culture. This not only has the effect of reducing all cultural practices to an effect of government; it also prevents a recognition of non-cultural contexts for museum as well as governmental practices. The total effect of these limitations is in fact an inability to conceive of the museum as an institution that may not be always concerned with relations of power.

This chapter then sets out to question both the history of museums and approaches to theorizing that history. The aim is to open up a space in which museums do not always have to be understood in terms of power relations. To this end, the chapter demonstrates that continuities are found not only in the function of museums as an instrument of power but also in their place as a site of pleasure and consumption. It does so, first, by suggesting that the nineteenth-century museum had its 'irrational' moments when it rubbed shoulders with popular culture and with life in the streets. These moments, I want to suggest, were part of a wider development of a 'culture of looking' which also implicated the museum within touristic practices. Such a history resonates with present day attempts to popularize and build new museums within leisure and tourist spaces, suggesting that the notion of a radical break from the past cannot be sustained. In seeking to develop a more complex sense of the history of museums, I wish to suggest that contemporary developments amplify tensions that have always been there – between high and popular culture, between the rational aims of government and the 'irrational' pleasures of the populace.

The position I am advocating has two main advantages. First, it breaks a tendency in present discussions to see the association of museums within the tourist and leisure industries either as the death of the museum or its liberation. In moving beyond a form of explanation that demands a choice between two opposing poles, my position allows us to begin to think of culture and commerce in terms of complex relations. Second, it allows a more open, pluralistic sense of what museums are and have been. It becomes impossible to reduce the museum to a single function, either now or in the past.

To argue that present tensions may have their parallels in nineteenth-century museum practices is to suggest that there is more than one way of understanding modernity.[2] Foucaldian accounts of cultural practices and institutions tend to interpret modernity as the increasing regulation of culture by the state through various discourses of power. There are, however, alternative readings of modernity as animated through the rise of mediated popular culture (Hartley 1992), practices of consumption (Nava 1995) and the life of the streets (Berman 1988, Virilio 1991). There is ample scope for framing the museum in relation to these perspectives. The most important of these in the context of museum practices are the international fairs, the department store and the media.

Close encounters

The museum comes to the street: international fairs

Nineteenth-century international fairs have been interpreted, for the most part, as expressions of Western Imperialism and celebrations of capitalism. The work of Paul Greenhalgh (1988), for example, provides an excellent description of the ways in which these exhibitions displayed rivalries between nations in the race for empire, setting up oppositions between imperial centres and their colonies. Greenhalgh also describes how these fairs supported the growth of national manufacturing industries. Such a reading is supported by the work of a number of other writers, including Bennett (1988c, 1995) and Robert Rydell (1984). For Rydell, for example, the overriding characteristic of ethnographic exhibits, particularly those which exhibited 'ethnic' peoples, was to present in visual form a racial hierarchy along Darwinist lines. The Darwinist basis for anthropology at the time provided the theoretical framework for ethnographic displays both in museums and in the international exhibitions.

I do not intend to reject such a reading. Rather, I wish to suggest that it is perhaps too totalizing, erasing other meanings. International exhibitions created a sense of modern cosmopolitanism through the production of crowded street scenes in which the world was presented in miniature. Significantly, these displays, such as the Rue des Nations, the Rue du Caire in Paris and the Midway Plaisance in Chicago, were developed in the more popular zones of the exhibitions, close to the mechanical rides. While for critics like Bennett and Rydell the interactive dioramas created in these spaces are to be read within a narrative of progress with racist and nationalist overtones, contemporary commentary suggests that feelings *other* than pride in race and nation were also involved. These were popular pleasures such as physical or sexual excitement, the promise of strange foods and entertainment, of contact with the exotic. These intensities of feelings had more in common with popular culture – always regarded as feeding the baser instincts – than with the more abstract, moral values of high culture normally associated with the museum.

The association between popular culture and international exhibitions is recognized by a number of historians. Paul Greenhalgh, for example, has noted the association of the French and American exhibitions with popular culture, an alliance which he sees as both valuable and as missing in the British exhibitions (1989). He also comments that such links are not usually pointed out within British analysis of the exhibitions because of the English suspicion of pleasure and entertainment. Thus, the only series of exhibitions in England which did attempt to unite the educational functions of the exhibitions with popular pleasures in the White City series of exhibitions are almost excluded from critical analysis (Greenhalgh 1989: 77). Bennett, too, has recognized that the Great Exhibitions did reach into the sphere of popular culture, but he argues that narratives of progress eventually overcame these links, establishing the official culture as dominant (Bennett 1995: 83).

The possibility that such popular culture aspects to these exhibitions represent something other than an imperialist or Social Darwinist view of society is suggested by Meg Armstrong's (1992) interpretation in her article 'A Jumble of Foreignness'. Armstrong suggests that the ethnographic displays at the Midway Plaisance, an ethnographic display at the Chicago International Exhibition, cannot be entirely reduced to a Darwinian narrative of progress. To begin with, the very spatial arrangement of the Midway prevented a linear narrative from developing. As she says in a footnote on the Midway, the 'progression is from Bedouin Encampment to the Hungarian, the Lapland, and Dahomey exhibits and then to Old Vienna' (Armstrong 1992–3: 243). These are odd juxtapositions that randomly intersperse African groups with European ones in a non-linear flow. The point was made by contemporary writers such as Julian Ralph, who had this to say about the Midway:

> It will be a jumble of foreignness . . . a bit of Fez and Nuremberg, of Sahara and Dahomey and Holland, Japan and Rome and Coney Island. It will be gorgeous with color, pulsating with excitement, riotous with the strivings of a battalion of bands, and peculiar to the last degree.
>
> (in Armstrong 1992–3: 199)

Such comments suggest an absence of logic governing the choice of cultures represented. It is the singularity of the representations which is of interest not their place within a wider narrative of progress. Despite the use of dioramas as a technology of display, these exhibits refer not to the scientific exhibitions of the nineteenth century but to the cabinets of curiosity in the sixteenth and seventeenth centuries. Mr Malony, a literary figure in Thackeray's poem about the Great Exhibition of 1851, also comments on this 'jumbled foreignness':

> Amazed I pass
> From glass to glass
> Deloighted I survey'em
> Fresh wondthers grows
> Before me nose
> In this sublime Musayum!
> Look here's a fan
> From far Japan
> A sabre from Damasco;
> There's shawls ye get
> From far Thibet
> And cotton prints from Glasgow!
>
> (in Armstrong 1992–3: 191–192)

It can be added here that the exotic is associated with sensory adjectives – 'excitement', 'riotous', 'peculiar'. As Armstrong says, 'the exotic is a chaos, a jumble, a sublimely grotesque and bawdy array of colors, sights, scents, and sounds' (1992–3: 201). In its reminiscence of carnival, it produced a space in which normal behaviours could be forgotten, as this English guide to the Paris exhibition of 1900 explained:

> It suggests sparkle, colour, sun-burnt mirth, and spiritual intoxication as volatile ether. Beautiful, artistic and Bohemian Paris! Who would not go that had the chance? Bright, light-hearted, merry Paris! The prospect of treading its mercurial pavement sends a subtle spirit of rapture tingling through the veins. Luxurious, wanton, and – aye, alas! wicked Paris! Still, the British are a brave people – we go.
>
> (in Greenhalgh 1989: 93)

Together, these two aspects of the exotic produced what Armstrong calls a modern cosmopolitan sensibility. This is a sensibility that has more in common with Baudelaire's and Benjamin's modernity of the streets and arcades, of the *flâneur* than the rational, classifications of anthropology or with governmental programmes for civic reform. Promenading and walking the fair's streets was in fact one of the main ways in which the exotic panoramas could be consumed as contemporary comments make clear:

> A man walked the length of the street. It was a good day for aimless prom-enading. . . . He saw first, high tiers of graceful statuary arranged under velvet canopies guarded by swarthy Italian marines. He saw men from Switzerland leading visitors through a fairyland of carvings and jewels. He

saw men from Norway and Denmark standing at the street doorways of their pavilions. Russians in solemn black coats, buttoned up to their heavy beards, lounged among the kiosks. He saw Belgium's heavy arches and France's magnificent doorways. Through them he caught glimpses of silks, bronzes, porcelains, golden ware. . . . He saw many more things through the glass stalls or wide doorways of the miniature places, yet the best thing he saw was the street itself.

(in Armstrong 1992–3: 202–203)

In the activity of walking, the fair-going *flâneur* can compose his/her own exotic museum, collecting images as he or she goes. And as Armstrong argues, 'in making this jumble his own, he is also painting a portrait . . . of himself as a true cosmopolitan: he has been everywhere, *at once*' (Armstrong 1992–3: 207).

Dioramas at the store

In presenting the world through dioramas, international fairs shared in the museological enterprise. But they also built a connection to the new department stores that were rapidly helping to define the ambience of the modern cosmopolitan city. As Rosalind Williams (1982) argues, department stores in this period frequently displayed consumer goods in exotic settings, copying the technology of the diorama as a means of encouraging the consumption of the material goods on display. This is a point also taken up by Chantal Georgel (1994) in her work on the metaphor of the museum in French popular culture during the nineteenth century. She points out how the technology of the diorama was used to organize the displays of the Dufayel store which began to display their objects thematically as if replicating a visit to the museum. Thus the shopper could pass from one exhibit to another, 'from one hall to the next: the comparative furniture exhibit, the hall of festivities, the hall of fashions, and so on' (Georgel 1994: 118).

Borrowing also went the other way, as department stores provided museums with their first technologies of display such as overhead lighting through cupolas and glass display cases (*vitrines*). As Georgel argues, the word *vitrine* was a 'term borrowed simultaneously from the vocabulary of interior design, commerce, the bazaar, and the department store. A constellation of signs that linked the museum and the *magasin* was taking shape' (Georgel 1994: 118).

The relationship between the international fair, department stores and museums then was one that, in stressing practices of visual consumption, closely linked these institutions with the development of capitalism. Museums, as Michael Ettema (1987) has argued, taught the general population to value objects in ways that supported the growing need to get people to consume. They taught the value of materialism. While museums might have attempted to do this within aesthetic, historical or scientific discourses that sought to reform the values of the working class, there were also clear economic imperatives. The governmental use of museums was not only cultural as Bennett argues – it was also economic.

21

Thus, for example, as well as teaching people to consume, museums also sought to improve the quality of the goods available in the new department stores. In response to the frightening realization that British Manufacture did not produce goods of the same aesthetic quality as its European counterparts, the British government established the Victoria and Albert Museum as one of the legacies of the Great International Exhibition. The pedagogical role of this Museum was quite complex. It was meant to teach the principles of good design through example to those involved in the manufacturing industry. It was also meant to teach consumers about the range of goods available and to look for quality. The aim of the museum was to encourage reform in the manufacturing industries as much as in social and cultural values (Burton 1999).

Looking, consuming, travelling

What was perhaps most important about museums in this period is that they were part of an emerging culture of 'looking' which was central to both capitalism and to modern urban life. Paris of course was the international capital for this new form of modernity. As Marshall Berman (1988) argues, Baron Haussmann's reorganization of Parisian streets gave birth to a new cultural system as well as highlighting the internal contradictions of modernity, contradictions captured, for example, in the poetry of Baudelaire and others. For Berman,

> the Napoleon–Haussmann boulevards created new bases – economic, social, aesthetic – for bringing enormous numbers of people together. At the street level they were lined with small businesses and shops of all kinds, with every corner zoned for restaurants and terraced sidewalk cafes ... great sweeping vistas were designed, with monuments at the boulevards' ends, so that each walk led toward a dramatic climax. All these qualities helped to make the new Paris a uniquely enticing spectacle, a visual and sensual feast.
>
> (Berman 1988: 151)

The making of the city and its cultural and commercial institutions into a location which focused the gaze of its inhabitants and visitors points to another aspect of the growing culture of looking – the emergence of tourism as a popular activity. The advent of Thomas Cook, the development of railways and the emergence of the notion of holidays clearly positioned cultural institutions such as museums within an emerging tourist economy. The important role of tourism as one of the contexts in which this culture of looking made sense is made clearer through the centrality of another metaphor in the displays of international fairs, museums and department stores – that of travel. For travel made the exotic closer. Going to the fair was in itself a metaphor for travelling the world as noted above. If the *flâneur* was able to take on a cosmopolitan identity, then this was made more real by the rides that were available to visitors at the fair, taking them from one display to another. For example, the Trans-Siberian Railway developed one exhibit in which the fair-goer was placed in a railway carriage that moved 80 metres from the Russian to the Chinese exhibits. A painted panorama of the Siberian countryside was unrolled outside of the window as the train travelled, giving the impression of a journey across the Siberian landscape (Williams in Armstrong 1992–3: 236).

Such associations between cosmopolitanism, display and travel were also present in the museum. As Barbara Kirschenblatt-Gimblett points out in her book *Destination Culture* (1998) the museum is itself a metaphor for the activity of travel. This happens not only through the display of the exotic but also through the display of 'home'. Museums, Kirschenblatt-Gimblett argues, have always had a relationship with tourism, providing a destination for travellers or being a form of travel in themselves through bringing the strange home and making home strange.

Back to the museum

What then, was the effect of this 'jumble of foreignness' on the museum? How did relations between new techniques of display, a growing consumer culture and tourism affect the museum? And what might these connections mean for an interpretation of museums that focuses on its role in supporting power relations? If, as Bennett states, there was an overlap between museums and exhibitions through the exchange of staff and exhibits (Bennett 1995: 83), was this overlap entirely shaped by a governmental understanding of culture? Or is it possible that the display of objects and people at the international exhibitions and in department stores changed the way in which museum exhibits were viewed? Were museum spaces used in ways other than those intended by government?

There is considerable evidence that museum exhibitions were sites with complex and contradictory forces. For example, James Fenton, in a poem about the Pitt Rivers Museum, comments not on the order of the display with its evolutionary classification scheme but on the singularity of the objects displayed. He rediscovers the exotic object as fetish, as the object of wonder:

> Entering
> You will find yourself in a climate of nut castanets
> A musical whip
> From the Torres Straits, from Mirzapur a sistrum
> Called Jumka, 'used by aboriginal
> Tribes to attract small game
> On dark nights', coolie' cigarettes
> And mask of Saagga, the Devil Doctor,
> The eyelids worked by strings.
>
> (Fenton 1984: 81–84)

Thus, while ethnographic displays in both fairs and museums supported imperial and colonial claims, they were also associated with the exotic and hence with seduction and irrationality. In displaying ethnographic objects museums could not completely control the seductive power of the exotic as the singular, the strange, in much the same way that centres of Empire could not completely control the representation of the colony (Coombes 1994). For the exotic, while in need of control, also gets its meaning precisely from maintaining its difference from the hegemonic.

This association of the museum with the exotic is still one of the most dominant images of the museum in the popular imagination – dark and musty places, full of strange objects. This is the representation, for example, of museums in film, such as in the Indiana Jones series.[3] It is not the narrative of progress that is remembered but the exotic, the strange – museums as houses of mystery. This association suggests that despite their role within hegemonic discourses, museums are also associated with danger, the irrational, the uncontrollable. This becomes clearer when we look at what happens when the street comes to the museum.

The street comes to the museum

If, as Bennett and others argue, the museum in the nineteenth century was seen as part of governmental programmes to clean the city, the object of those programmes, the working class, did not always respect the space of culture. In some cases, museums were treated like any other urban space, becoming a part of the new urban fabric being developed in the nineteenth century and open to the behaviour of the general public. Colin Trodd (1994) has pointed, for example, to the tension between governmental programmes which attempted to make the National Gallery in London a space for the production of citizenship through the visual consumption of art and the actual *use* of the Gallery by the working class as an extension of the street. The presence of the working classes within the gallery, according to one contemporary commentator, made it impossible to undertake an aesthetic appreciation of the collection and physically endangered the conservation of the pictures. According to Gustav Waagen, a German art historian, the National Gallery

> had all the appearance of a large nursery, several wet nurses having regularly encamped there with their babies for hours together; not to mention persons, whose filthy dress tainted the atmosphere with a most disagreeable smell. The offensiveness . . . from these two classes . . . I have found so great that, in spite of all my love for the pictures, I have more than once been obliged to leave the building . . . It is highly important, for the mere preservation of the pictures, that such persons should in future be excluded from the National Gallery. The exhalation produced by the congregation of large numbers of persons, falling like vapour upon the pictures, tend to injure them; and this mischief is greatly increased in the case of the two classes of persons alluded to . . . it is scarcely too much to require, even from the working man, that, in entering a sanctuary of Art . . . he should put on such decent attire as few are without.
>
> (Waagen in Trodd 1994: 42–43)

As Trodd argues, Waagen is here describing the National Gallery as a space of pollution rather than as an agent in the cleaning up of the city. The city has entered 'the language of cultural discourse and the space of the cultural institution via the collective form of the crowd' (Trodd 1994: 43). While the dominant discourse about art presents it as separate from, and above, the daily grind of work, industry and commercial activities, Waagen points to the way in which the physical presence of the working class within the hallowed halls of the gallery reproduced the identity of the modern city inside the domain of culture (Trodd 1994: 45).

Commentators at the time were also offended at the way the working class made use of the space of the museum. As an informant for the 1853 Government Report on the National Gallery, the Assistant Keeper, Thomas Uwins, informed the committee that he had

> seen many persons use it as a place to eat luncheons in and for refreshments . . . many persons who come, do not come . . . to see pictures . . . I saw some country people, who had a basket of provisions, and who drew their chairs round and sat down . . . they had meat and drink; and when I suggested to them the impropriety of such a proceeding in such a place, they were very good humoured.
>
> (in Trodd 1994: 44)

Uwins also described how on certain days the galleries just resembled the streets outside:

> Mondays . . . are . . . when a large number of the lower classes of people assemble there, and men and women bring their families of children . . . and they are subject to all the little accidents that happen with children, and which are constantly visible on the floors of the place.
>
> (Uwins in Trodd 1994: 45)

Similar material has often been cited as evidence that in the nineteenth century the museum was the subject of increasing governmental controls. However, it seems to me that what is most remarkable about descriptions such as Uwins' is the total indifference on the part of the unwanted visitors to the efforts being made to improve their behaviour. It is almost as if they refuse to be made aware that there is anything wrong with their use of the space. They are simply unaware of the semiotics of power. Thus Uwins tells of his total incomprehension at being invited to share in a picnic inside the museum, while he thought he was admonishing the group. The picnickers were not resisting the attempt to change them. They were simply unaware that such an attempt was being made.

To recognize this is to break down the tendency in contemporary cultural criticism to posit a structural opposition between bourgeois and working class cultural practices. As Seth Koven has argued 'placing bourgeois and working-class culture in binary opposition to one another obscures the ongoing and negotiated character of authority to define the meanings of cultural objects and products' (Koven 1994: 25). For Koven, the issue is not so much one of resistance as one of cross-class cultural exchange.

Koven's study of the Whitechapel exhibitions in London at the end of the nineteenth century indicates that it is not only in the behaviour of the crowd that the museum found it difficult to establish its authority. Problems also occurred in the sphere of interpretation. Thus, according to Koven, while the White-chapel exhibitions were designed to instill values and ideals that were foreign to the lives of East Londoners, with simple catalogues that attempted to teach how to 'see' the paintings on display, visitors, who came in large numbers, brought their own set of values. Sometimes, these values allowed them to formulate their own critiques of the middle class reification of art. Koven mentions one example in which a woman compared Albert Moore's painting of three classic maidens *Waiting to Cross* to a United Kingdom Tea advertisement. In this way, the exhibition organizers' concept of culture as the means to 'tran-scend the degradation of commodity culture' (Koven 1994: 38) was effectively undermined. Given the relationships between fairs, museums and department stores, it is not too surprising if visitors did treat displays of art in similar ways to the display of commercial goods.

What these examples show, then, is that the museum has always been a complex, contradictory site that is not always amenable to a reading based on a notion of power relations. This is the case irrespective of whether the notion of power is based on Foucaldian or ideology critique perspectives. It is simply not the case that the meanings produced inside a museum always represent the power of the elite over that of subjugated groups. The production of meaning is too complicated a process for that to be possible. Nor is it the case that alter-native meanings can only be understood in terms of resistance to a dominant culture. In a considerable number of cases they simply reflect an alternative culture.

The complexity of museums is partly a function of their relations with other sites of display. While these relations certainly worked to support dominant interests, such as the development of capitalism, their connection with the development of modern cities also meant a certain degree of 'irrationality'. A focus on these moments of irrationality bring to light a different museum than that recovered by those whose focus remains centred on the more rational oper-ation of power relations.

The following chapter will continue these arguments by bringing them up to the present. This will be done through a discussion of two Australian museums – the Australian National Maritime Museum and the yet to be opened Maritime Museum in Fremantle, Western Australia.

2

Floating the museum

Tourists . . . form a major component of this museum's visitor profile. They are, I suspect, a larger market for us than most other Sydney museums. This is hardly surprising, given the popularity of Darling Harbour with tourists. I also feel certain that tourists flock to us because our national status and Australia-wide subject matter make us a 'must see' destination for anyone hoping to understand our nation's history and self-image. After all, there's nothing more Australian in the eyes of the world than a surfer or life saver.

(Fewster 1993: 3)

Given the history discussed in the previous chapter, the association of contemporary museums with popular culture, consumerism and the economy should come as no surprise. Nor should the growing importance of tourism. Those things are not in themselves new. What is new, is the status of economic arguments as the *central* rationale for the building of new museums. From at least the 1980s with the development of the Maritime Museum in Liverpool to the late 1990s Guggenheim extravaganza in Bilbao, economic rationales have been a prime motivation for major new museum developments.

A good example is the background discussions to the development of the Australian National Maritime Museum in Sydney's Darling Harbour. As the following memo between the New South Wales State and the Australian Federal governments indicates, the museum was seen as a central anchor to the commercial strategy underpinning the redevelopment of a derelict harbour area near the centre of Sydney. 'The museum', the memo argued,

would be the drawcard that will attract people to the area and indeed in all the publicity material associated with the redevelopment project the Museum features as pre-eminent of all the projects in the area.

A decision by the Commonwealth not to proceed with the Museum would require the development to be re-planned and could delay progress beyond 1988. The commercial viability of the redevelopment could be in doubt.

(NSW Government n.d.: 71)

The question, then, is how one should interpret the centrality of economic arguments in these new developments. Do they suggest that Bennett's (1990) argument about the civic role of museums, discussed in the last chapter, is no longer applicable? In what ways can an economic rationale be accommodated within Bennett's governmentalist approach to thinking about museums? Are there any connections between the economic function of museums and their turn to popular culture? What is the relationship between the orientation of museums towards tourism and their claims that they are presenting more democratic, inclusive exhibitions?

These are questions that return us to the problems outlined in the introduction to this book. Do current changes represent a break with the past? Or do they simply represent the most recent way in which governments make use of museums? Alternatively, are there ways in which these changes serve both governmental and 'popular' interests and are there connections between them?

In line with my suggestion that contemporary developments need to be understood in terms of both change and continuity, I wish to argue that they involve a complex set of relationships. These include governmental desires to make culture an integral part of the economy as well as museum practices that connect with visitors rather than government. Museums play to national and civic discourses at the same time as playing to a series of contexts that emphasize global flows of tourists, goods and ideas. These new contexts, I want to suggest, can be interpreted as reconnecting with the earlier relations between museums and international fairs, department stores and popular culture. This emerges more clearly upon a closer analysis of what is entailed when museums are built as essential anchors to urban redevelopment projects that aim to turn former industrial precincts into tourist and leisure spaces.

Anchoring tourism in maritime museums

Museums, tourism and urban renewal

An analysis of the history of two recent museum developments within tourist complexes in Australia provides us with some of the coordinates of this complex web of relationships. While there are about ten years between them, the two developments – the Australian National Maritime Museum in Darling Harbour and the new Western Australian Maritime Museum in Fremantle – are governed by a similar set of circumstances. Both are the result of a political desire to situate the cities in which they are located within a global post-industrial economy by manipulating the opportunities created by new relationships between heritage, culture and the economy. And both are examples of the tendency for such developments to be located in proximity to water.[1]

The redevelopment of Darling Harbour as a cultural site was an important element in the wider strategy for positioning Sydney as a 'global city', and as a centre of consumption; a positioning which would serve both national and state interests. As Anthony King (1990) explains it, redeveloped inner city areas can be understood as part of the attempt to develop 'global' or 'world cities' in which the global financial and banking services and culture industries are concentrated. Such cities become nodes in the global flow of goods, capital and information and are therefore centres of power within a global rather than national economic system.

Many of these cities use the semiotic resources of nineteenth-century port environments, which in their day were also the centre of economic and political power. Sites like Darling Harbour, the emerging Victoria Quay in Fremantle, the Docklands in London and South Street Seaport in New York thus feature historical landmarks together with 'water exposure'. The effect is that they are 'consciously reminiscent of the nineteenth-century commercial world city, with its quay sides and urban produce markets replete with open stalls, colourful awnings, costermonger barrows, and nautical paraphernalia liberally scattered around' (Goss 1993: 23). They are also reminiscent of the international fair and the nineteenth-century city with its departments stores, cafés, restaurants, museums and parks. They are spaces for the contemporary equivalent of the *flâneur*. As a result, a space such as Darling Harbour produces a complex set of semiotic signs in which 'ethnic' markers like the Harbourside Festival Marketplace food stalls and the Chinese Gardens combine with cultural sites such as the Powerhouse Museum and the Australian National Maritime Museum to represent, at one and the same time, an international cosmopolitanism and a national rhetoric of multiculturalism.

Like the International Exhibitions of the nineteenth century, places like Darling Harbour offer spectacles through the production of carefully controlled liminal spaces in a carnivalesque atmosphere. These spectacles attract new forms of consumerism which are part of the symbolic capital needed to attract investment. This aim is obvious in the governmental rhetoric surrounding the building of Darling Harbour. Neville Wran, then Premier of New South Wales, summarized it nicely:

> the combination of exhibition convention facilities linked to tourist class and to luxury hotel accommodation means that Sydney will tap into this lucrative industry, by ensuring that the world's conventioneers and trade/business/professional exhibitors will for the first time visit and invest in this part of the global village.
>
> (quoted in Plummer and Young 1988: 12)

Attracting investment is predicated on having a world class tourist site with appropriate cultural and corporate facilities. A closed loop is set up in which initial investments by government are designed to attract an even greater amount of investment from private investors which will then keep feeding itself. Despite Wran's claim to the contrary, the claim is not entirely new. Almost one hundred years before, Sydney like many other cities hosted one of the Great International Exhibitions which, like Darling Harbour, was also designed to attract financial investment and international exhibitors within a space which was oriented to the pleasure seeker as well as the businessman (Dyster 2000).

This objective is also evident in the cost/benefit analysis carried out by the NSW Treasury in June 1986. While the analysis was criticized as rushed and biased towards development (Huxley and Kerkin 1988), its rhetoric became integral to the spectacle of Darling Harbour itself. As Huxley and Kerkin (1988) argue, rhetorics like those associated with Darling Harbour are part of a self-fulfilling prophecy, a prophecy which appears to be a necessary part of flexible systems of accumulation which are characteristic of post-industrial economies. The cost/benefit analysis argued that:

> In addition to the direct benefits, the Darling Harbour Development is providing a number of indirect benefits which, while difficult to quantify, are of considerable importance to the community as a whole. Importantly, by promoting Darling Harbour as a unified development, the tourism potential and other benefits and attractiveness of the total development are considered to be significantly greater than the sum of the components if developed separately. Darling Harbour will be a major development which will help to reinforce Sydney's role as a tourism, trade and finance centre, both within Australia and the Asia/Pacific region.
>
> (New South Wales Treasury 1986: 6)

Economic considerations were also evident in the plan to redevelop Fremantle's waterside into a maritime cultural precinct. While it did not share in the hyperbole and international pretensions of Darling Harbour, the Victoria Quay redevelopment also aligned new museum developments with other cultural facilities and retail spaces along the water's edge as an opportunity to attract new investment. The architects pointed out that as well as providing a much needed civic amenity, the proposed redevelopment of this area of Fremantle's harbour would 'attract investments to the Fremantle waterfront and to the west end of Fremantle' (Cox Howlett & Bailey Woodland 1998: 1) while promising to 'become a unique and vibrant setting for the residents of Perth and Fremantle and a must see destination for overseas and interstate visitors' (4). The development of a new cultural/leisure precinct was clearly intended to rekindle economic investment in the area, drive up rental prices for office space and make the area a premier location. The development was, in part, an attempt to bring Fremantle into the sphere of a post-industrial economy as its traditional economic base around the port continues to diminish in significance.

Discourses

The economic arguments for such developments make conscious use of the historical associations between museums, international fairs, department stores and the modern metropolis as a site of cultural consumption. They do so through the use of three discourses. The first is a well established discourse around the importance of the aesthetic in a city's major public buildings. The second is more recent and concerns the use of heritage to help sell the cultural value of the developments in question. It is the notion of heritage which markets these sites as being of cultural value in the global economy when they do not involve an art gallery. The third invokes the complex relationship between the street and the museum discussed in the previous chapter and plays on a rhetoric of 'the people'.

As the promotional literature associated with these sites indicates – and indeed with developments such as the Tate Modern and other new museum developments around the world (Blaswick and Wilson 2000) – it is the 'iconic' characteristics of these new developments that is pushed as a central legitimating factor in gaining public support. These developments are showered with media reports that glorify the work of the architects involved and attempt to place them within international, 'global', trends.

In the case of Darling Harbour and Victoria Quay, the rhetoric is produced by those initiating the development themselves as well as by the media. For example, the magazine *Darling Harbour – The New Dimension*, produced by the Darling Harbour Authority itself, used an aesthetic discourse to shore up the international significance of the development. In a section entitled 'The men who turn visions into reality', the architects Phillip Cox and John Andrews are described as creating structures of 'international significance'. While the architects themselves place their work within a cultural 'renaissance that will confirm Sydney as one of the great cities of the world' (Darling Harbour Authority 1986: 17) – presumably of equal stature to New York, London or Tokyo – the Darling Harbour Authority explains that the architects' work is 'destined to play a key role in the State Government's plan to make Sydney a major international commercial and tourist destination . . .' (Darling Harbour Authority 1986: 17).

In the case of Fremantle, the *Draft Masterplan for the Redevelopment of the Western End of Victoria Quay* (Cox Howlett & Bailey Woodland 1998) describes the proposed new Maritime Museum as possessing national significance and consequently as requiring 'an architectural solution of absolute excellence particularly in its resolution of the requirements for both a contextual response and a significant presence' (Cox Howlett & Bailey Woodland 1998: 17). The building, they promise, will be a 'landmark building', an 'iconic building of great international significance' (16). The rhetoric is repeated in local media reports.

Likewise, the adaptive re-use of obsolete areas through a marketing of their heritage value is also to be found within the literature selling these sites to both the citizens of the area and potential investors and visitors. For example, the magazine *Darling Harbour – The New Dimension* could be read as an advertisement both to financial investors and Sydneysiders. The magazine attempts to produce in its readership a sense of excitement, placing Sydney at the cutting edge. The cover of the magazine, with a simulated view of the appearance of the Festival Market Place, promises 'The first total view of Sydney's world beater'. Inside, we are taken on a historical tour of the precinct before being introduced to the world of the future in which the development is controlled via electronic technology. A glossy picture of the effects of Darling Harbour on Sydney's economy is presented, emphasizing the symbolic cultural capital the development will bring through a redeployment of the area's heritage:

> Darling Harbour is Sydney's opportunity to win back its waterside heritage. The change in cargo-handling techniques and the establishment of the container terminal offers the chance for a fresh approach. The scale of the opportunity is massive. And the result of the work now under way

to make the most of the possibilities promises a new dimension for the entire city.

(Darling Harbour Authority 1986: 9)

New forms of economic investment reinvigorate obsolete sites and in the process give back its historical significance in representational form. That this can be achieved at all is the result of a unique symbiosis between the heritage and tourist industries. As Barbara Kirschenblatt-Gimblett (1998: 151) puts it, 'heritage and tourism are collaborative industries, heritage converting locations into destinations and tourism making them economically viable as exhibits of themselves'. This becomes very explicit when the two come together as powerful agents of urban renewal, particularly in waterfront developments. As Chris Plummer (Plummer and Young 1988: 12) comments, 'there has been a remarkable coincidence of new waterfront "people places" occurring around the world as a result of recycling older and obsolete industrial waterfronts'. This coincidence is due to the 'dramatic changes in the technology and economics of maritime commerce' (Fewster 1991: 75). As Fewster points out, developments in containerization and bulk handling have revolutionized the waterfront, impacting on the social structure and physical geography of ports. 'What were once amongst the most bustling parts of most cities became depressed backwaters' (75). In Port Adelaide, for example, there were 2,100 waterside workers in 1958. In 1989 there were only 200 (81).

The story of a declining labour force as old industrial areas become redundant is a familiar one in sociological accounts which relate it to a shift from an industrial to a post-industrial economic system (Harvey 1985, Huxley and Kerkin 1988) in which cultural consumption is the basis for new forms of economic production. Urban renewal programmes that attempt to turn these redundant spaces into tourist sites by using their heritage value are one example of such strategies to encourage new forms of consumerism. The most widely known cases are South Street Seaport in New York City, the Boston Waterfront, Baltimore, Granville Island in Vancouver, and the Docklands in London. All of these developments include museums as an important part of their offerings. There are also examples in which former industrial waterfront sites are used for the development of new museums such as the Tate Modern in London's Southbank which utilizes a former power station. Other uses of former industrial waterfront locations include the construction of new buildings such as Bilbao's Guggenheim Museum. It would appear from this impressive list that a waterside heritage plays the same function as an art gallery – both provide opportunities for marrying cultural and economic activities in ways that support the post-industrial economy.

Politicians have also developed their own discourse on the desirability of these redevelopments emphasizing their availability for the people of the city/nation. For Laurie Brereton, for example, the Minister responsible for overseeing the Darling Harbour development,

> [t]his project is about giving a vital part of the Harbour back to the people, it's about reviving the centre of the city in a way which has never

been attempted before. It's about providing everybody, rich and poor, with a marvellous area for leisure, for cultural interest, for entertainment, for shopping, for fun. Sydney's going to be a better city and a more prosperous city for all of us. It will enrich all our lives.

(Darling Harbour Authority 1986: 23)

Phillip Cox, the architect of many of the 'iconic' buildings central to the development, has himself supported this notion, comparing the infrastructure of Darling Harbour with the development of a major exhibition complex in Kensington, London, itself the aftermath of the world's first International Exhibition in 1851. In an interview conducted by Hans Hallen (1988: 3), published in the *Architecture Bulletin*, Cox stated that

> the Darling Harbour area represents to me Exhibition Road in Kensington with its corresponding Victoria and Albert Museum, the Science Museum and other museums. It is being done at a time when the economy is buoyant and illustrates confidence in a cultural sense. It provides people with a cultural and entertainment centre that includes the Powerhouse Museum, the Entertainment Centre, the exhibition halls and Maritime Museum and Aquarium. Activities like these offer popular galleries for people.
>
> (Hallen 1988: 3)

It was important to the success of Darling Harbour, for Cox, that it draw 'crowds'. This is evident in the political rhetoric – 'a place for the people' – and it is reflected in the architecture itself, which, as John Docker (1994) points out, invites ownership by the people in the openness and inclusiveness of the buildings' spaces. The Festival Marketplace, for example, is

> a theatre without a separate stage. All could be players, so that when you are sitting in a restaurant or cafe at the front, you can not only look at the waterfront and the city but also the passing crowd as they are looking at the building and you.
>
> (Docker 1994: 99)

Victoria Quay too was marketed to the electorate as a new people's place. In this case, the emphasis was not only on the public nature of the site and its friendliness to pedestrians, but also on giving back to the people of Fremantle their own history. Thus the redevelopment was

> [a]n opportunity to establish a unique and vibrant precinct that is emblematic of Western Australia's maritime heritage and culture. A precinct that allows Western Australia to celebrate its maritime history from the ventures of the first seafarers, to the first landing of European settlers, to the military and economic contribution that Western Australia has derived from the ocean and the Port of Fremantle. The keystone of the precinct will be the new Maritime Museum of Western Australia whose centrepiece will be the display of the Australia II, the winner of the America's Cup and the boat that focussed the world's attention on Australia's yachting endeavours.
>
> (Cox Howlett & Bailey Woodland 1998: 1)

Clearly playing to a local electorate, the redevelopment attempted to reconcile local needs and feelings with the perception that new facilities were needed if Fremantle was to maintain and indeed grow its market share within the tourist industry.

Corporate panoramas – a round around Darling Harbour

The rhetorical use of 'the popular' for corporate and governmental ends is reflected in the architectural characteristics of spaces like Darling Harbour. Unlike the international fairs, however, the rhetorical uses of 'the popular' are not achieved by vantage points such as the Eiffel Tower which people can climb in order to gaze on the world below from a position of power. Instead, Darling Harbour is characterized by a series of horizontal vistas that involve the criss-crossing of freeways, the monorail, views to the city and building forms with a permeable interface between their interior and external spaces. Rather than recalling a 'panorama of empire' (Morris 1988a) through the use of verticality then, Darling Harbour appears to work instead through what can be called, after Morris (1988a) a 'touristic panorama', a panorama which encourages the tourist to pass *through* rather than possess.

Central to this understanding of the panorama is the possibility of constant mobility. Often taken as a metaphor for modernity (Lash and Urry 1994), mobility implies a potential to develop an aesthetic 'cosmopolitanism'. For Lash and Urry,

> such a cosmopolitanism presupposes extensive patterns of mobility, a stance of openness to others and a willingness to take risks, and an ability to reflect upon and judge aesthetically between different natures, places and societies, both now and in the past.
>
> (Lash and Urry 1994: 256)

Such an analysis recalls Armstrong's (1992) 'Jumble of Foreignness' and suggests ways in which Darling Harbour, and the museums within it, connect with an earlier history of displays.

Cosmopolitanism is signified through a number of aesthetic characteristics. The first is the futuristic aspect of the site, embodied mainly in the monorail which is smooth, quiet, gleaming and shaped like a high speed train. It moves in and out of buildings as if they had no walls, becoming part of the architecture itself. With the monorail there is no such thing as an entry to Darling Harbour for the monorail blends into it and is part of it.

This implies a radical change in architectural metaphors. Where once buildings implied solidity, materiality and permanence they now imply their opposites – viscosity, immateriality and impermanence. In the case of the Australian National Maritime Museum, the image of the temple or fortress is replaced by a glass and steel building which plays with maritime metaphors of sails. Such metaphors extend beyond the architecture of the shell as the museum is transformed into a technological space, a move which radically embraces principles of immateriality (as I argue in Chapter 5).

With its views from the monorail, Darling Harbour also shares in the aesthetics of film. While travelling on the monorail, tourists can see the city while in constant transit. Unlike the visitor to Centre Point, Sydney's tallest Observation Tower in the centre of the city, the point of vision for the tourist in the monorail is constantly changing, as is the object of the gaze. Tourists are viewing in perpetual motion. As John Docker points out:

> Going round the monorail permits perception at speed, allowing the passenger to be a *flâneur* above ground level, interpreting a 'variety of changing, juxtaposed orders', reflecting on times past, present and future in terms of architectural styles and modes. For a few minutes, passengers can inhabit a liminal space and time, lifting them out of the city as business- or purpose-oriented, allowing them to feel *as* if in a magical movie world.
>
> (1994: 97–98)

The touristic panorama

This 'magical' aspect of the monorail expressed in both its futuristic and touristic aesthetic represents a new image of corporate strategy. For both the monorail and Darling Harbour are liminal spaces in which there is an attempt to infuse the corporate world with popular culture. One of the ways in which this is achieved is through the establishment of a number of vistas or panoramas of the city itself and the place of Darling Harbour within it. The monorail helps in this by providing constant images of Sydney and Darling Harbour for the tourist. The vistas gained from a trip in the monorail are signifiers of Sydney – the harbour with its expanses of water, Darling Harbour itself, China Town and views of the commercial centre of Sydney – the city. In this way the monorail does act like the Eiffel Tower, providing perspectives which may not be possible from the ground. It is a vantage point, but the speed at which viewing takes place prevents it from becoming a possessive or 'imperialist' gaze. Rather, it provides snapshots, or an opportunity for glancing.

Such snapshots are also made available in the form of postcards which constitute one of the most successful forms of merchandise found in Darling Harbour (Docker 1994: 98). Through postcards, Darling Harbour emerges, above all, as a site of images – of Sydney, of itself, of tourists, of a holiday atmosphere. The images in these postcards produce Sydney as a modern cosmopolitan city by focusing on Darling Harbour as a vibrant nightspot and as a holiday location through views of the water, the presence of palms, sunshine, boats and crowds.

A system of glances and gazes

One of the most prevalent activities in Darling Harbour is strolling through its promenades. Walking is an important activity in Darling Harbour, so important that the architecture of one of its main buildings, the Festival Marketplace, was designed to be looked at from the pavement. In Figure 2.1, for example, it is possible to see that the Marketplace is not monumental. Its façade is broken up into a series of horizontal projections in which people can sit and eat and drink. These people then become a part of the spectacle offered to those walking on the promenades. Part of the object in walking around Darling Harbour is to gain a sense of pleasure from watching others consume, while knowing that you too can join them. Here it is possible to both look and be looked at by other people. As Docker points out:

> The Harbourside Festival Marketplace was designed to catch the eye of the stroller promenading in Darling Harbour by its impressive Crystal Palace-like galleria; as you get closer to it, an effect of its soft edges, its restaurants and cafes at the front, its balconies, and its various openings, so that the public feel it owns its spaces, can effortlessly move in and out.
>
> (Docker 1994: 99)

This also means that the boundary between outside and inside is permeable at ground level, just as at the higher level, the monorail can also enter and leave through a permeable membrane.

In character with its liminal qualities, however, these promenades are not only for walking and experiencing the feelings of being part of a crowd. They also afford views back to the city and of Darling Harbour itself. In Figure 2.2, for example, walkers at the edge of the promenade are looking back towards the city. The promenade thus offers the possibility for walkers to position themselves in relation to the corporate world represented in the views of the city.

Figure 2.1 Terrace outdoor eating areas.
Photographer: Mark Gibson, 1996.

These views or panoramas are made possible by the distance and sense of space provided by the expanse of water. It is also a distance which is small enough to enable the city and the corporate, financial interests it represents to be reflected in the glass walls of the Australian National Maritime Museum, as in Figure 2.3. This is a reflection which is embodied in more permanent form within the museum in the sponsorship and naming rights of the Mazda Gallery and the ANZ theatre.

Sidestepping the rhetoric

Everyday uses of Darling Harbour

While it is easy to establish how developments such as Darling Harbour support dominant interests, the very fact that these spaces are used by crowds of people opens up the possibility of 'irrational' behaviours within these spaces. The aim may be to foster consumerism, attract investment and represent history and culture in a triumphalist mode. But just as in the nineteenth century, there are ways in which the streets can come to the museum, ways in which public behaviours simply sidestep governmentalist and corporate aims.

Figure 2.2 Walkers on the edge of the promenade, looking back towards the city.
Photographer: Mark Gibson, 1996.

Figure 2.3 Corporate reflections on the Australian National Maritime Museum.
Photographer: Mark Gibson, 1996.

Such a possibility can be opened up by using Michel de Certeau's (1988) arguments in 'Walking in the city', a central essay in *The Practice of Everyday Life*. In this essay, de Certeau proposes that just as the everyday is different from the official, walking is taking possession from below rather than from the rational view of the planners, who look down on the walkers from above. For de Certeau, the two perspectives imply different models of power – one is to possess, the other to use. To look down on is to totalize, to erase difference and heterogeneity, to consider only in terms of the larger picture. As de Certeau put it, long before the advent of September 11 questioned the infallibility of rational modes of power:

> To be lifted to the summit of the World Trade Centre is to be lifted out of the city's grasp. One's body is no longer clasped by the street that turn and return it according to an anonymous law; nor is it possessed, whether as player or played, by the rumble of so many differences and by the nervousness of New York traffic. When one goes up there, he leaves behind the mass that carries off and mixes up in itself any identity of authors or spectators. . . . His elevation transfigures him into a voyeur. It puts him at a distance. It transforms the bewitching world by which one was 'possessed' into a text that lies before one's eyes.

(92)

By contrast, there is no possessive perspective from down below, from the street level. On this level there is only the everyday, the walker, the shopper, the worker. As de Certeau puts it, we are at this level 'below the threshold at which visibility begins' (93). Hence walkers can make use of places which are unseen and therefore unknown by the developer and city planner. Their lack of visibility also means that such places cannot be represented by them. Knowledge of places remains at the level of use rather than at the level of representation. Comparing walking to writing, de Certeau comments that 'the networks of these moving, intersecting writings compose a manifold story that has neither author nor spectator, shaped out of fragments of trajectories and laterations of spaces: in relation to representations, it remains daily and indefinitely other' (93).

Indifference to the gaze

Following de Certeau then, it is in the particular use of places by people that other possible meanings emerge, turning place into space.[2] Thus while some people do indeed stop and look at the view (as in Figure 2.2), others make use of the place for private practices, turning the public place into a private space. These spatial practices produce meanings that in many cases completely ignore the intended use of the place on the part of planners. In doing so, people take personal possession of public spaces, even if momentarily. In Figure 2.4, for example, a couple uses a bench designed for someone to sit and appreciate the view of the city to engage in a private expression of their relationship. They take possession of the bench as if this were not in a public space with other people looking on.

Such private use of public space is reminiscent of the social effects produced by the opening up of medieval Paris to Baron Haussmann's boulevards. As Marshall Berman (1988) points out, one of the unintended effects of the new boulevards was to create a space in which lovers could make the new excitement and joy of being in open public spaces part of their own private feelings for one another. In a discussion of Baudelaire's poem 'The Eyes of the Poor', Berman suggests that the boulevards

> created a new primal scene: a space where [lovers] could be private in public, intimately together without being physically alone. Moving along the boulevard, caught up in its immense and endless flux, they could feel their love more vividly than ever as the still point of a turning world.
>
> (152)

The boulevards were thus more than new thoroughfares which made possible the rapid movement of troops through the city, more than new economic units with the shops and cafés that lined their pavements or even a new urban aesthetic of sweeping vistas down tree lined streets to civic monuments – they were also spaces for the public display of private relationships and emotions. Darling Harbour's spaces evoke this same aesthetic in modern dress with its promenades, benches, cafés, shops and vistas. And likewise, it is also a space for the public display of private emotions.

Figure 2.4 Oblivion.
Photographer: Mark Gibson, 1996.

Other uses of the same place might include meeting friends, having lunch, catching a bit of sun in a lunch hour. This is the ordinary, everyday use of the space which simply ignores the corporate pretensions. As Adrian Mellor argues, in his study of the uses of Albert Dock in Liverpool, many visitors come 'not to do anything in particular' (1991: 107). Theirs is a more relaxed, less instrumental use of time. As Mellor says, 'most visitors to the Dock amble around relatively aimlessly' (107). The Dock offers a space for adults and families 'where "doing nothing" can go on safely and decorously. There people can talk, joke, share experiences, and reinforce the group and family ties that the weekday world denies or limits' (109). 'Doing Nothing' is actually encouraged in that part of Darling Harbour which is designed as an urban park and which does not have such good views to the city. In these areas, we find a children's playground, young families picnicking and generally having a day out. Thus activities which, in one part of Darling Harbour could be read as resistance to the corporate, consumer oriented perspective, are welcomed in other parts of the site, making for a complex fusion of corporate and popular perspectives. The fact that these activities spill from one area into another only adds to the contradictoriness of the site.

Tacky and popular

If the exterior of Darling Harbour presents a complex liminal space which fuses the interests of the corporate world with that of popular leisure activities, the interior of Darling Harbour, particularly the Festival Marketplace is not so ambiguous. Here there is no sense of distance or panorama. And, interestingly, there are no postcards of the interior of the Festival Marketplace. It is as if, in de Certeau's terms, the inside of the Marketplace was below the 'threshold of visibility'. And yet, careful planning has also gone into this space. As Docker (1994) documents in his analysis of Darling Harbour, the interior displays a rich profusion of signs, many of which are artistic renditions of historical and multicultural themes. For Docker, these signs firmly embed the Festival Marketplace in the history of Sydney and more particularly its maritime and multicultural history.

Yet these are also the signs that could be found in almost any harbourside, for maritime locations are by definition concerned with the city as a centre of trade and multicultural influences, a nodal point for global flows. The result is a tension between the local and cosmopolitan references. For Docker, this tension is evidence of a cosmopolitan postmodernism which he defines as popular in its aesthetics and local in its orientation. However, Docker's aesthetic analysis of the site never quite resolves the tension between Darling Harbour's local and international allusions. His interest in postmodernism as an aesthetic category prevents him from analysing the actual daily usage of the site. Had he done so, he would have seen that the postmodern interior decoration – the mosaics on the floors, the detailings on the walls – are in fact hidden in the profusion of tourist shop signs and displays, the cacophony of sounds and the almost constant consumption of food.

The interior of the Festival Marketplace consists of a profusion of signs which in the nineteenth century would have been associated with the worst aspects of

the fair and the cultural values of the working class – only here, these characteristics are aestheticized for the consumer. Thus, above the escalators, between
the two levels of the international food hall, a sculpture playfully turns
the space into a circus display (Figure 2.5). While the food available here is
cosmopolitan, it is available as fast food. You stand in a queue to buy it, you
eat it standing or if you are lucky find a spare table to sit at, removing the
remains of the last meal yourself (Figure 2.6).

The experience is, from the point of view of a corporate, cosmopolitan perspective, a tacky one. This is further reinforced by the presence of many tourist
shops full of tea towels, place mats, key rings and stubby holders, koalas and
sheep skin rugs (Figure 2.7). These are not exclusive boutiques catering for
the cultured tourist. The experience is not that of luxury made available to the
masses. This is a place for anyone, the culture of the everyday. There is no
privacy, no sense of exclusion from the masses. Instead, you are one of them,
listening to their conversations, watching them eat and drink, just as they too
can watch and hear you.

The inside of Darling Harbour then could be read as a takeover of the
'authentic' popular from the corporate popular found in the terrace cafés
outside – especially given the difference in prices. However, the sign of 'authenticity' was only made possible by the removal of the original working class
population of the area along with its traditional leisure sites, including pubs and
brothels.[3] The popular was reinvented in the name of the consumer. Darling
Harbour is not an exclusive leisure site but it was built from the point of view
of capital.

Floating the museum

Like the space surrounding it, the museum cannot be completely contained
within rational aims. The complex web of relations that characterizes contemporary museums as belonging both within civic, governmental discourses and
more global economic discourses has an impact on the way in which exhibitions are developed. As Fewster (1991) comments, changes in exhibition style
are not only due to changes in museology but are

> a result of the museums being developed within major urban renewal
> programs. The pressures and opportunities associated with being located
> within a tourist precinct have required museums to maintain a strong
> focus on their visitor appeal. While not ignoring traditional curatorial
> responsibilities, these maritime museums readily accept as part of their
> mission the need to attract a broadly based audience to the immediate
> area.
>
> (1991: 77)

Fewster's focus on maritime museums and urban redevelopment sites as the
centre of these changes can be understood as a specific articulation of a tension
between a terrestrial rhetoric of the nation-state and a maritime rhetoric of
transnational capital. This is a tension that is present in the very juxtaposition

Figure 2.5 The circus comes to town.
Photographer: Andrea Witcomb, 1996.

Figure 2.6 Eating takeaway.
Photographer: Andrea Witcomb, 1996.

of the words 'Maritime' and 'Museum'. For maritime is often a metaphor for a space of flows, for transcultural movements, whereas museums have traditionally been associated with stasis, centralization and the state.

Taking up anchors: terrestrial versus maritime rhetorics at the Australian National Maritime Museum

The association of the museum with the nation-state is, as already argued, one of the central themes of recent critical museology. Not surprisingly, it is also an association that is made in government policy circles. While critical museologists argue that this association suppresses cultural difference within the nation, policy makers use it with a positive value to establish national cultural identity. With this positive inflection, the 'nationness' of the museum was certainly present in the establishment of the National Maritime Museum, a presence that does not go unnoticed by critics of the Museum.

The Museum was first mooted in the recommendations of the 1975 Pigott *Inquiry on Museums and National Collections* to the Federal Government. Written during the nationalist Whitlam years, the report expressed a concern that Australia did not have an adequate museological representation of the history of the nation. As well as the establishment of the National Museum of Australia, the report argued that Australia also needed to establish a National

Figure 2.7 Tourist alley.
Photographer: Andrea Witcomb, 1996.

Aviation and a National Maritime Museum, as ships and planes had an important place in 'the history of an isolated nation' (Pigott 1975: 83).

Given that Australia already has a War Memorial, the recommendation could be read as a reduction of Australia's history to the role of its armed forces. For some, it was little more than a call for 'big toys for big boys' (Anderson 1991: 134). However, the contexts for the establishment of the National Maritime Museum suggest other interpretations. One of those contexts is the maritime theme of the museum itself and the other is its location in Sydney's Darling Harbour, a site which, as I have suggested, established Sydney as a cosmopolitan city and a node in the flows of transnational capital. Read against more traditional conceptions of museums, these contexts present a problematic relationship between territorial representations of nationhood and maritime representations of transnational movements of capital, people and objects, much in the way that I have argued was the case with the International Exhibitions of the nineteenth century.

In some ways the National Maritime Museum can continue to be understood as a monument to foundations. It is associated with the discovery of Australia, the Bicentenary Celebrations and the State. As the then Prime Minister Bob Hawke expressed it when unveiling a commemorative plaque, the Museum represents

45

the fruits of the co-operative efforts of the Commonwealth and NSW Governments in ensuring that the Heritage is commemorated in an exciting and accessible way. No more suitable or more impressive a site for the National Maritime Museum could have been imagined than the site here at Darling Harbour – the cradle of Australian maritime commerce. It is close to the site for the first European settlement in Australia and it borders one of the world's finest harbours.

(Hawke 1987)

In other words, it is both physically and metaphorically close to the birth of the nation.

These associations are all part of what Paul Carter (1987) calls 'imperial history'. This is a history of classification and taxonomies, a culture which can be readily assimilated to the history of museums. Museums traditionally represent stasis, a concern with classification systems and a belief in empiricism. Hence the importance of their orientation to objects and their image as mausoleums. The practice of classification is also a practice that Carter associates with the land rather than with the sea; with the botanist Joseph Banks rather than with the explorer James Cook. Thus it is perhaps not surprising that Australia's first museums were natural history museums in which the 'strangeness' of the Antipodes could be made known and conquered through scientific classification systems. Flora, fauna and people were subjected to intensive study in what can only be understood as an imperial, colonizing project.[4]

Yet the location of the National Maritime Museum in the maritime environment of Darling Harbour, in a liminal space of tourists and consumers, indicates that it is also linked into movement and flows, a link which is also articulated in its exhibitions. The association between maritime metaphors and a space of flows, networks and movement is developed by Carter as an alternative historical narrative not dominated by imperializing, territorializing figures such as Banks. I take it as an association that can liberate the museum from the territorial space of the nation-state. In this respect, it is interesting to note that Pigott, in his 1975 *Inquiry on Museums*, indicated that the new National Maritime Museum

should display and research not only the history of ships but their cargoes, ports, sea routes, and the working life and conditions of the men who manned them. It is our view that too many museums of the sea are antiquarian and stillborn because they see no further than the hull, rigging, and engine room.

(Pigott 1975: 83)

For Pigott, the National Maritime Museum would not be a traditional static museum. Rather, it would 'travel', establishing connections with other maritime cultures.

In displaying a concern with sea routes, rather than cultural roots, maritime environments question the nationalist paradigms for thinking about cultural history. As Paul Gilroy (1993) suggests in the preface to his book *The Black*

Atlantic, 'nationalistic versions of cultural history fail when confronted by the intercultural and transnational formation(s)' (Gilroy 1993: ix). For Gilroy, ships 'focus attention on the middle passage ... on the articulation of ideas and activists as well as the movement of key cultural and political artefacts/tracts, books, gramophone records, and choirs' (Gilroy 1993: 4). In a maritime museum, ships and related artefacts and images offer opportunities to present ways in which national cultures are shaped by constant movement.[5]

The Maritime Museum can be taken as a representation of the movement of ideas and activists as well as material culture across the Pacific; a movement which, when juxtaposed with some nationalist tendencies within other displays in the museum, provides a critique from the inside. For example, the nation/maritime tension is articulated between a display dealing with the Bondi lifesaver in the *Leisure* exhibition and an exhibition dealing with the transmission of Hawaiian and Californian surfing culture in the *USA–Australia Gallery*. The first speaks to a nationalist conception of Australia's cultural history. The Bondi lifesaver has a long history as an icon of Australianness, grounded within a terrestrial military iconography. The second exhibition speaks to a transnational flow of cultural goods and practices – to surfboards, beach record players and surf music, to the counterculture of the 1960s versus the consensual, repressive culture of the 1930s. In this display, the Pacific becomes a site of exchange in which identities are not fixed but are constantly mediated by processes of cultural exchange.

Another example is the *Passengers Gallery*, an exhibition that deals with the process of migration. Here, ships are indeed 'microcosms of political systems in motion', to use Gilroy's phrase. Through the migration process Australia is linked to the cultures of Europe and more recently Asia, to different political and religious systems. The exhibits deal with the material remains of the process of migration to Australia – with books, diaries, personal histories, photographs. It is an attempt both to recover the experience of travel and to document the range of influences that have shaped Australian cultures.

Taken together with the exhibition on the European Discovery of Australia, these displays also replay the history of museums as a form of travel (see Kirschenblatt-Gimblett (1991) for her treatment of this theme). James Clifford has proposed that travel encounters provide the opportunity to present 'constructed and disputed historicities, sites of displacement, interference, and interaction' (1992: 101). For Clifford, marginal figures in the anthropological field such as missionaries, merchants, explorers, prospectors, pilgrims, entertainers, tourists, migrant labourers, immigrants are travellers who give the lie to the anthropologist's belief they had found an 'untouched', 'authentic' society. These travellers are also the people who figure in all the six themes/exhibitions of the Maritime Museum: *Discovery, Passengers, Commerce, Leisure, Navy and the USA–Australia Gallery*. They are the means through which an implicit critique of Australian culture as singular is effected through a representation of the history of cultural contacts. As these examples show, many of the museum's displays deal with the process of cultural mutation, a process which defies authentic notions of culture so necessary for nationalist narratives.

The displacement of the citizen?

If all of these tensions affect the way exhibitions are constructed, how might they affect the way in which the museum is theorized? Can the complexity of these new developments be accommodated by an understanding of museums which prioritizes their role in establishing relations of power? More particularly, can they be understood within a framework which stresses the governmental nature of museums? Indeed, is such an understanding sufficient to account for the development of the public museum in the nineteenth century?

I would argue that both the history of museums and present day developments question the appropriateness of both understandings. The limitations are perhaps easiest to establish if one follows through the consequence of placing commercial imperatives as the central rationale for new museum developments. In the case of the Australian National Maritime Museum, this meant a governmental directive to impose an entry charge – the first for Australia. As the initial steering committee well understood, this was a radical change from the traditional understanding of museums as public institutions whose role was one of civic reform. The imposition of an entry fee undermined one of the main rationales for the existence of museums – that of educating the population. Instead, museum visiting was placed alongside the movies or the fun park. In doing so, it also weakened the notion of 'the public' as the main reason for the existence of museums.

The Interim Council recognized the need to develop new arguments to support continued public support for museums but was unsure about how to do this. Thus they tried to erase the difficulty posed by an entry charge by simply advancing the following proposition as fact:

> The educative role of museums is clearly within the brief of the traditional museum. The commercially aware museum realises its responsibility to fulfil that brief by using contemporary marketing tools. In conclusion, the commercialisation of museums is more a change in attitude than anything else, but it is a definite and sometimes dramatic change.
>
> (Australian National Maritime Museum 1987a: 3)

Knowing that the traditional argument for supporting museums relied on their educational value, the Interim Council was unwilling to publicly admit to the pressures of commercialization. Thus the breaking down of 'the public' into a series of market niches was explained away as a more effective way to reach the public. That the public was no longer defined as citizens was not on the table for discussion. As a consequence, neither the negative nor the positive effects of such a change in orientation towards their visitors could be examined.

In articulating its relationship to its audiences as a commercial one, the National Maritime Museum became the first Australian museum to challenge the notion that museums are civic institutions. Rather than defining its work as serving the Australian public, the museum began instead to talk about serving a number of separate 'market niches', many of whom were defined as touristic as indicated in the opening quote to this chapter. This change in orientation altered the way in which power relations were negotiated. The audience was no longer in a contractual relationship in which they gave up their individual identity in order to have it returned to them by the state in representational form (as in Bennett's model of the political rationality of the museum). Rather than 'the public', a singular entity bound by a common identity, 'museum audiences' are now described as representing different 'market niches', each with different needs and desires. The market orientation has forced the Australian National Maritime Museum to develop forms of representation which are polysemic and pluralist, a development which I will look at in Chapter 6.

The articulation between consumerism, tourism, new forms of capital investment and culture problematizes an understanding of museums as still essentially an institution for civic reform. For it is precisely its civic attributes that are questioned when the audience is understood not as citizens or 'the public' but as tourists. Despite the fact that the Maritime Museum is a national institution, its operating context is not limited to governmental policies that aim to create a singular national community. Its economic position within a maritime leisure and tourist development requires us to pay more attention to the way in which museums articulate with flows of capital, people and objects.

This does not mean, of course, that these new articulations do not have a governmental aspect. New museums are certainly, in part, a governmental response to changing economic circumstances. They are civic in so far as they aim to manipulate the positioning of cities within a global economy. But they are less oriented to reform or the instilling of a set of moral values. At the same time, they activate an earlier history of the museum in more informal connections between museums, and other sites of display and popular culture. While contemporary museums are going through a remarkable period of change, that change connects in interesting ways to relations established in the nineteenth century between museums and popular forms of display. These are relations which open up the possibility of irrational moments within the rational walls of museums.

With these connections in mind, it is possible to reread Kirschenblatt-Gimblett's analysis of the impact of tourism (1998) in relation to a longer history. For Kirschenblatt-Gimblett,

> [t]he type of museum that tourism produces is increasingly becoming the model for purpose built museums. Museums that orient themselves more to their visitors than to their collections now aspire to the vividness of experience, to immersion in an environment, to an appeal to all the senses, to action and interactivity, to excitement, and beyond that to aliveness. This reorientation, which owes much to travel experience and to the cinematic, has precipitated a crisis in the identity of museums as institutions and specifically in the role of its collections in exhibitions.

Tourism has certainly brought these issues to the fore, but they were active in the international exhibitions and in nineteenth-century department stores and museums.

In the next chapter, I am concerned to explore the consequences of the emergence of tourism as a dominant context for museums on curatorial culture. At the same time, however, I am also careful to avoid an argument which rationalizes these changes in curatorial culture purely in terms of the effects of a turn towards the market. Thus I attempt to theorize the current turn towards tourism as part of a longer history of concern with the relationship between public audiences and experts.

3

From Batavia *to* Australia II: *negotiating changes in curatorial practices*

> The Museum of the Future may not be recognizable, when you consider that it will have to be planned yet flexible, differentiated and integrated, use new technology but allow respect for the object and individual self-determination, and appeal to all while catering for niches. We have no choice but to reconcile what we have always thought of as opposites.
>
> (Janes 1997: 11)

In a presentation to Members of the Board and various advisory committees on the contents of the new Maritime Museum in Fremantle, various suggestions for possible multimedia interactives were put forward. One of these was called 'From Terror Nullius to the Land of the Long Weekend'. It is a suggestion that could be seen as a metaphor for the extensive changes going on in the identity of the Western Australian Maritime Museum as it builds a new branch as part of the redevelopment of Victoria Quay. For the title is more than a clever pun with the phrase *Terra Nullius*. It marks a historical shift from a perception of the West Australian coast as an empty landscape capable only of inciting terror to a coastline that invites leisure activities such as sailing. In doing so, it also unwittingly marks a change in the very identity of the Museum.

The new Maritime Museum is a branch of the Western Australian Maritime Museum. The parent Museum is essentially a maritime archaeology museum, internationally famous for its work on Dutch shipwrecks off the Western Australian coastline – the very ships whose sailors experienced the 'terror' referred to in the title. By setting those experiences in the past, the title marks the differences between the new and the old Museum – differences that were the subject of bitter discussions within the Museum itself. As indicated by the second part of the title – The Land of the Long Weekend – the new Museum has a strong orientation to contemporary popular maritime culture. Rather than the anchors belonging to the old shipwrecks, the new Museum is focused on the sails of leisure boats, particularly *Australia II* – an Australian icon following its win in the 1983 America's Cup.

The emphasis on sails was partly the result of the specific politics of the proposed new development – Premier Richard Court, who was himself an enthusiastic sailor, was personally involved in ensuring the return of *Australia II* to Fremantle and in pushing for a new museum to house it.[1] But it also followed from the orientation of the museum towards tourists. For many of the staff, the possibility that the existing Museum might become part of the new development was frightening. They felt that any such move would destroy the traditions they stood for. As one curator argued, the proposed museum forced a choice:

> Is it leading us to become part of a mass culture which sees leisure simply in terms of a cheap day's fun? Or do we wish to be part of a leisure precinct which provides 'quality leisure' at little or no cost, which people will enjoy and want to return to more regularly?
>
> (Stanbury 1997: 4)

Her preference was clear. The existing Museum, she argued, was sufficiently removed from commercial activities to offer a refuge from them:

> The commercial food outlets are close, but not encroaching; families picnic on the Esplanade lawns or on the beach; . . . The Maritime Museum is both part of the environment and apart from it; close but not too close, which seems to enhance its attraction.
>
> (1997: 3)

As this quotation indicates, the change in orientation reflected in the title of the interactive was a traumatic experience for most of the staff at the established Maritime Museum. The extensive changes in orientation and priorities raised a question mark over many of the established staff's most cherished assumptions. This chapter is an attempt to understand their reactions in order to draw some more general conclusions about the effect of new museum developments on traditional curatorial culture. While the pressure to change can be understood in terms of the commercialization of culture, this pressure is itself a symptom of much wider changes in the way knowledge is produced and communicated. Such changes are making it very difficult for public institutions such as museums to remain specialized, research-focused institutions. Understanding this wider process will give us not only a deeper insight into the contexts behind change; it will also provide a more nuanced interpretation of the debates around it.

The staff's response to the new museum concept can be understood in terms of what is, by now, a well established debate between those who seek to popularize museums and those who seek to preserve their traditional curatorial cultures, particularly the notion of research. It is a debate that has raged since the middle of the 1980s, especially in the Western world. Despite its geographic and temporal spread, it is a debate whose contours are immediately recognizable. Its shape is based on an opposition between 'culture' and 'commerce', between 'history' and 'heritage', between 'scholarly research' and 'pandering to the masses', between 'education' and 'entertainment'. Its most established point of reference is the 'heritage debate' in Britain in the 1980s and early 1990s.

My sympathies in this debate are divided. Robert Lumley (1994), Adrian Mellor (1991), Raphael Samuels (1994) and others have made strong arguments in support of popularizing tendencies. All point to the way in which those who criticize the heritage industry do so by pointing the finger at the effects of commercialization on elite values. For example, Lumley (1994) argues that the problem for many critics of the heritage industry is that heritage, and by extension museums, has come to be understood as an *industry*. For Lumley it is the collapse of a distinction between economic and cultural activity that frightens critics of the heritage industry into apocalyptic predictions and paranoid projections about the end of professionalism, morality, truth, objectivity, history, and the importance of the object. Mellor also tends to think that the apocalyptic tone is more strident in 'those instances where "heritage" meets "enterprise" . . . Real dismay is reserved for the conjunction of "history" and "commerce": for the moment of commodification' (Mellor 1991: 101). Thus he quotes Waldemar Januszczak who, in writing about the Albert Dock, feels that the Tate Gallery is misplaced amongst the consumerist ethic promoted by the leisure and entertainment precinct. The gallery, Januszczak says, 'must compete with the jaunty sea-faring mood that is being cultivated around it in the theme dock (the pizzas in the café opposite have names like The Trafalgar and Bosun's Surprise)' (in Mellor 1991: 101).

Mellor goes further, suggesting that this distaste for the incursion of market forces and the use of a moralist discourse is used to hide elite cultural values. As he sees it,

> [b]y the late 1980s . . . the omnipresence of 'nostalgia' had become the prime focus of educated concern, and was serving the current generation of the chattering classes in much the same way as their forbears had been served by the evils of gin, the decline of religious belief, horror comics, and juke-box boys.
>
> (Mellor 1991: 97)

At the same time, however, Lumley, Mellor and Samuels tend simply to invert conservative positions and so fail to explain changes currently taking place. Their approach is too reductionist, seeing the debates merely as a battle between conservative and democratic forces expressed as a dislike on the part of the 'educated' for the incursions of commerce into the sphere of cultural activity. The demand to make a choice between two opposing poles elides the possibility of a relationship between commercialization and changes to the way knowledge is produced and communicated.

The framing of the issue as an opposition between conservatism and democracy is also present in media reporting of new museum developments. The *Sydney Morning Herald*, for example, ran a number of articles in 1988, all with a similar tone. 'Museums blast from the past' ran one headline:

> As Government purse strings tighten, public institutions such as libraries, art galleries and museums can no longer sit quietly on their foundations and wait for crowds. Once-staid places have lifted their skirts and vie with a cheeky newcomer for image, audience and the precious corporate dollar.
>
> (Abjorensen 1988: 8)

In siding with new technologies, consumerism and marketing, it is suggested here, museums are overcoming their traditional stasis and becoming relevant. To change, to side with the new, had to involve a radical break with the past. Such positions can often be traced back to the senior museum administrators responsible for driving change. The *Sydney Morning Herald* report cites Des Griffin, for whom 'The days of museums being dull places full of stuffed dead things in glass cases are gone' (Griffin in Abjorenson 1988: 8). Margaret Coaldrake, then acting director of the Powerhouse Museum, is also quoted on the side of change:

> We must – and indeed, all museums must, as we enter the twenty-first century – respond to public needs. Marketing must identify these needs and pick up audience. . . . That's really the change that has come over museums both in this country and overseas in the last 20 to 30 years. That is, in recognising the audience and dealing with it as a consumer market using all the tools of the commercial world in selling itself. My main brief in charge of services and marketing was to ensure a widening of the traditional audience.
>
> (Coaldrake in Abjorensen 1988: 9)

This insistence on a choice between the old and the new can also be seen in more recent museum developments. In an article in *The Weekend Australian* discussing the soon to be opened National Museum of Australia, the museum's director, Dawn Casey, explained that this museum, like the recently opened Te Papa in New Zealand, would be a 'people's' museum. Casey 'wanted the museum to set the imagination alight, rather than simply house a series of dull but worthy objects' (Casey in Powell 2000: 16). Like Griffin and Coaldrake, Casey looked particularly to the use of multimedia as well as media techniques for storytelling. 'I went to the Museum of Civilization in Ottawa', she said. 'It was like walking through a film set' (16):

> Museums around the world are heading in the same direction; they have hauled themselves out of the days of dusty glass cases filled with exhibits painstakingly labelled according to scientific orthodoxy but with little regard for firing children's imaginations or igniting adult illumination. The National Museum will be an exemplar of all that is new in museology; with an emphasis on multimedia, on high tech electronic interactions, on all that is best and brightest in bits and bytes.
>
> (Casey in Powell 2000: 18)

While there is much to be said for this enthusiasm, I want to suggest that the issues are more complex than such analyses have allowed. The debate over the direction of museums covers a lot of terrain – the impact of tourism on museums and heritage sites, the changing structures of museum staffing, the diminishing importance of objects in exhibitions, the rise of 'interactive' media oriented displays, the loss of curatorial authority and questions of access, cultural diversity and representation. To describe the context for these issues only in terms of elite or populist perspectives is to simplify a complex situation to a point where nothing is explained.

As a first step in analysing the current situation it may be helpful to take a distance from the idea of a radical break between the traditional and contemporary museum. While museums are certainly undergoing change, they have also done so in the past. Nor is this the first time there have been conservative discourses around the proper role of museums. As Lowenthal (1998) has pointed out, the desire for roots, for the expression of tradition, is keenest at moments of rapid change. While he situates the desire for stability in contemporary global movements of people and the creation of a society of the spectacle (see also Appadurai and Breckenridge 1992), these movements are not new. They developed from the onset of modern forms of urban life in the nineteenth century, the very moment when the modern museum was born. As Marx famously put it, 'all that is solid seems to be melting into air'[2] (in Berman 1988). As argued in Chapter 1, the massive changes then occurring were associated with the new experiences found in the streets and in the department stores (Buck-Morss 1991). And even at that early stage, fears were held for the survival of 'culture' in art galleries and museums. At the very moment at which museums were emerging as public institutions, cultural critics were also posing questions about the appropriate relationship between tradition, aesthetic values and the needs of 'the masses'.

Like many commentators today, nineteenth-century critics sought to defend the values of tradition, scholarship and auratic culture. As discussed in Chapter 1, nineteenth-century art critics criticized museums and art galleries for allowing the culture of the streets inside the museum. Such contact was seen to contaminate the art works and make aesthetic appreciation almost impossible. Chief amongst the critics was Gustav Waagen whom we encountered in Chapter 1. Waagen argued that street people should be excluded from the space of the museum or at the very least that 'in entering a sanctuary of Art . . . he should put on such decent attire as few are without' (Waagen in Trodd 1994: 43).

The opposing position was also well developed in the nineteenth century as can be seen in William Buss' account of his visit to the national armoury at the Tower of London:

> the people were hurried through in gangs of from 20 to 30, and there was no time allowed for the investigation of any thing whatever; in fact, they were obliged to attend to the warder, and if the people had catalogues they might as well have kept them in their pockets; when they wanted to read them in conjunction with the object they saw, of course they lagged behind, and then the warder would say, 'You must not do that; the catalogues are to be read at home; you must follow me, or you will lose a great deal;' and I was peculiarly struck by that, for I thought it a very odd mode of exhibiting national property.
>
> (Report 1841, minute 2805 in Bennett 1995: 53)[3]

Buss' concerns clearly anticipate present day criticism of elitism and inattention to the needs of the visitor. If, in the nineteenth century, the debate was conducted around a perception that the values of the museum were not those of its visitors, the debate in the late twentieth century is not dissimilar. Issues of education versus entertainment are called into play alongside debates about the continued relevance of the material world and the values of scholarship and cultural authority. If, in the nineteenth century, the offenders were the people of the street, in the late twentieth/early twenty-first century the offenders are the media (especially television), postmodernists and the tourist industry.

An example is Charles Watkins' (1994) article 'Are museums still necessary?' Watkins expressed an intense dissatisfaction with a museological practice intent on providing pleasure and gratification of the senses rather than hard knowledge. He attributes this move to the new orientation to the market and charged it with a displacement of the object. In developing his arguments Watkins cast himself as defending the traditional authority of the museum in establishing frameworks for knowledge. To let go of this authority, he argues, is also to abandon professionalism, connoisseurship, and a regard for the authenticity of objects. So, for example, the problem with providing reproductions in the museum shop is that they 'prevent an appreciation of the original' and 'will eventually supersede the need for such an appreciation' (1994: 30). In a similar vein, Watkins questions the effects of the 'new museology' on the authority of the museum. He is especially concerned about a museology that deconstructs ideas of authenticity. It would be all right, he says, 'if all of this were simply hairsplitting by European academics . . . but there are examples of the practical application of such ideas' (1994: 28).

Rather than questioning the value of originals and the importance of authenticity, Watkins argues, museums should be teaching it to the population at large. A good exhibition is one which 'allows each visitor to learn how curators evaluate historic furniture for quality and authenticity' (1994: 27). An exhibition which is 'shaped by the visitor's experience, not the show's content' may be 'laudable from a sociological perspective', but 'tends to undermine the authority of museums and suggests that every person can ultimately become his or her own curator' (27–28).

Watkins represents perhaps a smaller cross-section of museum professionals than he might have done in the past. His arguments were severely criticized. It is significant here that not all of his critics were curators. This reflects the fact that curatorial work is no longer at the centre of museum practice. Educators, public relations officers and marketeers have an increasing role – one that was recognized by the same journal that published Watkins' article, *Curator*. Responses to Watkins' article were published in the following issue. David Resnicow (1994), a consultant, criticizes Watkins for his elitism, while Lisa Roberts (1994), a Public Programmes Manager, critiques him for assuming that leisure or recreation and education or learning are intrinsic oppositions.

The Watkins' exchange is interesting because of the way in which the debate is characterized by black and white positions, demanding that the reader take sides. It provides a reflection of the characteristics of the current debates. On the one hand there are those depicted as conservative and traditionalist, as supporting elite cultural values and as opposing the values of cultural diversity.

They stand for notions of authenticity, for the continued importance of the object, the need for curatorial authority, scholarship and the privileged space of culture. On the other hand, there are the progressives, who stand for cultural diversity, access, the compatibility of education with entertainment, the need for museums to engage with contemporary popular culture, particularly that of the media. Only then, they argue, can museums hope to survive and maintain some degree of cultural relevance (MacDonald 1991, 1992, MacDonald and Silverstone 1990, Wallace 1995, Weil 1995).

Yet the situation described is much more complex than these debates allow. As MacDonald and Silverstone (1990) suggest in their work on the Science Museum in London, the sense of crisis manifested in these debates is expressive of a wider set of concerns. 'These concerns – with problems of authenticity, representation and the active demanding reader/viewer/visitor – are central to current discussions in the analysis of other cultural industries' (176–177). My suggestion is that such concerns exist because the relationship between museums and visitors is again under review, just as it was when Waagen was writing in the mid-nineteenth century.

The relationship between museums and visitors can be understood as part of a wider question about the way in which public institutions address the audience they both produce and represent. This is a question that is as old as modernity. As John Hartley argues in *The Politics of Pictures* (1992), the development of modern society goes hand in hand with a belief in the existence of 'the public' – which both needs to be represented in the political sense but which also needs to be shaped according to the requirements of capitalism. According to Hartley, this faith in the existence of the public and the need to control it has led to the development of three major modern institutions – government, education and the media: 'All three have been organized around the belief in the public as blank sheets of paper on which moral, political, religious, commercial and other knowledges are to be impressed' (Hartley 1992: 120).

Government, education and the media have each developed a different strategy for tutoring the public – respectively democracy, didactics and drama. As Hartley puts it 'education gets the didactics, the media take the drama, government gets the democracy, and the public gets taught, entertained, governed, apparently, and often without much consultation' (120).

For Hartley, however, it is the media which has been most successful at popular instruction. This is because of the three institutions, media is the one which has 'retained and refined the strongest sense of integration of the three D's of democracy, didactics and drama' (121). The media are the first of the 'smiling professions' – those professions which function 'to create, sustain, tutor, represent and make images of the public – to call it into discursive being' (121–122). In the smiling professions 'performance is measured by consumer satisfaction, where self is dedicated to other, success to service, where knowledge is niceness and education is entertainment' (134). These professions include anyone who has contact with the public – from teachers, journalists, advertisers and publicists to waiters, receptionists and shop assistants.

As a metaphor for the kinds of values that are currently ascendant, the notion of smiling suggests that the public is fashioned and represented as much by the mode of communication as by the content:

> both government and education have had to take a leaf out of the media's book, learning that smiling is not incompatible with either politics or knowledge, but that Correct Ideas whether civic or civilized, are only ever as good as the media through which they're communicated. Smiling, in fact, is now the 'dominant ideology' of the 'public domain', the mouthpiece of the politics of pictures.
>
> (122)

Hartley's concept of 'smiling professions' does, of course, rely on a polar model as well. There is, in his description of the situation, a certain lack of sympathy for the situation 'experts' face in learning to smile:

> some professionals continue their disciplinary, classical, clubby and institutionalized maleness, as bastions of older notions of power, enemies of smiling, last of those who hate the public even if it is the object of their professional practice or the source of their income, protectors of binary oppositions and clear boundaries between authority, access, truth, and their opposites, or at least their others, outside(r)s.
>
> (135)

There is also the implication that experts can never be good communicators. To the extent that Hartley takes the position of batting on the side of the 'popular', his arguments suffer from the same problem of oversimplification as with those who defend current reforms to museological and heritage practices.

However, Hartley's idea of the rise of the smiling professions does allow us to rethink the effects of the incursion of the market into the museum as part of a broader phenomenon. The museum is faced with a similar question to other public institutions: what is the appropriate means of communication in the contemporary public sphere? To make this connection allows us to rethink the nature of museological work by placing problems relating to the incursion of the market into the museum as an instance of a wider problem of how to address audiences. This does not mean, however, that we won't, at the same time, need to face some hard questions about the long-term effect of 'smiling' on the production of specialized knowledge.

The effects of an orientation towards 'smiling' in museums can be illustrated by a 1993 marketing report at the Australian National Maritime Museum. The report warns the museum that a change in the curatorial culture of the museum must be achieved if it is to be successful in the market place. Richard McLauchlan, consultant to the museum, suggests that

> to achieve our objectives we would like to encourage the Museum to see marketing not just as a section title but rather an 'umbrella' concept which plays a fundamental part in all our planning and development. . . . In this regard, Marketing, Visitor Programs and Curatorial should be encouraged

to work closely together in order to maximise the visitor experience and maximise the promotional opportunities.

(McLauchlan 1993: 3)

At stake is a redefinition of the 'core duties' of a museum. Traditionally, these have been defined as collecting, interpreting and exhibiting – all understood to be curatorial and custodial duties. Current definitions of museums are more likely to use words and phrases like 'access', 'social responsibility' and 'community involvement'. As Geoffrey Maslen wrote for the cover story of the September issue of *Museum News* in 1988:

> In place of the ancient incantations: 'preservation, conservation, education', museum directors and their curators have been forced to learn a new litany, one that includes such terms as 'accountability, relevance, marketability'. More and more, the big museums and art galleries are being viewed by governments as key elements in the nation's economic strategy, their role crucial in capturing a larger slice of the world's tourism dollar.

(Maslen 1988: 33)

Maslen could have added that more and more museums are being required to smile, to find ways in which they can make themselves more appealing to a broader audience. The same point is made in another way by Stephen Weil who warns curators of the danger of continuing to believe that developing, managing and researching a collection provides museums with their rationale. Weil points, like Hartley, to the importance of thinking about modes of communication rather than simply the content:

> we have too often taken what is a necessary condition to the work of museums – the existence of carefully acquired, well-documented and well-cared-for collections – and treated that necessary condition as if it were a sufficient condition. In developing justifications for the public support of museums, we have too often forgotten that their ultimate importance must lie not in their ability to acquire and care for objects – important as that may be – but in their ability to take such objects and put them to some worthwhile use. In our failure to recognise this, we run the danger of trivialising both our institutions and ourselves.

(Weil 1995: 29)

The pursuit of knowledge for its own sake has now become associated with elitist value systems. It is thus not surprising that this new focus on the importance of communication, and by extension on the visitor, is generating a worldwide questioning of the value of specialists who are not regarded as good communicators. This questioning has been directed particularly at public institutions. Often, the result is the loss of specialists. As an editorial for the British journal *Museum Management and Curatorship* (1993) comments,

> the choices being made recently in order to allocate resources intended to increase visitor numbers and to place a greater emphasis on education and visitor services have led to a progressive loss of curatorial posts as research and museum-based scholarship was being downgraded.

(124)

The tension between specialist research-based knowledge and the need to communicate effectively with a diverse range of visitors is the subject of intense pain and soul searching in many museums. The need to learn to 'smile', to think about research in terms of its communication to a broad audience is one of the most pressing issues facing museums today. There is a desperate need to develop new management processes that recognize the extent of the changes being required of specialist staff and which provide encouragement for change while demonstrating an appreciation of the work specialists do. Such strategies can only come about if managers themselves take the time to understand the pressures their staff are facing – not an easy task when many of these new requirements are accompanied by tight deadlines, political pressures and financial constraints.

It is here that academic research may have a role to play. In what follows I offer a reading of one example of a current reform process in the Western Australian Maritime Museum in Fremantle. This museum has been undergoing a restructuring process since the middle of 1997, when it became clear that the State government would be investing a considerable sum of money in a new maritime museum. The new museum was conceived as a part of the redevelopment of the dock area in Fremantle known as Victoria Quay (discussed in the previous chapter). With the support of the Museum's staff and the directorate I have followed these developments by sitting in on staff meetings, being invited to contribute to workshops on the new development and sitting on the Maritime History Advisory Committee. This has allowed me an opportunity to study the impact of a new museum development on the culture of the old museum.

As part of the project I also held a focus group discussion. The aim of this discussion was to get the staff to articulate their understandings of what a museum is through a discussion of their perceptions of the role of the existing Maritime Museum. While the discussion required staff to put the new museum development to one side, it became clear throughout the discussion that the spectre of the new Museum was forcing a revaluation of the existing Museum and the work of its staff. The discussion was marked by a tension between pride in the Museum's profile in the field of maritime archaeology, a profile which was largely based on research, and the pain and confusion generated by an awareness that the existing displays did not communicate this work effectively. This tension is an almost perfect expression of the problems now facing public institutions as a result of the rise to prominence of the smiling professions.[4]

The origins of the Western Australian Maritime Museum

The Western Australian Maritime Museum is a branch of the Western Australian Museum. It was established in 1979, more than a decade after the discovery of two Dutch shipwrecks off the Western Australian coast – the *Vergulde Draeck* (*Gilt Dragon*), and the *Batavia* – in 1963. The Museum developed a unique identity around the archaeology of Dutch shipwrecks[5] based both on the displays at the museum but more importantly on the scientific research behind the preservation of the material itself. This reputation eventually led to a successful application to become a National Centre of Excellence. Such centres are funded by the Australian Government and represent a recognition of research excellence in a particular field. They are usually found in universities rather than museums.

What kind of institutional culture led to the development of such a high research profile? Why was there such a focus on Dutch shipwrecks? What impact did this specialization have on the curatorial culture of the museum? What values were embedded in this profile and how have they been questioned by recent developments?

The reasons for the research focus of the museum go beyond the obvious point that the Western Australian coast is littered with Dutch shipwrecks. It emerged from a complex web of factors. Externally, there was a political environment that fostered the development of knowledge about Western Australia's history, an environment that was reflected in the dominant historiography of the 1960s and early 1970s. There was also a strong diplomatic interest from Holland and therefore the opportunity to make international research links, as well as a fascination on the part of the media with shipwreck stories. Within the Western Australian Museum, there was an emerging research culture based on the natural sciences as well as a close connection to the University of Western Australia. All of these factors are important in understanding the curatorial culture of the Western Australian Maritime Museum at the moment of the proposed new development.

In 1963, when the *Gilt Dragon* and the *Batavia* were discovered, the Western Australian Museum was only just beginning to display an interest in the European history of the state. Until then, the Museum had been predominantly a natural history museum with some interest also in the material culture of Aboriginal society (Delroy 1991). This was not unusual in a country like Australia. From the nineteenth century until the late 1960s, most state museums were either art galleries, science and technology museums or natural history museums that also included ethnographic collections (Gregory Kohlsteadt 1983, Sheets-Pyenson 1988). As Tony Bennett (1995) points out, Australian history did not animate the Australian museum scene until the 1970s.

Up until the 1960s the Western Australian Museum had had a very checkered history. After the initial investment in buildings, collections and exhibits at the turn of the century, development came to a virtual halt during the First World War. The museum was then unable to command the government's attention until 1958 when funds were released for the first update of its galleries since 1907.[6] With the appointment of Dr George Ride as Director, the Museum took a new turn. Increased government funding allowed a modernization of exhibitions and an expansion in the quality of its research. Skilled scientists were employed to work on the existing collection as well as undertake fieldwork. The number of publications produced by the museum went up radically in these years. It is against this backdrop of an improving scientific research status that maritime archaeology emerged as a field of interest.

The discovery of the Dutch shipwrecks resulted in intense public interest. As Myra Stanbury suggests, this was because 'they provided tangible evidence of the early presence of Dutch seafarers on the west coast of Australia' and because of 'the fact that the vessels carried large quantities of bullion, coupled with stories of mutiny, rape and murder . . .' (Stanbury 1987: 105). While it needed to respond to such public interest, the Museum had no specialists in the field of history let alone maritime archaeology. There was no legal framework for the recovery of shipwreck material and indeed the Museum had no legal responsibility to act as a custodian for shipwreck material. There was a need, therefore, to establish an institutional framework to respond to the finds and to the public interest in them. As we shall see, it was the Museum's traditional scientific research paradigm which provided the foundation.

The first step was to change the Museum Act so that the Museum became the legal repository for all maritime archaeological material as well as responsible for carrying out research on the material itself (Museum Act 1964). This meant the Museum had to develop expertise in the area and seek outside advice in order to do so. It did this primarily on a scientific model, looking for advice on practical issues for raising, preserving and documenting the shipwrecks. Questions about the wider social significance of the material did not receive the same degree of attention.

The original Historical Material Advisory Committee was composed of archaeologists from the University of Western Australia, members of the diving community, museum staff from the indigenous and natural history areas as well as library staff. The members of the committee were carefully chosen for their technical expertise, particularly in adapting land-based archaeological processes to the maritime environment. The Minutes of the first meeting in December 1964 record that this committee was responsible for advising 'the Museum Board on practical issues which would arise as a result of the amendment to the Museum Act' (in McCarthy 1993). These responsibilities included the power to decide which wrecks should be added to the schedule of Historic Wrecks, devising the museum's procedures for recording and documenting all maritime archaeological material and working with the Museum to educate the general public on the new responsibilities of the museum so as to avoid looting of shipwrecks.[7] There appears to have been little concern with interpreting the historical significance of the material raised from the seabed or with how it might be displayed. That the Museum did not appoint a maritime archaeologist or even a maritime historian at this stage is indicative of their narrow approach to this material at the time.

In 1966–7, the Museum decided to restructure its departments, partly in response to the emergence of maritime archaeology. Accordingly, the Museum divided its research areas into two departments – the Division of Natural Science and the Division of Human Studies. The latter included Anthropology, Archaeology, Arms and Armour and History. According to its first head, Dr Jack Hinton, 'the most important field of History in which the Museum is interested at present is that of Dutch shipping and wrecks on the Western Australian

Coast'.[8] Throughout Hinton's tenure, however, the wreck programme was administered by technical rather than curatorial staff.

At the time of Hinton's retirement two issues emerged. The first was a realization on the part of the Museum that public interest in history had broadened beyond shipwrecks and that the Museum could not fulfil its responsibilities in this area through a single curatorial staff member.[9] At the same time, there was 'considerable press publicity' over the ability of the Museum to conduct fieldwork on the shipwrecks (Green 1979). The University of Western Australia became particularly active in questioning the Museum's ability to carry out its administrative duties in relation to the wrecks programme at this time (Green 1991). The University prepared the ground for greater involvement in the Museum's shipwreck programme by announcing a special research fund for research into maritime archaeology to be jointly managed by itself and the Museum.[10] The emphasis of this fund was on research on the preservation of maritime archaeological material – a highly specialized and scientific area of research.

The Museum responded to this pressure in three ways. One was to expand the staff of the Division of Human Studies. The second response was to change the make-up of the advisory committee and give it stronger powers. This would take into account the fact that the committee would now be 'co-ordinating research and the expenditure of its research funds'.[11] A new Joint Committee on Maritime History and Archaeology was inaugurated in June 1970. As well as stronger powers, the Committee increased its representation from the University of Western Australia.[12] In fact, it was answerable to both the Museum and the University.[13] Third, the Museum established its first branch museum in Fremantle, also in 1970. Located in a former mental asylum, this museum had a special brief to cover maritime history using the shipwreck material. Called the Fremantle Museum, it was described by Mike McCarthy, a senior curator in maritime archaeology in these term:

> its' [sic] exhibitions focussed, on the award winning building, it's [sic] former inmates, early Fremantle, life in the colonial period, life on the Swan, the pearling, whaling and port industries, including two historic boats in the courtyard. Three shipwrecks (one Dutch and two colonial) also featured. It was a very successful multi-faceted offering, presenting the history of Fremantle, maritime history and maritime archaeology in a holistic fashion.
>
> (McCarthy 1997a: 1–2)

This holistic approach was largely due to the efforts of the new history curator, David Hutchinson.

The Museum's efforts to professionalize its maritime archaeological programmes received a further boost when it decided to appoint a curator of Maritime Archaeology in 1971. This appointee was Jeremy Green. Under his leadership and with the help of the Committee, a much tighter focus developed. According to Green himself,

> In the 1970s the objectives of the Department of Maritime Archaeology
> was to establish an active maritime archaeological programme, to train
> Departmental staff in maritime archaeological procedures and to contain
> the problems relating to the on-going looting and interference of the
> Dutch wreck sites.
>
> (Green 1991: 2)

With the support of the Committee, Green was able to expand the staff, slowly
recruiting scientifically trained personnel to replace the former technical staff
(divers) (Green 1991: 2).

At the same time, the Western Australian Museum also created a Department
of Conservation located at the Fremantle Museum. While the department
served the entire Museum, it developed a special research interest in the preservation of maritime archaeological material. In an alliance which still exists,
maritime archaeology curators worked alongside conservators, developing a
number of innovative techniques for the conservation and display of shipwreck
materials. Their work on the preservation of *Batavia*'s timbers became internationally recognized. The results of this partnership are of paramount importance to the identity of the Maritime Museum, and are often referred to by staff
as central to their research focus as in the following example:

> The scientific research and development resulting from the conservation of
> maritime objects has been of substantial benefit to the Museum's natural
> science, history and ethnographic collections. Furthermore, by allowing its
> maritime archaeologists and conservators to participate in projects
> throughout Australia and overseas, the Museum has reaped the benefit
> of a wider source of knowledge and recognition of its own expertise.
> The latter, in itself, has played an important role in attracting research
> funding, bringing the appropriate cudos [*sic*] to the institution as a place
> of scientific research. . . . In addition, these same factors have enabled the
> Museum to participate as an educational and training facility for students
> at both primary and tertiary levels thereby increasing its status and func-
> tion as an informant and educator for the public.
>
> (Stanbury 1987: 111)

The focus on scientific research, cemented through the alliance between
maritime archaeology and the department of conservation, distinguished
maritime archaeology from history more generally and even from maritime
history. Part of the story of the rise of maritime archaeology was its effort
to distinguish itself from its closest competitor at the time, the Department of
History. Maritime archaeology was at first a sub-section of the latter. Hence
that Department's exhibitions at the Fremantle History Museum combined
Dutch shipwreck material with material relating to the settlement of WA as well
as colonial maritime history. The effect was to bring the Dutch material into a
wider story about the European history of Western Australia.

In the mid-1970s, however, the Department of History began to expand its
interests to the broader history of settlement. In 1976 an exhibition dealing

mainly with colonial history was opened in the main Museum itself. Inevitably, this meant competition for the public's interest as well as for institutional resources. At the same time, Maritime Archaeology was developing a strong reputation for its techniques of shallow water archaeology, new preservation techniques as well as the discovery of a number of other shipwrecks. This led to arguments about the need for specialized displays. The result was the creation of a separate branch Museum in 1979 for the display of maritime archaeological material and the separation of Maritime Archaeology from the Department of History.

In achieving a separate status, the maritime archaeology programme was now free to continue to develop its own programme without reference to the wider work of the Division of Human Studies. It did so primarily by defining maritime archaeology as a science concerned with the techniques of recovery and preservation. One of the effects was the loss of maritime history as a binding mechanism between maritime archaeology and history more generally. Even in the mid-1980s, when the Maritime Museum began to establish a collection of historical boats, this remained the case. While the Maritime Museum created a separate Department of Maritime History, this department was under-resourced, with only a shed for the purpose of storage and display. There was little or no dialogue between the two programmes, either at the level of research or in terms of exhibition programmes.

If this history establishes why research was such a strong part of the Museum's identity, it does not fully explain why the focus was on Dutch shipwrecks in its exhibitions. It is important here to consider the prevalence of a consensus model of history in Western Australia at the time of the Museum's development and the opportunities it provided Western Australia to fulfil a need to define a distinctive identity. The most important exponent of this model was Geoffrey Bolton, who was on the Museum's Advisory Committee. Bolton saw Western Australia's history as a narrative of progress largely lacking in conflict. As Tom Stannage has characterized it in this narrative, 'in Western Australia, unlike the eastern colonies, men and their families worked together harmoniously against an intractable earth and a tough climate ... social conflict was muted or entirely absent' (Stannage 1993: 1). It was an interpretation that celebrated narratives of discovery and exploration and glorified the process of settlement. Within this framework, the presence of the Dutch in Western Australian waters becomes a precursor to a long narrative about the development of this region through a European presence. This much was evident in the first museum in Fremantle which linked the Dutch shipwrecks to colonial history as Bailey (1979: 21) makes clear:

> Three centuries of Western Australian history was unfolded there; on the Ground Floor the story of the Dutch ships that came to these shores in the 17th and 18th centuries is illustrated with cannon, coins, pottery and other relics recovered from the *Batavia*, the *Gilt Dragon* and other Dutch merchant ships that foundered on this coast in the 17th and 19th centuries; old maps and engravings from Holland of the period will give

an understanding of our early link with Europe. The visits of sealing and whaling ships, the arrival of British colonists, and the convict era, and many developments of this century is also summarized in displays. A feature of the museum is exhibits on maritime history, from the days of sail to present times. Maritime industries such as whaling, pearling, and crayfishing are treated in displays on the upper floor.

As Tony Bennett (1988b) points out in his article 'Out of which past', early European explorers were very useful in elongating the European history of Australia beyond 1788. In historicizing the Australian landscape within European history, the focus on Dutch shipwrecks became a tool for the new national histories that were then emerging. But if they were useful to the nation, they were also especially useful to Western Australia giving it a privileged place as the site of the earliest European contact. This is in line with a long tradition within Western Australian public culture that emphasizes Western Australia's distinctiveness from the rest of Australia. It is a tradition which underlined not only a conservative account of Western Australian history but which also received public support through considerable resistance to the notion of Federation and an attempt to secede in the 1930s. By focusing on Dutch shipwrecks, then, the Western Australian Museum achieved two things – it developed a unique expertise, contributing to a significant area of historical research and it built a prominent place for Western Australia within Australian history. This is evident in the Museum's own attempt to articulate the significance of its focus on Dutch shipwrecks:

> Fremantle, 'gateway to the West', has witnessed the birth and growth of Western Australia. Dutch seamen saw the mouth of the Swan River, where Fremantle now stands, in the 17th and 18th centuries; and it was through Fremantle that settlers and cargoes came to the Swan River Colony even before settlements were established at Adelaide, the Port Philip District and Morton Bay.
>
> (Bailey 1979: 18)

It was a history worth celebrating when the Maritime Museum opened in 1979, Western Australia's sesquicentenary year.

Within the Maritime Museum itself, the importance of Dutch shipwrecks to Australian historiography has taken on something of a mythical status. Thus, in a 1987 article about the history of the Maritime Museum, curator Myra Stanbury argued that 'In its twenty five years of progress, the Museum has alerted the Australian people to the value of their maritime history. It has promoted a greater awareness of the maritime events concerning the European discovery, exploration and settlement of Australia' (Stanbury 1987: 104). More recently the importance of Dutch shipwrecks to the Museum's research profile and identity was reflected in the focus group discussions' answers to a question on the specific identity of the existing Maritime Museum. One of the most senior and long standing curators at the WA Maritime Museum claimed that the museum had established that it was the Dutch and not Captain Cook who had discovered Australia:

It's been the catalyst for . . . heightening awareness nationally and internationally about this subject of Australia, that it wasn't Captain Cook
who discovered Australia and my generation grew up with that. And while
it's not told in the gallery, it's been a catalyst for a lot of people to publish
a lot of material, both for schools, you know, primary, secondary, tertiary,
and then there's documentaries, books, and so it has acted as a catalyst,
very much, I think, in terms of stimulating other people outside of the
organisation to also incorporate that information into the curriculum for
schools.

(Focus Group Discussion, 20 May 1998)

Implications for the curatorial culture at the Museum

There are two main implications of this history on the culture of the Maritime
Museum. The first is a tendency to privilege scholarly modes of communication, a tendency that resulted in a relative lack of interpretation in the exhibitions. Second, the stress on Dutch shipwrecks made it harder for the museum
to keep up with changing historiographies and museum practices. This was a
problem that also made it difficult for the existing museum to respond to the
need for new historical narratives. This problem has become particularly severe
as Western Australia, and particularly the Perth/Fremantle region, has been
increasingly oriented towards a post-industrial global economy.

The focus on research meant that museum staff were completely occupied by
recovery, documentation, preservation and scholarly interpretation. Their
attention was turned almost exclusively towards professional issues. One of the
few exceptions to this is the Museum's wreck trail programme in which wreck
sites are identified for divers and on the coastline for other visitors. In this
programme wreck sites are almost considered part of an open-air museum. The
overall narrowness of the Museum's focus, however, is evident in a remark
made in response to a request to define the value of museums in general at the
focus group discussion with staff:

I think we shouldn't forget about us, all the people who are actually doing
things in a museum. I think perhaps the very most important thing about
a museum is the process that everyone gets involved in and that's not just
us who are paid staff, but it's also the volunteers and . . . other people who
get involved in any way. It's only through that involvement that a museum
is of any value, I think.

(Focus Group Discussion, 20 May 1998)

It is the internal activity of the museum and the way in which this activity
brings people together which is of significance, not necessarily how this
activity is communicated to others or even understood by others.[14] The highly
specialized nature of the work conducted within the museum generates its
own sense of community, a sense that extends to those who decide to participate in the museum's dream. The romanticism attached to the field of maritime

archaeology and the aura of shipwrecks generates a group of people who are completely committed to their work, to the material they raise from the seabed, and who have a sense of a joint enterprise. For them, the museum is special because the nature of their enterprise is so specialized and different from that of other museums.

Such a focus was sustainable while there was a public culture supporting the notion that public institutions such as museums were there to educate and develop specialized knowledge. The production of knowledge was understood to be a separate activity that did not require direct contact with the public. With the change in public culture, however, the weaknesses of the Museum's public programmes began to become more apparent. In the late 1990s there was an increasing expectation that museums would be entertaining, up to date and relevant to diverse cultural groups. At the same time, curators were expected to be specialists in exhibition development, a task that increasingly involves particular communication skills. The specialist museum had become something of a luxury in an environment where communication meant everything. Some of the staff became aware of this in the focus group discussion I held in May 1998, at the height of debates within the Museum about the future relationship between the Department of Maritime Archaeology and the proposed new museum. They pointed out that the Museum's exhibitions were aimed at gathering support for the professional practice of maritime archaeology rather than communicating the results of the research as historical narrative:

> I think what this museum's done far more is promote maritime archaeology, our profession basically, what we do – recover objects and try to discover something about the past from those objects. But really it has promoted maritime archaeology, it hasn't done much to promote the maritime history of Western Australia. That's something that's been going on – the books – well Graham and especially Frank Broeze, that have tried to emphasise that this place wouldn't have existed if it hadn't have been for the ships coming here – it was absolutely crucial to the existence of Western Australia. And we haven't actually addressed that in our displays or whatever and yet those ideas have been growing over the last quarter of a century.
>
> (Focus Group Discussion, 20 May 1998)

In prioritizing research over exhibitions, the Museum also prioritized scholarly genres over more popular forms of communication. Their contribution to Australian historiography was felt not through exhibitions but through publications and documentaries. This meant that while it was significant, the impact was also dispersed. This made it difficult for staff to point at their exhibitions and say – look, there it is, there is our contribution to Western Australian history and to Australian history more generally. As another staff member commented in support of his colleague's statement that the Museum 'hasn't done much to promote the maritime history of Western Australia':

> I don't think this museum actually does that – it doesn't actually give them a story about it, it doesn't actually tell them. It gives the evidence but it

doesn't actually give them the story about it, it doesn't actually say the Dutch were here first or the French were here first or whatever. There's evidence of it in the collection, but there's no story that's telling people.

(Focus Group Discussion, 20 May 1998)

In valuing research above communication, or in Hartleyan terms, didactics over drama, the Museum failed to keep track of the wider context in which it was embedded. Its scholarly publications gave it an international standing and Federal Government funding for research, yet it failed to maintain full public and political support for its shipwreck programme.

If the prioritizing of research over other museum functions resulted in an institutional culture that found it difficult to tell 'stories' through exhibitions, the prioritizing of Dutch shipwreck archaeology as pre-eminent within the field of maritime archaeology also had long term repercussions. In essence, its continued priority over time eventually put the Museum out of step with changes in museological practice as well as historiography. From the 1970s, Australian historians developed research interests on labour, gender and race issues as well as the history of popular culture. This took them away from historical narratives of discovery towards an examination of the process of settlement and nation-building. In part, the difference was an explicit politicization of historical narratives. The focus was now on ordinary people and their experiences as articulated through the categories of class, gender and race.

This change in historiography tied in very well with the new museology and its concern to establish more meaningful relations between museums and communities, a point not lost on Mike McCarthy, the curator responsible for colonial maritime archaeology. In raising and preserving the engine of a steam iron ship called *Xantho*, he and his team had already made their mark through scientific developments. As a pamphlet on the museum proclaims, 'the Museum's excavation of the SS *Xantho* and the successful recovery and conservation of its engine has proved that iron and steam shipwrecks are an equally valuable field of study' (n.d.). McCarthy perceived, however, that the *Xantho* had a significance beyond the archaeological process itself. It lay in the history the engine could be used to tell. According to McCarthy, 'The *Xantho*/Broadhurst story has much more to offer than the archaeological and conservation breakthrough that it represents. From it we are led to an extraordinarily wide range of relevant issues' (McCarthy 1996: 1).

The *Xantho* story afforded an opportunity to address Western Australia's colonial maritime history through maritime archaeological remains. In a discussion paper that put forward his vision for interpreting the engine through public display, McCarthy suggested that it could be used to interpret a wide range of themes: 'The process of European settlement, Sea transport in the colony, The pearling industry, Aborigines and the sea, The introduction of Malay labour, Steamship owning and operating' (McCarthy 1996: 1). He was also open to involvement from the Department of Social History in displays on colonial maritime history. Sadly, his proposals came to naught as the Museum decided to develop a travelling exhibition in partnership with Holland on Dutch explorers. An opportunity to link maritime archaeology with maritime history on post-settlement themes was missed and with it an opportunity to bring the museum's exhibitions up to date with contemporary historiography and museology.

The focus on the pre-history of the state made it very difficult for the museum to demonstrate how it represented the maritime history of the state and its culturally diverse population. This omission became particularly important as cultural tourism developed. As I argued in the last chapter, the marketing of place has become an important marker of cultural capital. Achieved either through renowned art collections or through claims to represent a society's cultural identity, this is part of a complex strategy to redevelop backwaters into places that attract international investment and new populations from amongst the professional class. Museums are important not only for attracting tourists but also for attracting new residents in search of a distinctive sense of place.

In the case of history museums, such a strategy requires a focus on people and their experiences. This did not fit well with the Maritime Museum's under-standing of maritime archaeology, a point that emerged in the Focus Group Discussion. For one staff member, maritime archaeology was a set of skills and scientific knowledge which enabled them to bring up objects and parts of ships from shipwrecks, conserve them and display them:

> For me, maritime archaeology is a profession, a trade, a science even. It's a series of processes that recover material, certainly the research for mate-rial, but it's also the process of doing it, of gaining information, and gaining material in particular.
>
> (Focus Group Discussion, 20 May 1998)

The staff also showed some awareness that this approach placed them outside of current developments. Referring to the increasing practice in some museums to deal with what they termed 'controversial issues' they pointed out that they themselves remained apolitical in their interpretations:

> I think in a sense that maritime museums have been one of those groups that's been out of the political controversy area and therefore what's tended to happen with maritime museums is we're right at the extreme of the group that doesn't get involved in controversial topics.
>
> (Focus Group Discussion, 20 May 1998)

When pushed to explain this statement a little more, the staff member quoted here argued that the nature of the objects on display did not lend themselves to political or social analysis. Maritime archaeological material, especially Dutch shipwrecks, was inherently apolitical:

> A shipwreck is not something which gets heavily political in terms of Liberal or Labor or any such thing and so we've tended not to encounter really controversial issues. I suppose if we were to deal with, let's say, a slave ship, and have a strong emphasis on what's going on with that industry there, something like that would get us into controversial social

issues and so forth, but so far, with the Dutch shipwrecks, which has been the emphasis of what we've got, I suppose in terms of themes about humanity, were . . . the Dutch who went onto the Abrolhos sort of a typical group or not . . . there's not been any sort of depth of analysis of the people concerned, I think that's true.

(Focus Group Discussion, 20 May 1998)

Such an institutional orientation placed the Department of Maritime Archaeology in a very difficult position when plans for a new maritime museum with *Australia II* rather than the *Batavia* as the 'jewel in the crown' emerged. The problem was that the 'people' had become a crucial rhetorical point of reference. This was especially clear in governmental discourses about the need for a new maritime museum to represent more recent history, a greater diversity of communities and most importantly to be oriented towards a tourist market, which, in their minds, necessitated both popular content and popular modes of address.

The proposal for a new maritime museum argued the need for a broad 'peoples' history of Western Australia but in a difference sense from that which animated the revisionist historiography of the 1970s and 1980s. Rather than dealing with historical experience through the lenses of class, race and gender, the proposed museum centred on a conservative narrative of progress focused on leisure. Hence the important place of *Australia II* as the motivating force behind getting the new museum established. As the title of the interactive with which I began this chapter put it, the development of the state was one that saw the displacement of hardship and the emergence of the long weekend.

The new museum, it was argued, would centre on understanding people's experiences of the sea, exploring the various ways in which they engaged with and were affected by it. In this context, the museum was to be not only about people, it was also for the people. This was in line with the overall concept for the redevelopment of Victoria Quay, a concept that attempts to develop the cultural infrastructure of Fremantle for both tourists and the increasingly professional or middle class population. This meant that the existing museum suddenly found itself out of favour in both content and mode of address. The model of historiography which had animated the Museum's research culture was not capable of responding to new populist demands. It dealt with the origins of the nation rather than the experiences of its people. The Museum was being asked to redefine the special nature of Western Australia in ways that focused on more recent experiences and on narratives of success. At the same time, the value placed on entertainment made its research focus seem alienating. The Museum was being asked to change the way in which it communicated with the public.

Existing curatorial staff responded angrily to these developments, understanding them as a move away from education towards entertainment, from culture to popular culture, from a public facility to crass commercialism. In order to understand how this was the case, it is necessary to outline something of the proposal for a new museum and the response from the maritime archaeological staff.

Celebrations of Western Australia

One way to begin to understand why the proposed new museum became the focus of so much anger within the Museum is to explore the metaphorical associations produced around the centrality of *Australia II* as the rationale for the new museum.

Australia II is the Australian yacht which won the America's Cup contest in 1983. The yacht was built in Fremantle and funded by a local business entrepreneur, Alan Bond, who became one of Australia's most famous businessmen, not least because he ended up in prison for embezzlement and fraud. The yacht is also significant in local history because its success at the 1983 Cup led to the next contest being held in Fremantle during 1987, the first time in 150 years that the Cup races had been held outside the USA. Both races were defining moments for Western Australia and helped to define its difference from the rest of Australia. The hosting of the 1987 America's Cup led to the revitalization of Fremantle as a modern tourist-oriented city, capitalizing on a rich nineteenth-century streetscape and proximity to the ocean. The America's Cup offered a golden opportunity to project the city into the new global space discussed in Chapter 2. Just as in Darling Harbour, the proposed new museum was to be part of a revamped maritime precinct, oriented to tourists and day trippers, the only difference being that Victoria Quay is located within a still functioning port. It was also a means for the Premier to put Western Australia on the global map by showcasing a special achievement of the state.

This aim is reflected in the literature associated with the new museum which promoted it as an icon building, right at the entrance to Fremantle's Harbour, and as the flagship of the Victoria Quay redevelopment. While emphasizing the significance of local history, the rhetoric also borrowed consciously from that of Darling Harbour as is evident in the *Draft Masterplan*:

> The plan brings the city closer to the waterfront and provides it with a new focus. . . .

> The plan's centerpiece, a new Maritime Museum, will provide Fremantle with an international symbol of Western Australia's rich maritime history and one of the very few museums built as part of a major commercial port.
>
> (Cox Howlett & Bailey Woodland 1998)

The use of *Australia II* to define Western Australia was of course quite controversial, particularly given its association with the disgraced Alan Bond. A Fremantle city councillor, for example, had this to say:

> I like many others have no interest in seeing *Australia II* interpreted as a pinnacle of sporting endeavour. It is only one aspect of Fremantle's long maritime history and is an eloquent statement of the 80s including the close collusion of government and business.
>
> (Councillor Thompson, Fremantle City Council Minutes, 15 June 1998)

The rhetorical framing of the new museum as an exciting global drawcard had two important consequences for the existing Museum. The first was that it became characterized as a 'shipwreck' museum. Behind the new name was the implication that it was behind the times. Not surprisingly, many staff resented this characterization and moved to argue against it. The second was an increasing exposure to global comparisons. Many staff began to associate the new museum development with an attempt to emulate other maritime museums. This was often equated to 'pandering to the masses', becoming completely tourist oriented and developing displays without any meaningful research. For the Department of Maritime Archaeology, in particular, such a move was regarded as a death knell. Let's deal with each of these issues in turn.

The emergence of a 'Shipwrecks Museum'

The emergence of an unofficial new name for the existing Maritime Museum was a response to the need to develop a clear identity between the two maritime museums, even though, institutionally, they were one museum. Its practical effect, however, was twofold. First, it effectively separated the two departments of the museum – Maritime Archaeology and the much smaller Maritime History Department – into two separate museums, making it easier to avoid any need to rethink the enterprise of the museum as a whole. Second, the door was left open for a definition of the Shipwrecks Museum as lacking a clear notion of history and hence without a strong platform of public relevance. The positioning of the Museum as irrelevant to the main story that needed to be told was foreshadowed with the Director's attempt to raise the level of excitement about the new museum while supporting the Premier's vision:

> I will talk about my vision for the new facility. There is a need for the WA Maritime Museum to tell the West Australian story – to raise issues about those industries, lifestyle interests and heroes so well known in the history books and newspapers but not represented in any museum. The Shipwrecks Museum is about the beginnings of European involvement with the continent – an exciting story about a remote and distant past – but the story we have yet to tell is about local people. It will also explore questions about how we relate to the outside world. Trade, the port, the Navy, shipbuilding, recreation, immigration, fishing, oil and gas, the State's place in the Indian Ocean: these maritime themes we will deal with from a social history perspective. While avoiding a narrow technological approach, the new museum will address the importance of maritime technological developments to this State. . . .
>
> So we have a highly successful but exotic Shipwrecks Museum, and the aspiration for a directly relevant modern maritime history museum: the Maritime Industries Museum.[15]

> (Henderson 1998: 43–44)

History and present day politics come together in these passages. At one level, they reflect a marginalization of a specialized research culture. To be exotic is to be a luxury, serving no rational aim. The new museum, by contrast, does serve a rational aim. It narrates the progress of the state as a function of its maritime history. The celebratory nature of the historical narrative invoked in these public pronouncements, however, illustrates how this museum has effectively bypassed the revisionist historiography of the last twenty years and is merely updating the consensus model of history. An important consequence is the lack of an opportunity to establish links between the two departments within the new museum. For example, the 'Shipwrecks Museum's' activities in colonial maritime archaeology are not represented in the public rhetoric about either site.

It was difficult, however, for Museum staff to recognize their own implication in these problems. Occasional statements indicated momentary glimpses but these were lost in the general effort to preserve the research orientation of the Department of Maritime Archaeology. In one discussion, for example, a difference emerged as to the role of exhibitions in ensuring the long term survival of maritime archaeology. One staff member suggested that 'exhibitions count. They will ensure survival of the department.' Others, however, discounted the suggestion, even going so far as to suggest that 'at the end of the day we must ensure the survival of department – exhibitions don't matter' (Maritime Archaeology Meeting, 12 May 1998). What mattered, in the words of a junior member of staff, was that the Department should make a 'strong push for process of research here' (ibid.). In their eyes and in those of some of the senior members of staff, exhibitions were not part of the research culture they were fighting for.

Attitudes towards the new museum

In defending research as the proper focus of the museum, there was a tendency among staff to deride the new project. In line with other contemporary museum developments, the new museum adopted a thematic approach. From the perspective of maritime archaeology, this looked incoherent. What was positively described by the promoters of the new museum as a smorgasbord with something for everyone was, in the eyes of others, 'a real hotchpotch' (Maritime Archaeology Meeting, 19 May 1998). The new museum's orientation to local stories was further interpreted as merely a variant of narratives available elsewhere. 'Only the names of the local "heroes" differ' (Stanbury 1997: 1). 'This is the boat that Jack built; wasn't he clever. He lived in Western Australia' (2).

These criticisms substituted for reflection on the limitations of the existing focus on Dutch shipwrecks. Little thought was given, for example, to the need to think about modes of communication and their appropriateness for different types of audiences or the need to indicate an awareness of the political implications of historical narratives. In failing to engage with revisionist history, many museum staff were unable to reflect on the historiographical implications of existing and proposed exhibitions. The result was an inability on the part of maritime archaeologists to contribute to exhibitions as well as an inability on the part of the museum as a whole to engage with the political nature of the new proposal and to develop strategies to deal with the problem. An opportunity to develop a broader, more reflexive understanding of maritime archaeology and integrate it into Western Australian history was lost. In effect, their response was simply reactive.

The result is that maritime archaeology has been pushed to one side. While the Shipwrecks Museum continues to exist for now, the institutional resources, financial and otherwise, are focused on the new development. The long term future of the Shipwrecks Museum and its programmes is unknown.

Conclusions

If this case study has shown how suspicious responses to changes in museums are about a lot more than the incursion of market forces into the sphere of culture, it has also raised questions which are very difficult to answer. There are some serious issues in the revolt against change I have just described. It is not simply that the staff were being asked to develop exhibitions in areas in which they had no expertise. Nor was the revolt simply about historiographical concerns. At a more fundamental level, traditional forms of expertise were themselves in question. An internal focus on research and collection development was no longer sufficient. Instead, curators were being asked to become expert popular communicators. One example of the importance of communication to the new museum enterprise was the early decision to employ the Museum's head of education as the curator of the Leisure gallery whose main focus was *Australia II*. None of the maritime archaeologists ended up working for the new exhibition development team. And very little, if any, of their collections and expertise has made it to the new museum. Other indicators are the fact that almost none of the new curators are experts in maritime history, and few have extensive experience as curators. Instead, the museum appears to be relying on an external firm of designers to ensure that the new museum has the appropriate tone. Early indications are that the museum will be visually exciting and dynamic, and that the design will be an important carrier of a celebratory narrative. This is despite considerable efforts to attend to issues of cultural diversity, particularly in the museum's interpretation of Western Australia's fishing industry and in the attempt to place Western Australia within the Indian Ocean region.

Is it possible to preserve research communities in a climate in which public forms of communication are increasingly taking on spectacular forms? What is the future of specialist knowledge in museums if curators are now required to be generalists (at least in history museums) and be communicators rather than experts in a specific discipline? Should there be a distinction between curators (experts) and exhibition content developers? Should we be thinking about ways to establish relationships between experts and 'smilers'? Or can experts learn to communicate to those outside their field? What can traditional forms of knowledge production based on a research model offer?

If these questions indicate a sympathy for some of the negative implications of current changes, another set of questions indicate a sympathy with those who argue for the need to change. There is, at the very least, a need to think seriously about the ways in which knowledge is produced and then communicated. Some of these questions might be:

- What strategies would ensure that research institutions remain vibrant and relevant?
- What is the role of public institutions such as museums in the process of knowledge production and dissemination?
- How can we ensure the communication of expert knowledge to as wide an audience as possible in ways that are relevant to them?

A related set of questions concern management processes:

- Very simply, how did this museum, and no doubt many others, become so alienated?
- Why was it allowed to drift for so long in a direction which was ultimately a dead end?
- Could the process of change have been better managed?
- Are there ways in which specialists can be turned into translators without losing their own sense of who they are and what they stand for?

The politics of any one situation may make it difficult to operate within a set of guidelines based on general principles. Nevertheless, there are some useful lessons that can be abstracted from the specific experiences of the Western Australian Maritime Museum. These have to do with the general policy contexts in which proposals for new developments occur, specific management strategies for dealing with change and the need for advocacy.

One of the problems of this specific development was the way in which it occurred within a general museum policy vacuum. In the state of Western Australia, state museums come under the Ministry of Arts and Culture. In recent changes, the directors of these state museums are directly responsible to the Minister, making it very difficult to preserve the principle of arm's length from party political processes. The problem is further exacerbated by the lack of a state-wide museum policy. There is no framework within which proposals for new museums can be assessed. Nor is there a policy framework to advance the cause of museums more generally, by, for example, having a state-wide government grant system. The result of this lack of policy at a state government level was not only the pressure to respond to the Premier's vision. It was also the lack of pressure to rethink the nature and purpose of the Maritime Museum as a result of the proposal for a new museum. The Maritime Museum was never forced to either merge the two sites or to think through their relationship to one another. This was both intellectually and economically irresponsible. A general recommendation then is the need for museum professionals everywhere to ensure that there are museum policies at a governmental level which impose the need to critically assess new developments.

These problems were not helped by a lack of clear directives from within the museum – both on site and from the parent body which has ultimate responsibility for the new development. In fact, the managerial problems between the Maritime Museum and the Western Australian Museum were so intense that the government decided to put the whole development in the hands of the Government Property Office. This made it even more difficult to provide a framework within which the museological issues surrounding the new development could be discussed. Clear directives from within the museum management were clearly needed to ensure that the relationship between the two sites, as well as between traditional research orientations and the new demands to 'smile', were negotiated.

To expect such directions is not to underestimate the difficulties that might arise as a result of giving them. As Robert Janes (1997) indicates in his account of managing a process of change at the Glenbow Museum in Alberta, Canada, managing the move from a collections oriented institution to a public programmes oriented one is not an easy process. The difficulty of the process, however, is not an excuse for not attempting it. As he says,

> it is foolish to expect that the organizational changes at the Glenbow will not anger, frustrate and disappoint people. This is especially true when the changes go far beyond cosmetic tinkering. We are insisting upon new ways of thinking and acting which will make the organization more responsive to the communities we serve. The real question is whether or not the emotions associated with change, be they rage or elation, and the energy these emotions require, can be redirected toward the transformation of Glenbow.
>
> (Janes 1997: xvii–xviii)

What, then, might be some of the strategies that could have been used at the Western Australian Maritime Museum? The first suggestion is the need to put in place a strategy for open discussions. Such a strategy would need to be based on a clear articulation from management of the terms of the new proposal, a revision of the vision statement and mission of the museum and a very clear explanation as to their impact of the structure of the museum. These proposals would then need to be debated throughout the museum. This necessitates forums within which such discussions can take place within departments, across departments, with and without the director. It also means that there must be an opportunity to articulate anonymous responses to the proposals to avoid public showdowns between directors and their staff. Final decisions need to be taken by a group composed of senior staff once everyone has had an opportunity to play a part in the discussions. As Janes (1997) argues in relation to his experiences, it is important that all staff feel they own the process of change.

An important foundation to this strategy would be the need to spend some time reflecting upon the museum's history, discussing its present culture and weighing up both its positive and negative aspects. It is only within the context of a more reflexive museum practice that questions about the relationship between research and its communication can be discussed.

What this makes clear is that good museum management needs to be based on a sound understanding of museum histories as well as the range of current pressures on museums. Both managers and museum staff need to develop a more reflective approach to collecting and exhibition development, one that thinks about the political or ideological nuances of what is being said. Such an approach would empower curators to argue back, to recognize more clearly what is being asked of them and to develop appropriate strategies for dealing with new situations.

As well as strategies that force a complete reevaluation of the museum and its purpose, there is a need for strategies that encourage cross-disciplinary research and public programmes. The best known of these is the team approach. In some museums, this is limited to the process of exhibition development. An exhibition team is put together which includes curators from across a number of relevant disciplines, education officers, designers and conservators. While this approach helps to unify the work of various departments across a museum's public programmes and ensures that voices other than the experts are heard, it does little to challenge or modify the research culture of a museum. A more radical approach would be to completely reorganize the departmental nature of museums, so that all work was organized according to the institutional priorities and the way in which these were operationalized into specific programmes. This is what Janes (1997) calls a 'team-based' and 'project-based' organization. As he points out, it is only by reorganizing inflexible departmental structures that new ways of thinking can be implemented. Such a strategy would recognize the value of specific forms of expertise. At the same time, however, it forces these experts to communicate with others outside of their field. This is the case not only within the work teams themselves but also in terms of their work objectives – to communicate with those outside of the institution.

At the same time, all of these strategies need to be supported by specialized training, particularly for staff in senior positions. It is unreasonable to expect staff whose experience has been limited to their professional expertise to suddenly understand and support the requirements of an institution focused on public programmes. They need training in project management, interpersonal communication skills, conflict management resolution, as well as the opportunity and the encouragement to develop a reflective approach to museological practices.

While these suggestions are not exhaustive they represent a step towards managing the process of change in ways which do not exclude staff. It is important to recognize, however, that attempts to include and make joint decisions do not necessarily result in compliant staff. There will always be those who resist change in the belief that the values they hold dear are more important. If those values are a threat to the survival of the institution and its public relevance there may well be a need to develop strategies for implementing redundancies.

The next chapter moves from a focus on understanding and managing the internal community of the museum in a context of change to a focus on relations between museums and communities.

4

'A place for all of us'? Museums and communities

'A place for all of us'?

One of the ways in which contemporary museums are attempting to challenge dominant views of the museum as a site of power relations is to invoke and encourage new relations between museum and communities. As a movement, this phenomenon can be broadly defined as the 'New Museology'. It has adherents across a variety of museums but is especially strong in contemporary art galleries and in museums based in the disciplines of anthropology and history. It also has supporters amongst museum critics writing from outside the museum.

New Museologists question a museology that focuses on museum processes and ask instead for a focus on the political dimensions of museum work (Karp *et al.* 1992, Vergo 1989, Weil 1990). Quite often, this political dimension is encapsulated in a call for a greater focus on the relation between museums and communities. The centrality of 'community' in these accounts of the purpose of museums tends to associate the concept of community with radical democracy and resistance to the dominant culture. Communities tend to be understood as existing outside of government and even in opposition to it. By placing 'community' at the heart of the museum enterprise, the argument runs, it will be possible to overcome the role of museums as hegemonic institutions. In giving voice to the powerless, a process of self-discovery and empowerment will take place in which the curator becomes a facilitator rather than a figure of authority. It is a position which is succinctly summarized by Viv Szekeres (1995), Director of the Migration Museum in Adelaide, who claims that her museum strives to make 'A place for all of us'.

This call to bring communities into the space of the museum is criticized by Tony Bennett (1998a) in his book, *Culture: A Reformer's Science*. Bennett's criticisms are based on a questioning of the way in which this call relies on an opposition between the community and the museum. In querying whether 'museums should be transformed into instruments of community empowerment and dialogue', he is intent on suggesting that we recognize instead that museums shape and regulate the population in 'ways that reflect the genesis of cultural politics from within the processes of government' (Bennett 1998a: 195).

In wanting to dislodge any hint of an opposition between the interests of the community and those of government, Bennett is aiming to remove the connotations of resistance which attach themselves to the notion of community. The intent is to offer a more positive reading of the cultural work of governmental institutions such as museums. For Bennett, the history of museums is one of civic reform. Museums are pedagogical institutions that play a role alongside the penitentiary, the police force and slum clearance in reforming newly formed populations into a modern citizenry. While this role was developed in the nineteenth century, in the context of a rapid growth of industrial cities, it remains relevant today even if the specific aims of reform have changed. If, in the nineteenth century, the aim was to instill a sense of morality and good behaviour in the hearts and minds of citizens, the aim today is to foster an acceptance of cultural diversity.

There are two implications of Bennett's argument which need to be drawn out in the context of a discussion of the relations between museums and communities. The first is that it becomes impossible to maintain an opposition between cultural and governmental practices. Cultural workers, such as intellectuals and museum curators, can be seen, according to Bennett, as 'cultural technicians', as people who work within government rather than in opposition to it. Rather than 'seeing government and cultural politics as the *vis-à-vis* of one another', Bennett argues, we should 'locate the work of intellectuals within the field of government' seeing their political role as 'being committed to "modifying the functioning of culture by means of technical adjustments to its governmental deployment"' (1998a: 195). The work of museums is to tinker with 'practical arrangements within the sphere of government – that is, the vast array of cultural institutions, public and private, that are involved in the cultural shaping and regulation of the population' (1998a: 195).

The second implication is that museums need to be understood not as institutions which represent communities and cultures – which create a 'place for all of us' – but as institutions which actually *produce* the very notion of community and culture. This argument goes back to an earlier article 'The political rationality of the museum', discussed in Chapter 1. Bennett argued in that article that the very aim of achieving equal representation is based on a faulty logic (Bennett 1990, 1995). The desire to achieve equal representation can only *remain* a desire, he argues, for there will always be some group who will find itself unrepresented. As a consequence, museums will always be open to the charge of being unrepresentative and therefore undemocratic. It would be better, he suggests, to understand their role as producing a culture that supports the political principles underpinning the very notion of representation.

Bennett's recent work on museums (1995, 1998a) is part of a larger intellectual project within Australian cultural studies which, during the late 1980s and early 1990s, sought to transform cultural studies into *cultural policy* studies. Developed mainly out of the Key Centre for Cultural and Media Policy Studies at Griffith University in Queensland,[1] advocates of the cultural policy position sought to move the discipline of cultural studies away from what they considered to be a romantic legacy which emphasized a revolutionary rhetoric of opposition. Like others in this school (for example, Hunter 1988, 1994 and

Cunningham 1992) Bennett opposes this legacy as reducing government to 'the interests of a ruling class or of patriarchy' (1998a: 194). He proposes that it is possible to develop a critical perspective *within* institutions that are habitually perceived as representing power or cultural authority.

Bennett's refusal to demonize the museum is a breath of fresh air in a field in which many museum practitioners find themselves besieged by critics even when trying to change museum practices. His arguments are also valuable in recognizing that museum practices involve processes of cultural *production* as well as representation. They offer a more appropriate explanation of the context of relations between museums and communities (as well as a more accurate description of curatorial work), than that offered by the model of curator as facilitator. I will demonstrate this by applying Bennett's arguments to an exhibition I curated on the Portuguese community in Perth called *Travellers and Immigrants: Portuguêses em Perth* held in the Community Access Gallery of the Fremantle History Museum and to my work as a museum consultant with local museums in Queensland.

However, I will also point towards some serious limitations in Bennett's position. Bennett's determination to do away with romantic notions of community led him to ignore dialogue between actual communities and museum policy makers and curators. There is an increasing body of work that points to the need for museums to recognize their own cultural frameworks as well as those of their audiences. There have also been numerous attempts to address this need (Burton 1999, Hooper-Greenhill 1997, 2000, Karp and Lavine 1991, Karp *et al.* 1992). One notable example has been James Clifford's work on museums, particularly the latter's essay 'Museums as contact zones' (Clifford 1997: 188–219). It is a useful example as it is one with which Bennett has openly engaged. In the course of this engagement the limitations of Bennett's arguments become clear.

This chapter considers the issues raised by the Bennett–Clifford debate. I begin in sympathy with Bennett, using his arguments to explore how the community access gallery reflects a governmental desire to *construct*, rather than simply *represent*, a culturally diverse society. Then, I explore the limits of Bennett's arguments by discussing the actual process of developing the exhibition. Here I contrast his approach with Clifford's, utilizing their points of difference to explore some of the practical issues I have encountered in my own museological experiences. I suggest that one way of avoiding romantic notions of community, while also recognizing that museums are engaged in dialogue, would be to think of museums *themselves* as communities. Finally, I demonstrate how this perspective is useful in developing policy frameworks for museums as well as in curatorial work itself.

Teaching 'civic reform': the uses of community galleries

As the most explicit manifestation of the attempt by museums to allow communities to represent themselves, community access galleries are an excellent example for testing Bennett's general arguments. Within museological circles, the established understanding is that they offer a place within the museum building in which community groups can mount their own exhibitions rather than the usual practice of allowing the museum to represent them. In some cases, community groups use the museum collection, but they more often locate their own materials, particularly in history museums. The idea is to displace the authority of the museum and to foreground *people* rather than objects. In a roundtable discussion chaired by Margaret Anderson, a number of prominent Australian curators with responsibility for community access galleries defined such spaces as giving specific communities 'an opportunity to promote themselves' (Jane Scott in Anderson 1993: 4), and to 'run things themselves' (Kevin Wilson in Anderson 1993: 5). Community galleries, like the museums they are part of, are firmly understood within a framework of access to representation (see also GLLAM 2000, Hooper-Greenhill 1997).

As Bennett might argue, however, community galleries are as much about *producing* the notion of a culturally diverse community as they are about representing it. They have almost always been initiated by museums themselves, and can easily be used to illustrate that the notion of community is produced from within government rather than being something outside of, and in opposition to, it. This is sometimes quite explicit. The Western Australian Museum (1995) outlines the aim of their community gallery at the Fremantle History Museum as demonstrating a commitment 'to providing space and facilities . . . for community groups to mount their own exhibitions reflecting the social and cultural heritage of Western Australia' (Western Australian Museum 1995). In this way the Museum hopes to 'encourage a sense of community ownership of the Museum and to foster acceptance and understanding in Western Australia's culturally diverse society' (Western Australian Museum 1995).

Policy statements such as these are not purely a response to community pressure but spring from governmental discourses of access and equity. They reflect, in Bennett's terms, an agenda of civic reform. The call to 'foster acceptance and understanding in Western Australia's culturally diverse society' is both descriptive and proscriptive. The aim is not just to achieve equal representation in museums. It is also to instruct the community on the value of cultural diversity.

Access galleries also aim to teach the communities who use them. The Western Australian Museum attempts to facilitate equal access to representation by transferring professional skills to the communities concerned. The information sheets on the use of the gallery stress that 'Museum staff work co-operatively with community groups which have booked the Community Access Gallery to ensure that exhibitions are well planned and researched, that they focus on Western Australia's social cultural heritage, and that they are well presented' (Western Australian Museum 1995). It is not only the themes of the exhibitions with which the museum is concerned. The groups which have so far used the space also reflect the same interest in the project of civic reform, representing as they do various ethnic communities, women, the disabled and so on. As well as exhibitions which have focused on the Italian, Muslim, Irish and Portuguese communities, there have also been exhibitions on coping with breast cancer, on people with Down's Syndrome and on the Country Women's Association.

Despite the rhetorical separation of the act of representation from the activity of producing that representation, the Museum and its client groups are co-producers in the imagining of community. The development of *Travellers and Immigrants* at the Fremantle History Museum's community access gallery provides an example of this process.

Representation versus production

The variety of audiences for *Travellers and Immigrants*, alone, makes it difficult to see the exhibition as simply about facilitating access to representation. It was required, from its conception, to serve a *number* of communities. There was the Portuguese community as a whole, the museum community, the university for which I worked at the time and of course the visitors to the museum including tourists, local residents and members of the Portuguese community. The exhibition had to serve the interests of all these groups, and also those of the sponsors – the Australia Foundation for Culture and the Humanities and the Western Australian Lotteries Commission.

For the Museum, as its explanatory notes on the access gallery make clear, the principal interest was to be seen to be relevant and accessible to diverse cultural communities as well as to educate the general public in the principles of cultural diversity. For the Portuguese Community Council, the exhibition was an opportunity to utilize the skills of a curator. While not ethnically Portuguese, I was born in Portugal, speak the language, have contacts within the museum community and the ability to attract financial resources not available to them on their own. For the university, the exhibition was an opportunity to demonstrate the curatorial and research skills of its staff, to attract grants, provide training possibilities for students, and gain a higher public profile. For the visitors, the exhibition was an opportunity to learn something about the Portuguese in Western Australia and thereby undertake an act of ethical self-improvement called for by the project of civic reform.

All of these interests affected the way in which the exhibition was developed. Begun as a project that had, as its main aim, the representation of an ethnic minority in a public space, the exhibition became an exercise in producing a notion of community with which everyone could be satisfied. How and why did this change in orientation occur? The answer to this question lies both in the history of the Portuguese community and in the nature of the curatorial process itself – a process that challenged the idea that representation was a natural rather than a constructed process.

The role of history and its impact on the curatorial process

In starting with a group of people rather than a pre-existing museum collection, my first step was to get to know the community I was dealing with and to gain their confidence and interest in the project. This I did with the aid of the

Portuguese Community Council who introduced me to the Portuguese Club, arranged interviews on Portuguese community radio, gave me lists of contacts and invited me to official community occasions. My ambiguous status as an insider/outsider – born in Portugal but of English speaking parents – generated some interesting results. As I got to know various people and groups I began to notice a number of important characteristics in the Portuguese community. To begin with, there was little sense of a unified ethnic community. Rather, there were different interest groups, sometimes distrustful of each other but all with some claim to being Portuguese. Some of these distinctions would also be common to other migrant groups – distinctions of class, educational background and time of arrival. But there were also geographical distinctions which pointed to a larger history than simply that of nationality. For the patterns of immigration to Western Australia closely followed political and economic situations in Portugal and its overseas provinces. I was dealing with the history of an empire as well as with Portugal itself.

The first wave of Portuguese migrants to Western Australia began arriving in 1952. They were from the island of Madeira and almost exclusively involved in the fishing industry. The population of Madeira at the time was more than the island was able to support. With little in the way of industry, those who could not get jobs as fishermen or as farmers had to look for work elsewhere. In the 1960s, people began to arrive from Portugal itself, driven mainly by the desire for greater economic security. In April 1974 a revolution overthrew the right wing dictatorship which had ruled Portugal since 1932. The aftermath was political upheaval, economic insecurity and general instability alongside a process of democratic reform. In the colonies, the 'Revolution of flowers' meant independence, followed shortly after by civil war. In Angola, Mozambique, Guinea Bissau, Cabo Verde and East Timor, thousands became homeless, lost their properties and savings and were politically persecuted. Many of them sought refuge in Portugal, or migrated elsewhere. The late 1970s and early 1980s, then, saw another wave of migration to Western Australia, of people who had very different experiences from those who had migrated earlier. Many of them were highly educated, having been involved in colonial administration.

It also emerged that all of these waves of migrants were people who had a long family history of migration – both internal to Portugal and its empire and to other countries. Portuguese people, as the title of the exhibition indicates, have a long history of travelling, of dwelling in places that they do not call home.

This history makes it very difficult to understand the Western Australian Portuguese community as a single ethnicity or unified cultural group – a difficulty that affected the nature of my curatorial task. Rather than providing a medium between the museum and the 'community', simply facilitating representation in a public space, my task became one of producing a notion of community. One which most people of Portuguese background could accept but which, at the same time, explained something of the historical context in which such a disparate group of people had come to Perth. I had to produce a notion of community for both the Portuguese and the Australian audiences while securing the confidence of all groups, assuring them that no one group was in control – a task that was only made possible by the fact that I was an outsider. The problem I faced was more than just recognizing that any given individual can belong to multiple communities at the same time, or that any community has differences of opinion within it. The problem was that I had to work within a notion of community that could be recognized by all but which was also attentive to the cultural work which it would do – to explain a group of people to outsiders as well as to themselves.

So far, then, my experiences support Bennett's arguments that the role of the museum is to provide a pedagogical space that supports the governmental aim of civic reform, in this case the recognition of cultural diversity. As Bennett suggests, part of this role is to produce the notion of community within a discursive space based on the principle of equal access to representation. If looked at in this way, this understanding of the role of 'community' in exhibitions also highlights the more general argument made by advocates of the cultural policy position that the role of public institutions is, in great part, about fashioning a framework in which different groups can get on with one another.

However, the steps I had to take to negotiate between the community and the wider public began to show the limits of Bennett's arguments. In wanting to reject oppositions between culture and policy, Bennett reduces culture to government. He then extends this argument to make the claim that communities and their sense of self are also an effect of government. For him, this means that the manner in which

> cultural forms and activities are politicised and the manner in which their politicisation is expressed and pursued – are matters which emerge from, and have their conditions of existence within, the ways in which those forms and activities have been instrumentally fashioned as a consequence of their governmental deployment for specific social, cultural or political ends.
>
> (Bennett 1998a: 195)

The logical extension of this argument is that the interests of the community should coincide with those of government. Any resistance is in fact a playing out of a governmental rationality inscribed within the project of civic reform.

If this argument held, I would not have had a problem in producing a representation of the Portuguese community which served both the interests of the community and those of government. Those interests should have been the same. Both should have had a reformist or pedagogical agenda. That, however, was not the case. As I quickly learnt, there was a very different understanding about the purpose of the exhibition between myself as a representative of the museological/governmental perspective and some members of the Portuguese community. These differences emerged over the way in which objects were understood. As I talked to various people in the community I became aware that some people could not understand the need for a contextual narrative which would interpret their experiences through the display of particular objects and images. As far as they were concerned there was no need to interpret the objects. They were not interested in coming to know themselves in order to demonstrate their difference from other ethnic groups or the dominant Anglo-Saxon majority. From my perspective, however, the narrative produced by such an interpretation was the means not only to give 'voice' to the community but also to offer an explanation of one community's experience to another. In other words, interpretation was the means to achieve the pedagogical aims of the museum as an institution for civic reform – an achievement which relied on an explicit articulation of the notion of community.

Community versus museum: empiricism versus abstraction

At the heart of my problem, I began to realize, was an assumption common to New Museologists that in order to develop a more democratic curatorial practice it is necessary to think of museums as 'ideas based' rather than as focused on objects (see, for example, Weil 1990). The basis of this claim is an argument that museums need to overcome the belief that because they work with *objects*, their knowledge claims are necessarily *objective*. The aim is to recognize the ideological basis of all museum work. The result has been a prioritizing of narrative. Objects are understood to be mute unless they are interpreted. Not to interpret has come to be seen as elitist and anti-democratic (Witcomb 1997a).

As a curator who identifies with the New Museology, I wanted *Travellers and Immigrants* to be attentive to the problem of 'voice'. I wanted it to reflect the meanings Portuguese–Australian people themselves gave to the objects as symbols of their own migrant experience. My initial intention, therefore, had been to conduct oral history interviews with each person who offered to lend an object or a photograph for the exhibition. I felt that in this way, the exhibition would reflect a personal rather than an institutional viewpoint, the oral histories providing the narrative themes of the exhibition. The interviews would also provide an aural element in Portuguese for those who could not read the English labels based on the interviews.

Despite these intentions to be more democratic, to include the voice of different interests within the community, and to use oral history as the source of the exhibition's narratives and main ideas, I found that not everyone was comfortable with oral histories or even with having their experiences interpreted in a museum. This was not a question of language – most interviews were conducted in Portuguese. Nor was it a problem of reluctance to participate in the exhibition. I only spoke to those who either called me or whose names were given to me by their friends as people I should talk to. The problem appeared more to be one of trying to explain the purpose of story telling in an exhibition. There was resistance, on the part of some, towards abstraction. In fact, some even said it was enough to have just the objects. What did I want stories for?

On a number of occasions I arrived in a home to do an oral history interview and discuss the possibility of lending objects, after making an appointment by phone and explaining the purpose of the exhibition, to find the entire family assembled to greet me, the television on, and a wish to talk to me within the family group. In these situations I never even got the tape recorder out. The expectations of the situation were just too different. I chose instead to be guided by them, allowing them to show me books, photographs, and ornaments while sharing a coffee and cake. This provided them with an opportunity to reminisce, to remember their home, their village, family associations or even return trips. All the references were very specific to their immediate family or original neighbourhood. The strong preference was for concreteness – a preference that was reflected in the material culture of their homes, which were filled with memorabilia displayed on shelves and cabinets.

Any attempt to investigate further and get them to answer questions as to why they came, what the situation was in their home country, how they found Australia on arrival, what structures of support they had and so on were met with short, noncommittal answers. They were far more interested in reminiscing about their *terra* (birthplace), or in telling me about particular folkloric customs or ways of cooking food. Discussion of social conditions, politics or economics was resisted. In many ways their approach to the objects was an empirical one – the objects just *were*. They did not necessarily represent anything other than a sense of belonging.

Their response to my attempt to interpret their objects points towards the importance of recognizing what Eilean Hooper-Greenhill has called 'tacit' responses. As she defines it, 'tacit knowledge can be understood as all that is known by individuals, minus all that can be said' (Hooper-Greenhill 2000: 116). While tacit responses can be extremely influential in terms of people's behaviours, attitudes and values, Hooper-Greenhill suggests that their power is to some extent reliant on them remaining unexamined. To attempt to interpret the objects I was offered in terms of a more abstract narrative, then, would have been insensitive to the feelings of those who were lending them. It would have rendered those objects mundane and even, perhaps, profane.

Not to abstract, not to provide an explanatory framework would be, however, to turn my back on the culture of the museum. I had, therefore, to find a way to mediate not only between the museum and the community, but also between the needs of different sections of the community. I needed to provide a space in which this personal, concrete and familial approach to objects could be represented and at the same time explain, both to the community itself as well as a non-Portuguese audience, the different experiences of groups within the community and provide some sort of historical context. I needed to find a way in which the private nature of people's experiences and memories could be told and respected in a public space with a mission to educate – a mission which necessitated some level of abstraction and explanation.

The solution I developed was to provide an interpretative framework around the walls through the use of images, media and interpretative text. The objects were placed in the centre of the exhibition. For the most part, the only interpretation provided here was a short biography of the lenders rather than a formal interpretation of the objects themselves. This hopefully allowed the visitors to respond to the objects on display at the level of their tacit meanings rather than through a more abstract interpretative framework which situated those objects within public political, economic and social histories or within a more traditional stylistic interpretation.

Bennett's description of the relation between museums and communities did not offer an answer to my problem because his approach does not recognize that there can be a number of different interests. Bennett is so intent on erasing an oppositional politics in cultural analysis that he is unable to recognize a use of the notion of community which does not invoke a politics of resistance and opposition but which simply recognizes different interests and histories. The problem is that in throwing out the notion of community, Bennett loses the ability to recognize the co-existence of different cultures. This means that he is inattentive to the way in which museums are also sites for cross-cultural dialogues, for this requires the ability to recognize government as a community in its own right, with its own interests and cultural traditions.

It is the ability to relativize the museum (or in Bennett's terminology government) which, I shall argue, distinguishes James Clifford's (1997) essay 'Museums as contact zones' from the governmentalist position, offering an alternative understanding of the relations between museums and communities. Further, I shall argue that Clifford's approach does not involve a romantic notion of community, despite Bennett's arguments to the contrary. Indeed, it is the ability to relativize the museum which allows Clifford to account for relations between communities and museums without invoking a revolutionary politics. There are ways in which Bennett and Clifford share a common dislike for binary oppositions and are working towards similar aims. Their difference is over their conclusion, not, as Bennett claims, over the identification of the problem.

Like Bennett, Clifford wishes to read museological practices sympathetically. While his work engages with the difficult history of relations between museums and colonized peoples, he looks for moments within this history when the outcomes included positive experiences or the potential to change relations for those who came into contact with the museum. Clifford is careful to recognize the unequal power relations of such encounters, but he does not read the encounter within a simple binary system in which the imperial centre is always in a position of dominating power *vis-à-vis* the colonial periphery.

Clifford's arguments are also unusual within discussions about the relations between museums and communities because he attempts to describe those relations in ways which take the discussion beyond the question of parity in representation. His key concept here is that of a 'contact zone' which he borrows from Mary Louise Pratt (in Clifford 1997: 192). The term is developed by Pratt in the context of colonial history where she uses it to get away from understanding colonial encounters within a centre/periphery model. For Clifford, the term becomes a means of opening up the meanings of both colonial and postcolonial museological encounters from both sides so that both positive and negative implications can be explored. The focus is on cross-cultural experiences. Clifford also focuses on the temporal meaning of 'contact', pointing out how colonial experiences are ongoing ones with repercussions in the present.

In taking the term to the museum context, Clifford is interested in showing how it helps to shift analysis of the relations between museums and colonial peoples away from a binary system of meaning towards one which sees meaning as being shaped along a continuum of unequal power relations. The model of a contact zone is set in opposition to the model of the frontier. In the latter, the museum is a centre of accumulation, collecting from the frontiers of empire and controlling the process of making meaning. When seen from the perspective of 'contact zones', however, museums become 'an ongoing historical, political, moral *relationship* – a power-charged set of exchanges, of push and pull' (Clifford 1997: 192). The relationship is two way, involving two different cultures, two different communities. While the majority of Clifford's examples are from the present, he is careful to point out that even the nineteenth-century museum, while operating most of the time on a 'frontier' model, could and did at times become a contact zone.

The consequence of this approach is that Clifford is able to analyse specific instances of relations between museums and communities as cross-cultural encounters in which the museum, as much as the community, needs to make adjustments. Rather than understanding the museum as a static, monolithic institution at the centre of power, it is read as an unstable institution attempting to come to grips with the effects of the colonial encounter, an attempt which has both positive and negative affects on those involved. While Bennett would also view museums as unstable institutions – any movement on the part of museums is seen as a reflection of small tinkering manoeuvres to enable the reform of the citizenry according to the requirements of government – Clifford's arguments interpret this instability, by contrast, as a result of an engagement between two different communities, two different cultures.

One of Clifford's strategies for exemplifying the shift from a centre/periphery or frontier model to a contact zone perspective is to point out the limits of 'consultation' as a concept to adequately describe the range of encounters between museums and communities in contemporary museum practices. While consultation is the adjective currently used in describing attempts by museums to democratize, Clifford suggests that it belongs to the centre/periphery model in which museums collect information or advice from communities but are nevertheless relatively free to do as they wish with it. Actual experiences, however, indicate to Clifford that, quite often, something more is going on, that museums are being required to take into account community perspectives and radically alter their way of operating. Such a requirement is not, I would argue, simply a result of opposing interests, but is, if the notion of a contact zone is to be taken seriously, a result of contact history.

An example here is a process of 'consultation' undertaken by the Portland Museum of Art with Tlingit elders in reinterpreting its Rasmussen Collection of Northwest Coast Indian artefacts. When the Tlingit elders told their stories using the Rasmussen Collection of the Portland Museum, the museum became entangled not only in the past history of the colonial relationship but also in present relations:

> What transpired in the Portland Museum's basement was not reducible to a process of *collecting* advice or information. And something in excess of consultation was going on. A message was delivered, performed, within an ongoing contact history. As evoked in the museum's basement, Tlingit history did not primarily illuminate or contextualize the objects of the Rasmussen Collection. Rather, the objects provoked (called forth, brought to voice) ongoing voices of struggle. From the position of the collecting museum and the consulting curator, this was a disruptive history which could not be confined to providing past tribal *context* for the objects. The museum was called to a sense of its responsibility, its stewardship of the clan object.
>
> (1997: 193)

What is remarkable about this passage and the discussion that accompanies it, is that both the museum and the Tlingit elders are treated as 'communities'.[2] The museum is also understood as having a tradition, a way of doing things, a culture, which came into contact with Tlingit culture and which has not recovered its former hegemonic status in that process. This is clear in Clifford's description of the encounter from the perspective of the curators (Clifford 1997: 188–192). The expectations of museum staff – namely that the objects in their collection of Northwest Coast Indian artefacts should be given their meanings by the elders of the tribe – is not fulfilled. In using the objects as their starting point and telling 'contact' stories in the presence of museum staff, the tribal elders challenged curatorial approaches to the collection and made it impossible for museum staff to ignore contemporary political struggles over land use. The result was a cross-cultural dilemma for the museum itself:

> Staff at the Portland Museum were genuinely concerned that their stewardship of the Rasmussen Collection include reciprocal communication with the communities whose art, culture, and history were at stake. But could they reconcile the kinds of meanings evoked by the Tlingit elders with those imposed in the context of a museum of 'art'? How much could they decenter the physical objects in favor of narrative, history, and politics? Are there strategies that can display a mask as simultaneously a formal composition, an object with specific traditional functions in clan/tribal life, and as something that evokes an ongoing history of struggle? Which meanings should be highlighted? And which community has the power to determine what emphasis the museum will choose?
>
> (191–192)

For Clifford, then, the questioning the museum faced from the Tlingit community was a product of a long history of contact between them. It was not simply that the community came knocking on the museum's doors demanding change.

For Bennett, however, Clifford's account of the relation between museums and communities suffers from a romantic understanding of community, seeing it as outside of, and in opposition to, government. Bennett develops his criticisms by making two moves. The first is to indicate that there were two frontiers in the nineteenth century. The first one, as Clifford identifies, is that of the colony. The second one, however, is internal to the nation and it involved both regional centres and the working class. For Bennett, this second frontier means that museums were centres of 'dispatch' as well as of accumulation and that they have a long history of involvement with communities.

While he thus raises a question mark over Clifford's historical account which only mentions relations between museums and national communities as a twentieth-century phenomenon, the main point of his argument is that these relations were and continue to be relations of government rather than of exchange. Bennett argues his point by describing how, in the nineteenth century, museums used objects in a governmental programme for the reform of populations. Such a programme, he suggests, still continues today, although of course the actual reform agenda has changed to encompass the principles of cultural diversity. The notion of a contact zone, he argues, is only an effect of such a governmental programme. It is nothing more than an expression of the governmental values of cultural diversity.

The effect of Bennett's criticisms is to negate the possibility of an open dialogue between two distinct communities. Any suggestion of different interests is immediately suspected as invoking a binary system of meaning and an oppositional politics. That differences do not have to be read in terms of oppositions, however, can be demonstrated by using the very same set of historical facts that Bennett uses against Clifford. It is possible to understand Bennett's account of nineteenth-century relations between museums and communities as also a product of contact history – only this time the contact was not between colonizers and colonized at the fringes of empire but between agents and objects of domestic governmental reforms. The effect of this reinterpretation would be to reverse Bennett's argument. Rather than his suggestion that the notion of a contact zone is an effect of government, it might be possible to suggest that governmental relations with communities are only one instance of a complex contact history between different communities.

Clifford's application of the notion of contact zones to museums provides an illuminating set of coordinates for the situation I faced in curating *Travellers and Immigrants*. The mutual incomprehension I observed over the communicative role of objects in exhibitions is similar to the problem faced by the curators at the Portland Museum discussed by Clifford. How could I reconcile the community's approach to the objects with a museological approach that prioritized ideas over objects? How could the culture of the community be reconciled with a curatorial culture?

The problem is also discussed by Hooper-Greenhill in her book *Museums and the Interpretation of Visual Culture* (2000). Hooper-Greenhill argues that in order to produce polysemic exhibitions curators need to recognize the existence of multiple 'interpretive communities'. The term is borrowed from work in Media Studies over the last twenty years. In borrowing it, Hooper-Greenhill wants to highlight that interpretation is socially based and the result of a two way process – one that both produces and represents that which is being interpreted. The sociality of the process means that interpretation always takes place within a community: 'Individuals share interpretative strategies with others who share the same frame of reference, the same cultural references and the same positions within history' (Hooper-Greenhill 2000: 120). Such communities, Hooper-Greenhill argues, are recognizable through

> their common frameworks of intelligibility, interpretative repertoires, knowledge and intellectual skills. These will include specific uses of words and things, and particular textual and artefactual strategies. Attitudes, values and beliefs will become evident in those recurrently used systems of terms deployed to characterise and evaluate actions and events.
>
> (2000: 122)

In taking this idea to the museum, Hooper-Greenhill is arguing for the need to contextualize and relativize both the interpretative community of the museum itself and those of the audiences it hopes to attract. Only then, she argues, can exhibitions become sufficiently polysemic to attract the respect of multiple communities.

In the case of *Travellers and Immigrants* the solution was to develop a structure that catered for the various 'interpretive communities' that comprised its audience. The role of explanation, which defines the community of the museum, was based not on objects but on oral histories and archival research. This was in line with the more abstract historical nature of themes such as reasons for migration, religious practices, working life, and the history of Portugal and its empire. This explanatory role of the exhibition had to be portrayed mostly by photographs, use of media articles, interpretative labels and oral history recordings. The theme of continuity and cultural tradition, however, was based on objects and a personal perspective. As already argued, this enabled more tacit forms of interpretation to occur. The mix of the two modes helped to establish a bridge for those who did not belong either to the museum or to the Portuguese community.

That the exhibition worked on these different levels can be seen through some of the comments in the visitors' book:

> We learnt a lot about ourselves.
>
> It was nice to see so many objects from Madeira.
>
> Fantastic!! We arrived in 1972 from Madera [sic] and we love Perth Western Australia. But we are proud of where we are from.
>
> Being a child from a whole Portuguese family who has lost touch with their heritage, I have found this exhibition very informative as I have never been to Portugal but my mother and father are from Madeira. I also understand why for a Portuguese person living in Perth/Fremantle would not feel that this exhibition does their culture justice because a lot of history is lost and they are probably coming to this exhibition to be taken

'home' once again – perhaps some more photos and talk of other places in Madeira such as Paul de Mar. But congrats on the good effort, please do more like this in the future.

The entire time whilst perusing this exhibition, I had tears of joy and sadness in my eyes. Joy – being proud of my heritage. Sadness – knowing that my father Manuel B. Andrade, had passed away so tragically from this earth, but also knowing that he chose Perth as his home. To my dad (Para of meu Pai 1921–97, Fremantle 1957–97).

Such comments are an indication that such exhibitions are important for this group of people both because they can recognize themselves through the display of objects and photographs but also because they see themselves in a new light, as if from the outside. For quite a few, the exhibition also served as a memorial and a thank you to those who made the decision to come to Australia.

For those who did not belong to the Portuguese community, the exhibition provided a form of self-recognition in so far as it touched on experiences which all migrants have in coming to another country. But their comments also reveal the importance that such exhibitions have in providing some context within which to understand other cultural groups. This importance can be understood in terms of Bennett's role for museums as institutions which promote 'civic reform' as well as Clifford's notion that museums offer a space for cross-cultural dialogue:

A Western Australian:

> It's nice to learn about the background of all the Madeira women I worked with in the Sea Food Factories in Carnarvon in 1992. I always wondered how they ended up there.

An English tourist:

> It's a fascinating display, very well laid out, clearly explained and interesting. I loved the old photographs.

A tourist from the eastern states of Australia:

> As a migrant myself to Australia I appreciated your exhibition in order to gain knowledge and insight into your past as I too remember my own. It enables us all including our original settlers the Kooris to go on together to form a true Australia.

Dialogue, of course, cannot occur without some strategies for translation. Curatorial work is in many ways trying to develop appropriate strategies for the medium of exhibitions. In the example of *Travellers and Immigrants*, this translation work was achieved by allowing some objects to stand without an abstract interpretation but at the same time finding other media with which to provide the historical context and explanatory frameworks. Other strategies included the use of Portuguese in the titles for many of the labels, a catalogue which, while mainly in English, also included extracts from the oral histories in Portuguese, and a compact disc, with edited extracts from the oral histories which was played in the background on a continuous loop for those visitors who could not read English. The latter also had the effect of marking the space as 'foreign' to English speakers and putting them, even if only slightly, in the position of the stranger.

Dialogue and cultural policy

It is not only in the context of exhibition development that Bennett's arguments need to be tempered with a closer attention to the process of dialogue. The need is also there in the field of cultural policy. In some ways cultural policy is the ultimate test for Bennett's arguments. If culture is indeed a product of governmental strategies, there should be no problem with attempts to implement cultural policy. It should be possible, as Bennett plainly expects it to be, to reform society through the means of an effective deployment of cultural policies. While Bennett recognizes that

> there is still a good way to go before satisfactory frameworks, customs and procedures will have been devised that will prove capable of managing complex and highly different forms of cultural diversity which characterise the relations between the Anglo-Celtic, multicultural and indigenous populations of Australia

> (1998a: 104)

he fully expects that it is possible to design and implement them. For Bennett,

> culture still indefatigably tries not to make what each raw person may like, the rule by which they fashion themselves; but to draw ever nearer to a sense of what is indeed a liberal, plural, multicultural, non-sexist tolerance of diversity and to get the raw person to like this.

> (Bennett 1998a: 104–105)

Bennett's expectation that policy can achieve civic reform seems to be based on an understanding of the individual as formed entirely by governmental programmes. Hence his belief that people are 'raw', without culture until they come into contact with government. There seems to be no space for other formative experiences. That this position cannot be sustained, let alone supported, is the point of my next case study, based on my experiences working as a consultant with local museums in Queensland. Employed to teach local museum volunteers the values of the new museology through a grants programme devised as part of a raft of new museum policies at state government level, I found that my attempts to institutionalize the values of cultural diversity were not welcomed. As I shall argue, what I needed but did not realize at the time was an understanding of the need to dialogue and negotiate the values I was representing with the values of those I was working with. There was no such thing as a 'raw person' or group of people waiting for the imprint of government. For it is simply not the case that the imperatives of government can be easily matched with those of various communities. Policy will not, on its own, bring about a pluralistic society.

Like community galleries, local museums are another site in which a rhetoric of access and equity to representation is used by governments as a means to achieve civic and cultural reform. Excellent examples can be found in *Future Directions for Regional and Community Museums in NSW* produced for the NSW Ministry for the Arts and *Hidden Heritage* for Arts Queensland. Both reports illustrate Bennett's arguments that cultural policy makers use the rhetoric of community representation for purposes of cultural reform. Recommendations for funding are supported through a rhetoric of facilitating community self-representation. As *Future Directions for Regional and Community Museums* put it, local museums 'should be capable of truly reflecting the community back to itself in ways which illuminate complex, social, political and environmental issues' (NSW Ministry for the Arts Advisory Council 1994: 6). The Queensland version, *Hidden Heritage*, concludes with the statement: 'as we approach a new millennium and the Centenary of Federation, Queensland's Community Museums should be resourced to accept the challenge of promoting a distinctive sense of place and culturally diverse community' (Lennon 1995: 112).

The subtext of these reports is that representations in local museums should be brought into line with government policies on multiculturalism, gender equity and reconciliation. If read within the wider context of government policy, certain phrases become a code, meant to indicate the links to policies on multiculturalism and equity. For example, in return for a commitment to strengthening infrastructure, the NSW government hopes for 'strong museums [which will] create a strong sense of identity . . . foster awareness about an area's or a people's history of settlement, relationship with indigenous peoples and the land, technological and cultural achievements' (NSW Ministry for the Arts 1994: 6). Similarly, a 'culturally diverse community' in the *Hidden Heritage* report can be read as shorthand for multiculturalism. The policy objectives outlined by these reports are not only to support local museums – they are to extend governmental control of their representations. In short, cultural policy has become a pedagogical tool, a political intervention, in the process of redefining social and cultural values.

Hidden Heritage is particularly clever in furthering this agenda. Rather than just offer financial resources to local museums by means of small grants to buy equipment (such as storage shelves, a photocopier, or a computer) as in the past, such grants are tied to a pedagogical programme to improve conservation, documentation and interpretation. A rhetoric of crisis is used to support the recommendations in the report. Local museums 'are the protectors of our local, regional, state and national cultural and historical heritage' (Lennon 1995: 2).

> There is an urgent need to capitalise on the energy and dedication of volunteers who have established these museums for the benefit of all peoples, not just those in their local community . . . the collections are at a crisis point in management and assistance.
>
> (Lennon 1995: ii)

Instead of a grant system to support capital expenditure the report set in place a programme under which professional training for the museum volunteers had to be built into an application for funding. Under the Museum Development Programme, then, the category of Individual Projects is available to 'assist in the professional development of individuals working with Queensland collections' (Arts Queensland 1996). The other major category, Organization Projects, is designed to 'support professional museological management of Queensland collections of moveable cultural heritage and art. Priority will be given to projects which initiate professional management and innovative interpretations of collections' (Arts Queensland 1996).

The context for these changes in museum policy are not limited to those of cultural reform. There are also important economic contexts that need to be considered. These reports were written at a time when rural and regional economies were collapsing due to the impact of globalization, falling commodity prices and changes in farming techniques such as increased mechanization which decreased labour demand. In the case of Queensland the economic situation was exacerbated by a major drought. The small example of Mitchell, a town of about 1,000 people in south-west Queensland, provides a snapshot of the impact such changes can have on communities.[3] Falling market prices for wheat, wool and beef, the drought and changing farming practices all combined to create unemployment on the land. Young men could not find work and left town. The major source of employment for women – local business – also declined, as Roma, a larger town further east, expanded and became the service centre for the area. There was no longer a supermarket in Mitchell and banks were closing. Women who once worked as book-keepers and secretaries were superseded by computers in those businesses which had survived. This meant there was a dwindling source of off-farm income. It also meant that women no longer met together in town as they once did. They had no reason to come in to town – work or shopping – and many of them could not afford the fuel. It also meant that the population of the town was ageing rapidly. All of these changes impacted on the local community as memberships for various groups dwindled. The local choir, for example, felt the effects of people leaving town as well as the inability of those living in the district to come into town for rehearsals.

The story is similar throughout regional Australia, putting pressure on governments to find alternative sources of economic development and to find ways of keeping a growing number of unemployed people meaningfully busy. One of the strongest possibilities is cultural tourism. The sites are already there – local museums and heritage centres. They are run by a large army of volunteers which cost the government little. But to be attractive they need modernization – both in what they present and how they present it. This is the context for reports like *Hidden Heritage*, which won government support for its recommendations by arguing that government should be interested in helping to establish a 'coordinated museums industry' in Queensland because, amongst other things, this would create jobs in regional centres, diversify the economic base of regions, explain and reinforce regional and local identity, and foster cultural and heritage tourism (Lennon 1995: i).

If we were to follow Bennett's arguments we would expect these policies to be welcomed by the communities they invoke, since they seek to implement neces- sary cultural reform, provide the structure for increased resources and affirm the value of local cultures. But my own experiences as one of the cultural tech- nicians charged with 'professionalizing' local museums tells me that this is not always the case.

While living in Rockhampton, a regional city in Queensland, I was asked to act as a museum consultant to a small local museum, run by volunteers in Marl- borough. The museum had just received a grant to improve their displays and catalogue their collection. They needed a museum professional to show them contemporary practices and techniques.

The history of the museum is not unusual. A committee of six people had inher- ited a museum from a private collector, who had entrusted its upkeep to them before he died. While realizing that the museum could not remain static, the committee was unsure what to do. Some thought it was enough to pay the rates, hold an annual fête and keep the doors open. Others thought they should be doing more with the collection and applied for a grant with the aim of cata- loguing the collection and improving the display.

My job then, was to give the museum some direction and introduce them to contemporary documentation and interpretation practices. As I quickly realized, this involved much more than teaching them a set of techniques – how to accession, collect information about an object, classification practices, legal responsibilities of managing a collection and so on. It involved a new way of looking at history and at their community. I began by showing the museum committee and the other volunteers that, if they knew a little more about the objects in their collection, they could use the objects to tell stories about the history of the local community. They could develop narratives based on the strengths of their collection, selecting some objects for display while storing others for 'changeover exhibitions'. This in turn would enable them to attract the local school to use the museum, something they had not been able to do. Changing the look of the museum would also attract town people in.

The group decided that they would take some of these ideas on board and began to develop thematic displays based on the existing collection. Those objects that did not contribute to the stories went into storage. The volunteers researched each object that went into an exhibition, setting up a manual collec- tion management system so that they could accession the object and keep a file of information on it. Often this involved going back to the original donors, as the collection had grown since the death of the first collector, in order to get them to sign an official gift form as well as to find out further information about the object. The group developed three exhibitions in the space of two years – a remarkable effort. They divided into teams, some responsible for conservation, others for research and writing, others for accessioning. We thought that in turning standard museum tasks into part of an exhibition project everyone would feel part of the team and no one task would become boring. I took a number of workshops on preventive conservation, collection management, exhibition development and label writing.

Over time, however, cracks began to appear. I began getting phone calls from frustrated members of the committee: 'So and so is undermining the exhibition'; 'They are not pulling their weight'; 'They don't see why we should be doing exhibitions'; 'They just want to run the annual fête'; 'They don't think we should be doing an exhibition on women's work'. Some members stopped attending the workshops, even though they signed the cheques which paid me. Open conflict between two different factions in the museum became entrenched. In the end, those who wanted to return to the old ways simply destroyed the exhibitions everyone had worked on. The result for the museum was catastrophic – half of the committee left and the other half did not have the skills or the willingness to look after the collection according to professional principles. Both the collection and the community suffered as a result.

How are we to understand what occurred here? And, more importantly, what might be the solutions?

At one level the conflict was a result of specific local contexts. For example, the committee of six was composed of people who lived in town as well as those whose properties were further out. Those who lived in town formed the executive because they could get to meetings more regularly and were 'on the premises'. However, their social and economic status was not as high as the 'out of towners'. They lacked tertiary education and sometimes even upper secondary. These issues probably led to a feeling of insecurity and eventually resentfulness on the part of the executive. They had formal power but were unable to play as full a role in the new processes of documentation and interpretation.

The executive group was also the group who wanted to limit the museum's activities to an annual fête and ensuring the door was open. This section of the committee regarded their role in the museum as a sign of their social status in town. The museum was one of their projects, much in the same way as they looked upon their membership of the Country Women's Association or their involvement in the Church. Their involvement was part of the way in which they established their social position and networks.

But I think the issues involved in this museum's conflict go much deeper than what could be described as issues of class or 'cultural capital' or even the role of museums as centres for social networking. The physical destruction of the exhibitions indicates, I think, a real discomfort with the kind of narratives, the kind of history, the museum was now involved in constructing. For a thematic approach to collecting and exhibiting had precisely the effect that the new cultural policies were designed for – to introduce principles of cultural diversity. It was these principles which were being resisted.

The first exhibition on Chrisoprase mining in the district was a challenge because it required the museum volunteers to recognize that museums did not only deal with the distant past. The display was an exercise in contemporary collecting as an attempt to bring more recent residents in the district to the museum. The strategy worked but in so doing it also brought people who were interested in developing thematic exhibitions which dealt with issues such as women's contribution to settling the district. The new volunteers were younger, had higher levels of education, an urban background and a different understanding of Australian history. The result was a group of women who were far more open to the possibility of extending the available narratives about the past. Supported by the collection, another two exhibitions were developed – one on an earlier dairying industry and the other simply entitled *Women's Work*. While not exactly revolutionary, these exhibitions did challenge conventional pioneer narratives by bringing in a gendered perspective on what is usually an implicit masculine narrative. Instead of the traditional themes of opening up the land, hard physical labour, technological and agricultural innovations, pastoralism and mateship between men, these exhibitions focused on domestic industries, the role of women on the farm and the difficulties of home life in a pioneer context. The introduction of other narratives into the conventional pioneer story also highlighted the fact that pioneer history was a form of narrative in itself, a narrative which could be told differently. This was a challenge to an older generation who assumed their version of history to be 'true'.

The negative response to these exhibitions on the part of the executive is not an isolated one. As the rapid rise of Pauline Hanson indicates, there is ample evidence that 'the bush' is in the midst of a revolt against the values of a mainly urban elite. As many media commentators keep reminding Australians, there is an increasing split between the urban and rural political landscapes. The cultural values each holds dear are increasingly poles apart. The division is, in part, over different perceptions of Australian history and cultural identity. While urban elites tend to be more cosmopolitan, valuing the cultural experiences made possible by the increasing multicultural nature of Australian society and the effects of globalization on the flow of cultural goods, regional and rural Australians are mourning what they perceive as the loss of the dominant Anglo-Saxon culture. Much of this culture is expressed for them in the traditional pioneer narratives, particularly the notion of 'mateship' and its associations with other traditional Australian values such as a 'fair go'. These are values which are also central to the historical experiences of the urban industrial class, a class which is now disaffected, like those involved in primary industry, as a result of globalization. Both of these groups tend to express this disaffection with isolationist and racist discourses. The fact that the major conservative party feels the need to accommodate this revolt in order to neutralize the 'Hanson effect' is also an indication of its extent.

Where to now?

What, then, is the solution to this disjuncture between community and governmental responses to social change? Is it possible to develop a response which does not produce antagonisms? And is it possible to develop a notion of community which does not gain its meaning from an opposition to government?

For Bennett, the solution to such situations is merely to continue to work at refining the normative and reformative characteristics of cultural policy. Recognizing that 'the race debate unleashed in the aftermath of the 1996 election has shown there is a good deal further still to go before an acceptance of such goals will be firmly secured in "mainstream" Australia' (Bennett 1998a: 104). Bennett has no qualms that a 'normative mechanism remains at the heart of what is still a reforming endeavour' (104). True to his view that there is nothing outside of government, this is an answer which effectively takes the community out of the equation. Yet it seems to me that the root of the problem in reports like *Hidden Heritage* was an inability to think of cultural policy as an exercise in cross-cultural negotiation. Bennett worries about the tendency on the part of cultural critics to invoke a romantic notion of community which sets the latter in opposition to government. However, government technicians are themselves using a romantic notion of community as a naturally desiring community to erase the distinction between government and community. The problem here is not the assumption of *an opposition* between community and government but precisely the opposite – an assumption that they are one and the same. The result is a mismatch between the idealized governmental expectation that local museums 'should be capable of truly reflecting the community back to itself in ways which illuminate complex, social, political and environmental issues' (NSW Ministry for the Arts Advisory Council 1994: 6) and the reality that the values which communities want to represent may not be those associated with cultural diversity.

Clifford's focus on 'contact zones' as both a description and a prescription might offer a way out. There is, to put it simply, a need for more 'talk' which starts from a recognition that government is also a culture with a different set of interests from those of the communities it seeks to govern. A starting point, from this perspective, would be a recognition of the different interests involved. At one level, we have a variety of groups which have an interest in defining, preserving, documenting and interpreting their cultural heritage for themselves and others. At another level we have a governmental interest in cultural heritage – both as a means of shaping cultural values in the present and as an economic resource. And finally we have the interests of the heritage profession – with their values of the importance of preservation and the proper documentation and interpretation of collections. The differences between these 'communities of interests' or 'interpretive communities' need to be laid on the table for discussion.

For example, any attempt to professionalize the local museums sector needs to be explicit about the full agenda. Local museums need to be aware that in accepting grants they are also making a choice to 'reform' and to become part of a governmentalized public culture. This requires that cultural technicians argue the case for change. It involves discussing differences in cultural values, explaining professional attitudes as well as pointing out that public assistance comes with a system of accountability set by government. In some ways our task becomes that of explaining the options available and what the consequences of each may be. The downside of this approach is that we have to respect the right to choose *not* to learn professional ways of doing things or *not* to follow the values of cultural diversity. This means accepting that cultural diversity might need to include those who do not accept those very principles. We have to be more open to internal contradiction in our positions – we cannot use a rhetoric of community self-representation without accepting that many communities may have different ideas of history.

What are the implications of these case studies for thinking about the relations between museums and communities? Certainly we need to take on board Bennett's criticisms of current ways of thinking about this relation, particularly naive understandings of communities as outside of and opposed to the museum. The consequences of this are considerable. To begin with, curators can no longer be seen just as facilitators, enabling access to representation. Their role is a more demanding one which involves responsibility for actually defining the community being represented. This responsibility is not to be seen as a repressive exercise of power but as a positive one of civic reform, educating the public in the principles of cultural diversity. Such an understanding of the curatorial role does not assume that there is a community 'out there' that the museum can represent. This has a number of further consequences.

First, we need to reject the idea of an 'authentic' representation, including the belief that community groups must only represent themselves. Of course, the problems with these ideas are discussed by curators themselves. As many community gallery curators have argued, the representations that result in community galleries are those of particular *sections* of the community (Anderson 1993; Szekeres 1995). However, their answer has mostly been in terms of finding ways to achieve a 'truer' representation. Some curators advocate direct involvement in order to prevent 'inaccurate' or unbalanced representations, while others warn against interfering so that communities can decide how to represent themselves. The limits of understanding the situation in this way need to be better understood.

On the other hand, there is also a need to relativize the museum and avoid defining the representations purely as a result of governmental discourses and strategies. This does not mean that communities must be set in opposition to the museum but rather that the curatorial process is seen as the result of a set of exchanges between *different* communities.

This, I think, is the value of Clifford's work on museums. It tempers Bennett's exclusive focus on the effects of governmentality. Clifford's perspective enjoins us to engage also with the culture of the museum (and of government) and even to value some of its traditions. A dialogic perspective prevents a situation in which the only 'community' exhibitions which are valued are those which are perceived as having little or no input from the museum or 'curator'. By bringing the governmental and the dialogic perspectives together, it is possible to create a role for museums which focuses on their ability to translate between different groups without seeing this process as merely one of facilitation.

5

Beyond the mausoleum: museums and the media

> The German word *museal* (museumlike) has unpleasant overtones. It describes objects to which the observer no longer has a vital relationship and which are in the process of dying. They owe their preservation more to historical respect than the needs of the present. Museum and mausoleum are connected by more than phonetic association. Museums are the family sepulchres of works of art.
>
> (Adorno 1967: 175)

In this short quotation from Theodor Adorno's article, 'Valéry Proust Museum', is embedded a set of ideas which until recently provided the dominant intellectual response to the museum, in an intellectual tradition which reaches back to Quatremere de Quincy and forward to Adorno and more recently Douglas Crimp (Sherman 1994). It is a tradition which links the museum with the more stultifying aspects of modernity, representing it as an anti-democratic institution. As Andreas Huyssen describes it, the battle against the museum by those on the left and in the avant garde has been a long one. For them, the museum has

> stood in the dead eye of the storm of progress serving as a catalyst for the articulations of tradition and nation, heritage and canon, and has provided the master maps for the construction of cultural legitimacy in both a national and a universalist sense.
>
> (Huyssen 1995: 13)

While this intellectual tradition has a more popular face in the image of the museum as a temple or treasure house – an image which reinforces the idea of a separation from the present – it is also an image which points to the central importance of objects, to the material world, in constructing narratives of cultural authority. The materiality of objects seemed to provide an empirical basis for nineteenth-century ideas of civilization as material progress at the same time as supporting ideas of authenticity and originality which were essential to the construction of a notion of tradition. By studying the fabric of objects, museum curators could classify and order them into taxonomies in what appeared to be an objective manner. These classifications and taxonomies were themselves supported by a historical framework that used the exhibition space of the museum to popularize a narrative of Western society as the pinnacle of civilization. As Tony Bennett argues, the emergence of a historical frame for the display of museum exhibits was concurrent with the development of an array of disciplines and other practices which aimed at the life-like reproduction of an authenticated past and its representation as a series of stages leading to the present.

(Bennett 1988c: 88–89)

Order was imposed on heterogeneity.

As a consequence of this focus on the material qualities of the object, museums laid themselves open to critiques, such as that of the Frankfurt School, which accused them of commodity fetishism and elitism. These critiques have recently been extended by the emergence of the 'New Museology', a field of study which critiques museum practices in relation to their social, economic and political contexts. New museologists criticize the traditional museological notion that objects possess inherent moral, aesthetic characteristics or reflect an objective, empirical representation of the social world (Jordanova 1989; Kirschenblatt-Gimblett 1991; Saumarez Smith 1989). They argue that this notion has been part of a hegemonic discourse in which claims about knowledge are presented in absolute terms.

Such criticisms are themselves a reflection of the changing contexts within which museums now have to operate. It is a context in which the cultural authority of the museum is increasingly being questioned by communities of people who want a say in how the museum represents their culture, by governments which demand increasing levels of accountability in a context of diminishing faith in the cultural contribution of public institutions as well as an ever increasing number of competitors in the cultural field itself. These are contexts which make it impossible to continue a museological practice which fails to recognize the politics of making meaning.

Another development which is threatening traditional attitudes to objects in museums is the introduction of electronic technologies and the impact, more generally, of media. Museums have been strongly affected by discourses around electronic technologies and a sensitivity to media has brought widespread changes to contemporary museum practices. One of the most notable effects has been on the status of objects within museums. Their authority to 'speak' within a hegemonic system of representation is increasingly being questioned.

At a practical level, exhibitions now include non-objects – particularly mock-ups, audio-visual technologies and interactive computer information points. They also use other media such as film, television footage, magazines and newspapers. At a discursive level, these inclusions can be understood, from a certain postmodernist perspective, as making the museum continuous with modern media forms. The use of media within the museum connects it with global flows of ideas and information, preventing meanings produced within the museum from remaining enclosed within it. As Roger Miles (1993: 27) suggests,

> modern multimedia exhibitions reflect not the international world of museums as repositories, but the external world in which museums now find themselves. This is the world of our post-industrial society –

dominated by technology, with pervasive media and advertising industries, and instantaneous electronic communications; a society with a pluralistic culture in which the boundaries between high art and mass culture have broken down.

The inclusion of media, particularly electronic media is seen by commentators such as Miles, as breaking the association between museums and objects and, in the process, transforming an elitist museum culture into a more democratic and popular one. The tendency is to associate the introduction of 'virtual' technologies with the end of the material world. In this process, the argument runs, the association between museums and mausoleums is also broken as the museum becomes embedded within contemporary culture.

In engaging with this argument, this chapter will suggest that the history of association between museums and the media points not so much towards the end of the material world as to a democratization of social relations. To put it another way, the effects of electronic technologies have not entirely displaced objects but rather brought into question absolute claims about their meaning.

The argument will be developed through a number of steps. The first is to outline the range of contexts which enabled the emergence of a museological practice defined by an exclusive focus on objects. An understanding of this history enables us to understand the reasons for some of the more millenarian rhetorics surrounding the possibilities emerging from the introduction of electronic technologies into the museum space. Second, I will locate this discourse of change within the influential tradition of Canadian communication studies around the work of Harold Innis and Marshall McLuhan. This tradition has been very influential in the development of the Canadian Museum of Civilization around which much of the initial discussion about museums and electronic technologies took place.[1]

Third, I will situate the relation between museums and electronic technologies within a genealogy of the more general relation between museums and modern media forms. The connection between modern media – especially electronic technologies – and attempts to popularize the museum has a longer history which tends to be forgotten by both modernist and postmodernist perspectives on museums. Recognizing this history enriches the base for engaging with the use of media in museum displays. It also allows us to clarify the relation between museums, the media and more democratic forms of cultural production. Finally, I will describe these relations by providing examples of some of the ways in which the traditional status of museum objects is being displaced by electronic technologies and by media more generally.

Materialism and the temple as a treasure house

As already indicated, the image of the museum as a mausoleum is firmly linked to the idea that museums enclose objects, separating them from the life-forces which gave them their original social and political meanings. While this is an idea that has most currency within the more avant-gardist discourses surrounding the art museum (for an example see Douglas Crimp 1995), it has a more widespread force in the image of the museum as a store-house, a centre for the accumulation of material objects. These are images that are firmly embedded in nineteenth-century ideas of civilization as material progress. As Michael J. Ettema (1987) argues, the nineteenth-century museum can be understood as the embodiment of a view of history as material progress. Put simply, this was the view that those civilizations which had the most complex objects were the most advanced. In displaying the objects of various cultures, museums taught a hierarchical understanding of cultural development and instilled the values of materialism. They linked objects to a system of values which supported the ideas of technological progress, individualism and aesthetics. These values were perceived as the basis for modern civilization.

While Ettema is writing within an American context, there is a sense in which these ideas can be applied to all Western countries in so far as they saw the attempt of the new middle classes to establish their hegemony in the developing industrial capitalist system. Museums, in their focus on objects, were advancing the cause of capital. In the nineteenth century, the idea of progress seemed evident in advances in all areas of society – in transport, communication, industrial technologies and new consumer goods. Museums were thus ideally placed to represent these advances to the 'masses', convincing them of the advantages of industry and capital. In this way, they were very similar to the new department stores, as I have suggested in Chapter 1.

But as Ettema and others argue, this function was only made possible by a set of ideas about the nature of objects which became widespread in the nineteenth century – the belief that objects embodied the essence or spirit of the people who made them and that they contained abstract moral qualities which could be read through their physical characteristics. Thus objects from a primitive society would empirically prove the 'backwardness' of that society, both in material and moral progress. Western societies, as the most materially advanced, were also the most 'civilized'. This was perhaps most clearly set out in the large International Exhibitions throughout Western Europe, America and Australia. As Bennett (1988c, 1995) points out, within the theme of civilization, there was always a special place for the nation which hosted the International Exhibition as the apex of material progress.

The close relationship between museums and the large nineteenth-century international exhibitions confirms the link between objects, ideas of progress and capital. As Ettema suggests,

> these vast assemblages of both producer and consumer goods were designed to inspire the public with the material beneficence of modern technology. . . . By simply displaying the vast array of goods becoming available, human progress would be made self evident. Moreover, technological museums could educate the public in new types of goods available for purchase as well as the relative virtues of manufacturers' wares.
>
> (1987: 70)

These social and economic imperatives depended on the belief of the inherent capacity of objects to communicate abstract values.

At the same time as signifying capital, however, museum objects also have iconic value, a value which was described by Walter Benjamin (1973) as 'auratic'. For Benjamin, aura stems from the object's association with ritual, an association which was broken by the technology of mechanical reproduction. In museological terms the evidence of this quality was the 'patina' of an object, the traces of use through time. In contrast to this, Benjamin argued, modern reproduction techniques allowed the separation of an image from the object and hence from its particular place in space and time. In making possible a dislocation of the sensible attributes of an object from the object itself, reproduction threatened aura:

> The authenticity of a thing is the essence of all that is transmissible from its beginning, ranging from its substantive duration to its testimony to the history which it has experienced. Since the historical testimony rests on the authenticity, the former too is jeopardised by reproduction when substantive duration ceases to matter. And what is really jeopardised when the historical testimony is affected is the authority of the object.
>
> (Benjamin 1973: 221)

Benjamin's theory of the effect of mechanical reproduction on the status of the art object enables us to pinpoint another logic operating in nineteenth-century museum practices. This is the opposition between a copy and its original, an opposition which privileges the original as more important, more precious, than a copy.[2] Traditionally the 'authority of the object', to which Benjamin refers, has been the very basis for the museum as a social institution. The task of the museum was to provide a context in which people could view objects as originals. Originality could no longer be taken for granted. It had to be constructed and guaranteed. Although viewing the object meant being in its presence, the viewer was also distanced from the object. Semiotically this distance was represented by glass cabinets and the red cordon, physically putting up a barrier between viewer and artefact, between subject and object. At the same time, however, this barrier also served to signify the monetary value of the artefact, thus mixing auratic with monetary values, aesthetic with commercial values. For originality also came to be associated with rarity. The temple and the treasure house were the Janus-like face of the object, giving the lie to the belief that it is only now that the ground of 'Culture' is being undermined by the forces of commerce.

The concept of an original substance in the object and its direct link with the memory of an original creator was also important in sustaining narratives of authenticity, tradition and the universality of art. The cult of the artist, in particular, and the importance attached to authenticity, ensured that certain objects became icons enshrined within the museum's walls. Cultural concepts like aura and authenticity were established as absolute truths through the link with the physical existence of the original fabric. This was supported by a museological practice which emphasized the importance of classification systems and taxonomies which attributed meaning to the object according to its physical characteristics. Ideas of materiality, or a notion of a 'trace', were indelibly linked with those of authenticity. It was the physicality of the object which was important and which provided the basis for a quasi-scientific approach to the study of objects. As David Goodman (1990: 20) argues, the nineteenth-century museum was based on a 'subordination of other senses to sight, by its attachment to the classificatory table, and by its rejection of theatre and "show"'. Collecting was a scientific endeavour. Hence, the nineteenth-century museum 'stressed system rather than event' (Goodman 1990: 29).[3] The system was used to provide the object with a transcendental status in which its objectivity was both unique and universal at the same time. In this, nineteenth-century museology was not unlike other disciplines which also attempted to gain scientificity and thus universality through a positivist epistemology.

Objects and power

As well as supporting a narrative of materialism, objects were also important in supporting new claims to knowledge. For the museological discourse on authenticity, originality and presence supported a claim to knowledge on the part of museum curators. By studying the fabric of these objects, museum curators could classify them and order them into taxonomies. These classifications and taxonomies were themselves supported by a historical framework which used the exhibition space of the museum to popularize a narrative of Western society as the pinnacle of civilization. As Bennett argues, this historical framework 'constituted a new space of representation concerned to depict the development of peoples, states, and civilisations through time conceived as a progressive series of developmental stages' (Bennett 1988c: 88–89). While this space was one of universal time, the museum also instituted a special place for the emerging nation-state. For as universal time was increased by pushing historical time further and further back via archaeology, the 'recent past was also historicised as the newly emerging nation-states sought to preserve and immemorialise their own formation' (Bennett 1988c: 89). As Bennett goes on to explain, this led to 'universal histories being annexed to national histories as, within the rhetorics of each national museum complex, collections of national materials were represented as the outcome and culmination of the universal story of civilisation's development' (Bennett 1988c: 89). The result was a display of power in which the cultures of others were given meaning only within histories of Western civilization. As Negrin (1993: 100) points out, 'European culture in the nineteenth century was unique in being able to appreciate the relevance of other cultures to its own'.

It is not surprising, then, that this attempt at making order out of heterogeneity is associated with centralized forms of power and representation, a form of power which is neatly encapsulated by the notion of museums as treasure houses in the large metropolitan centres of empire.[4] The Louvre, for example, was extended during the Napoleonic period largely out of the spoils of war. The

presence in Paris of art works from all over Europe was used to establish a relation between universal and national history and, at the same time, between the
centre and the periphery – a relationship which I would describe as a 'territorial mode' of power relations (Gibson 1994, Virilio 1986).

This territorial mode of power relations can still be seen in museums today.
Despite continued critiques, an object focus continues to hold at governmental
and institutional levels. For example, the discussion paper *What Value
Heritage?*, produced by the former Department of the Arts, Sport, the Environment, Tourism and Territories in Australia, defines museums as 'our collective memory which reinforces our sense of place, being and community'
(DASSETT 1990: 7–8). The responsibility of museums according to the document is to 'serve society as custodians of their movable cultural heritage' and
further to 'interpret and communicate that heritage' (11). Central to this
conception of the role of museums is a belief in the fundamental importance of
material objects: 'It is the objects themselves, with their intrinsic values, which
are the principal means of linking the past with the present' (11). For
DASSETT, objects provided stable points of reference which enabled a culture
to fix its position and orientation within the coordinates of space and time.

What Value Heritage?, then, continues to view museums and their place in
society according to the positivist epistemology outlined above. The museum
has a central, controlling position from which it defines the identity of a unified
community, a community that can be spoken of as one. Moreover, this central
position is based on a belief in the ability of objects to represent a wider reality,
to stand in for the world. A positivist epistemology, together with an evolutionary view of history, provide the framework for an authoritative claim to
knowledge, a claim which situates the curator as a rational subject in a position of control over a homogeneous, mass museum public.

From treasure house to touch screens: the displacement of the object

It is this history of the relationship between museums and notions of materiality, and especially its association with centres of power, which much of the
rhetoric around the introduction of electronic technologies into museums is
seeking to displace. One of the clearest examples of this rhetoric is the discourse
found around the introduction of electronic technologies at the Canadian
Museum of Civilization. It is a discourse that borrows very heavily from the
rhetoric associated with the work of Marshall McLuhan.

McLuhan himself sits within a well established Canadian tradition in communication studies. This tradition has made two contributions to the discussion
about the relationship between media technologies and society. The first is the
argument that technologies can be understood as having cultural effects
through their form as well as through their content. The second is the suggestion that electronic technologies are radically different from previous media

technologies in that they set up a non-hierarchical space of communication which encourages social interaction.

Both Harold Innis and Marshall McLuhan argued that communication technologies have cultural effects as a result of the very medium which they used. For Innis, any civilization would be prone to what he termed a particular 'bias of communication' depending on whether its dominant communication technology led to the control of space or of time (Innis 1973). So, for example, ancient Sumeria was a civilization which had control over a small geographical space over a long period of time because its dominant form of communication was clay tablets. Ancient Egypt, by contrast, had control over a larger geographical expanse because it developed the technology of papyrus, a technology which enabled it to develop a relatively more rapid system of communication from the centre to the periphery of its empire. Both biases are concerned with communication as an expression of hierarchical systems of power.

For McLuhan, the uniqueness of electronic technology is that it overcomes both biases, erasing both time and space through speed (McLuhan in his Introduction to Innis 1973). In *Understanding Media*, McLuhan suggests that the

> obsession with the older patterns of mechanical, one way expansion from centres to margins is no longer relevant to our electric world. Electricity does not centralise, but decentralises. It is like the difference between a railway system and an electric grid system: the one requires railheads and big urban centres. Electric power, equally available in the farmhouse and the Executive Suite, permits any place to be a centre, and does not require large aggregations.
>
> (McLuhan 1967: 45)

For McLuhan, the political implications of this decentralization are enormous: electric speed is

> bringing all social and political functions together in a sudden implosion which has highlighted human awareness of responsibility to an intense degree. It is this implosive factor that alters the position of the Negro, the teenager, and some other groups. They can no longer be *contained*, in the political sense of limited association. They are now *involved* in our lives, as we in theirs, thanks to the electric media.
>
> (McLuhan 1967: 12–13)

For McLuhan then, electronic technologies force interaction by flattening social hierarchies and territorial boundaries through the inclusion of previously separate groups within the one space of communication.

Most commentators have seen this political claim as far too wide and naive. While agreeing that it is not empirically sustainable, I would like to appropriate some of the associations made by McLuhan and modify them a little. For McLuhan, modern forms of electronic communication indicate the possibility of a more democratic society by encouraging a greater degree of social interactivity. This notion of interactivity is provocative as it is much wider than the common idea of pushing buttons on computers and involves the bringing together in one space groups previously held apart. Indeed, it can be abstracted further than McLuhan does himself by seeing it as applying to media in general. Useful support for this can be found in John Hartley's (1992) book, *The Politics of Pictures*. Hartley argues that the rise of the modern media, particularly journalism, produced a popular readership establishing a basis for new social relations. By taking this argument to the museum, it becomes possible to analyse the museum around questions of *articulation*, focusing on how the museum is connected into, and operates through, other channels of communication such as television, the internet and film. If we follow this line of argument, the museum is not a closed repository, a mausoleum, but an institution that is closely connected with other sites of cultural representation. Moreover, it has always been so – in the nineteenth century as much as in the twentieth and twenty-first.

Modernity, popular culture and journalism

For Hartley, it is the media, and specifically modern forms of journalism, which produced a modern public sphere where new forms of social and cultural relations were possible:

> Journalism has a real and an imagined power to affect other systems, actions or events. It is said to affect individuals and bring down governments, to expose evils and wreck lives, to be the defence of democracy and the cause of decline, to extend knowledge and spread ignorance, all at once, all over the world.
>
> (1995: 20)

The argument has similarities to McLuhan's claims for electronic technologies. Yet journalism is associated with the central experiences of modernity – the development of exploration, scientific thought, industrialization, political emancipation and imperial expansion – as well as with its principles – notions of freedom, progress, and universal enlightenment (21). Both 'are associated with the breaking down of traditional knowledges and hierarchies, and their replacement with abstract bonds of virtual communities which are linked by their media' (21). As with McLuhan, the interest is in forms of articulation and the way in which these might facilitate social interaction and exchange.

For Hartley, this articulation and interaction takes place above all through *pictures. The public* is increasingly displaced from any actual public space into the realm of representation in the pictorial press. This entails an increasing social mediation in which 'political contestations have moved ever more decisively into the realm of visual representation' (Hartley 1992: 6). So much so that the popularity of any medium is defined by the availability of pictures.

The argument can easily be applied to museums. The recent association between popular culture and the museum has a lot to do with the use of media pictures through film, magazines, posters and so on. But the association can also be found in the nineteenth century. Moreover, it is an association whose significance lies precisely in a contestation between museums and their emerging publics as mediated through the print media.

The museum and the popular press: an Assyrian tale

In his article 'The times and spaces of history: Representation, Assyria, and the British Museum', Frederick Bohrer (1994) describes the role of the press in applying pressure on the British Museum to make the new Assyrian collection more widely available to the general public during the 1850s. As Bohrer describes it, the arrival of the Assyrian collection in the British Museum, as the result of an extensive and very public archaeological expedition, presented the museum with a series of quandaries. The museum regarded the new objects as a nuisance, not knowing how to classify them. They were not easily assimilated into an art historical discourse, as this was centred on Greco-Roman sculpture. The public, however, loved them, due in no small part to the role of the media in promoting the collection – a situation which eventually forced the museum to build a special gallery for the collection in answer to their critics.

Much of the tension between the general public and the museum was a direct result of the way in which the print media represented the museum and its audience. In effect, the media brought together two social groups which had previously been held quite distinct – the traditional upper class clientele of the museum and an emerging middle class. In the process it educated the museum into rethinking its relationship to the general public as well as introducing the museum and its culture to their readers. Much of this mediation developed around the concept of access. For example, the *Illustrated London News*, a magazine of the period with a lower to middle class readership, served as an organ of information on the Assyrian collection for people who found it hard to gain access to the collection itself. It also criticized the museum for its lack of cooperation in this task. A virtual war developed between the British Museum and the *News* over who had the right to depict the collection in the public domain and thus control its meanings. Representing its stand as a war over access to information, the *News* even went so far as to reproduce images of objects which were not available in the public galleries of the museum. For example, a cuneiform slab was reproduced in graphic representation in the journal's pages by accessing the drawings and records of the archaeologist responsible for the finds, Austen Henry Layard. There were no examples of cuneiform slabs in the gallery itself.

The same attempt to provide access to the inaccessible was evident in graphic representations of two of the collection's most famous objects – the winged bull and lion. While in the museum itself these large sculptures were protected from the public by a large fence, the *Illustrated London News* pictured them without a fence and placed a couple near the statues looking up in awe. The meaning is clear – the journal not only provided better visibility and hence access to the objects in print than in reality, it also had more faith than the museum in the ability of its audience to behave appropriately. Interestingly, the existence

111

of the fence is never actually mentioned within the text. It is almost as if the *News* dealt in the production of virtual museums, simulating the experience of access. In the end, the collection's representation in pictorial form within the popular press ensured that the British Museum was forced to display the collection in a purpose built gallery, contributing to the process of opening up the museum to wider cultural influences. As the trustees said,

> they would not have proposed this addition to the other estimates of the year, were it not for the peculiar circumstances attending the discovery and acquisition of the Assyrian sculptures, and the natural anxiety of the public to have the means of convenient access to them at as early a period as it can be provided.

> (in Bohrer 1994: 205)

Tales of Paris

Another way in which museums became articulated with the popular press was through the production of popular journals and magazines based on the metaphor of the museum. Chantal Georgel (1994), in an article entitled 'The museum as metaphor in nineteenth-century France', describes how publishing houses took up the metaphor of the museum as an encyclopaedic accumulation of knowledge and applied it to the production of magazines on almost any topic. Between 1806 and 1914, Georgel argues, 'more than seventy newspapers, journals, and albums carried the word *musée* (museum) in their titles' (Georgel 1994: 113). As she goes on to suggest,

> this fact alone suggests an interesting relationship between, on the one hand, the world of the press, with its retinue of money, publicity, and advertising – what John Grand-Carteret, in 1893, called 'the century's modern forces' – and, on the other hand, the museum as a privileged exhibition space.

> (113)

Georgel notes a similar association between modernity and the press as Hartley. What is more, she is also interested in the link between popular and elite cultural forms, a link which she also locates in the popular press.[5]

The connection between the museum and the popular press allowed a democratizing rhetoric to inflect the metaphor of the museum. Thus the idea of the museum as an encyclopaedia of knowledge was made available to all through the printed word and, as Hartley might predict, through illustrations. The common man, woman or child could become collectors by purchasing magazines and, by extension, the objects through their representation in illustrations. Some of the more successful magazines prefigured Malraux's (1967) museum without walls, providing comprehensive illustrations of paintings by genre. These illustrations could be cut out and framed giving the ordinary person an instant gallery. Thus, readers of the *Musée de l'histoire, de la nature et des arts* (1830) could look forward to 'the advantage of possessing within a few years and at very little cost a beautiful collection of lithographs, which they might seek to acquire in vain by other means' (*Musée de l'histoire, de la nature et des arts*, no. 1, 6 June 1830 in Georgel 1994: 114).

With this history in mind, it is possible to reinterpret what sometimes appears as a rather naive and utopian narrative around electronic technologies. The social effects of the latter can be seen as part of a much longer articulation between museums and the media, an articulation which has always promised a more democratic culture. Claims that electronic technologies have brought about a radical break begin to appear more as a rhetorical function than a serious attempts to claim a new empirical reality. This is not to deny the importance of rhetoric as it clearly has a role in enabling practices to change. When added to other pressures on the museum to democratize, the rhetoric around electronic technologies begins to look as one end of a wide spectrum of cultural change inside museums. Its usefulness lies perhaps in the very self-consciousness, even if this sometimes makes it appear shrill.

'A museum for the global village'

These other pressures are very evident in the arguments of George MacDonald, one of the most articulate advocates within the museum world for the possibilities afforded by electronic technologies. As director of the Canadian Museum of Civilization, MacDonald[6] explicitly took up on McLuhan's argument that electronic technologies bring different groups of people together in the one space, thereby offering the potential for a more democratic form of communication.

For MacDonald, electronic technologies offered a way to make the Museum of Civilization accessible to Canadians outside of the Ottawa–Hull area as well as to the rest of the world. Accessibility is of course an increasingly important objective for museums who need to develop ways of proving their relevance to the modern world both in cultural and economic terms. Describing the museum as a museum of the 'information society', and as a 'museum for the global village', MacDonald saw his work as an attempt to make the museum responsive to the new social structures and values emerging out of the shift from an industrial to an information society. For him, the 'values, attitudes and perceptions that accompany the technological transition from industrial to information society can make it possible for museums to achieve their full potential as places for learning in and about a world in which the globetrotting mass media, international tourism, migration, and instant satellite links between cultures are sculpting a new global awareness and helping give shape to what Marshall McLuhan characterised as the global village' (MacDonald 1992: 161).

One of the ways in which electronic technologies can help to disrupt the stasis suggested by the metaphor of museums as mausoleums is by breaking the association between objects and institutional authority. Thus, for MacDonald, museums are about the dissemination of information rather than a central repository of objects: 'all museums are, at the most fundamental level, concerned with information: its generation, its perpetuation, its organisation, and its dissemination' (1992: 161). In replacing objects with information, MacDonald is clearly attempting to associate the museum with the speed of global media flows, with contemporaneity rather than stasis. Objects are only important in so far as they contain information which can then be communicated using a variety of different media. From an information perspective, for MacDonald, there is no difference between an object and a photograph or an oral history tape. All three represent information. His argument is not unlike that of Walter Benjamin who argued, as we have already seen, that mechanical means of reproduction made possible a democratization of access to the arts, precisely because of the decreasing importance of the materiality of the art object.

For MacDonald, the notion of information also enables museums to break away from the social status based on the ownership of commodities or objects of value. In making this move, MacDonald uses Robert Kelly's argument that in the information society 'information and experience replace commodities as the basis of wealth ... people in the information society draw their status from the experiences they have and the information they control, rather than the wealth objects they possess' (Kelly in MacDonald 1987: 213). For George MacDonald,

> museum visitors responded in kind and attended quality shows for their information, and blockbusters for the experience (shared with others) which they provided. Where layers of glass signalled the monetary value of museum treasures in the past, the new visitor wanted more 'experiential' exhibits where the object was not separated from the viewer.
>
> (MacDonald 1987: 213)

Within this new framework of information and experience, according to MacDonald, it is the traditional focus of museums on the object that has to be changed. 'Collections have suddenly become something of a burden to museums. Most museum directors now feel like directors of geriatric hospitals whose budgets are devastated by patients whose survival for another day depends on expensive, high-technology support systems' (MacDonald 1987: 214).

For MacDonald, the information society brings with it a new social class and a new type of visitor to the museum (MacDonald 1992: 158–181). He argues that

> [the] features of this new visitor group that are important for museums include its inclination to reject traditional, low-tech, interpretative technologies that employ academic jargon with which they have no familiarity; its preference for new information technologies, with which many people feel comfortable and in control, and which allow them to query more; its greater interest in behind-the-scenes technical operation; and its demand for non-collections-based facilities and services, such as lounges, restaurants, and film presentations.
>
> (MacDonald 1992: 169–170)

The requirements of this new group of visitors mean, for MacDonald, that 'the challenge for museums is to be relevant to this new social group, or else face being defined out of its list of leisure activities' (MacDonald 1992: 170).[7]

MacDonald's position might be criticized as a rather deterministic perspective on recent developments. The information revolution is seen as a radical break from past practices, a break which the museum must also make in order to survive. MacDonald's language heightens the difference between the present and the past, seeing these differences in absolute terms. He is not, of course, alone in producing such a rhetoric. Many other commentators on the information society tend to assume that these new developments signify a complete break with the past (see for example, Castells 1989, 1996 and Poster 1990). There is no space in their analysis for recognizing continuities or extensions of past practices, or indeed for noting the continued relevance of older modes of communication. This also means that the only social group they concern themselves with is that of the new information class. The continued existence of groups for whom the new mode of information is either irrelevant or simply not part of their cultural landscape is dismissed as of little consequence.

The shift MacDonald describes towards valuing objects for their information is not just a result of changing technologies. It also has an institutional context. Financial cutbacks in museums have meant that museums no longer have the purchasing power they once did. There is also a move away from a tradition of connoisseurship towards a social history approach in which objects of little monetary value are collected. As Kenyon (in Fahy 1995: 84) argues, this shift has also involved a prioritizing of information above the value of the object to the point objects with no accompanying information or provenance are not collected. Sometimes, *only* the information is collected.

Yet, if all of this suggests that MacDonald overstates the role of new technologies, he is certainly correct in believing that they are important and have some real effects. In order to adapt to the 'information society', museums have had to change their architecture in order to accommodate the new technology. This has meant the development of a new museum technology which opens rather than closes the space of the museum to outside influences. In the nineteenth century, the architectural challenge was to allow an increasing number of people to view objects as well as to view themselves in the process, so as to institute self-regulation and enable constant monitoring (Bennett 1988c, 1994). In the twentieth and twenty-first centuries, it had also to address the circulation of information. Thus the walls and floors of the museum have to be built to contain electronic cables, the museum has to develop its own backup power supply, and display spaces as well as work spaces have to have facilities for computers.

At the Canadian Museum of Civilization galleries even double as television studios making the collection accessible to anywhere in the world. In the future, it will be possible to organize an event anywhere in the museum and to have it broadcast live. This is in line with MacDonald's belief that the museum must break its association with stasis, of being by definition a non-event. By introducing the museum to the media in this way, he is making a place for the museum within global information flows. The way to achieve access and reach national and global audiences is, he argues, to have 'television production facilities within the new museum, capable of providing a "header end" for educational and special interest television – much as sports domes feed a wide electronic audience today' (1987: 214). His plan in 1987 was

> to start with mini-productions for internal use and for what I see as a new market for cultural programs (the television magazine format). Spaces in the new museum, from exhibits to theatres, have been designed for television production with satellite link-ups that can allow simultaneous and interactive program between ethnic groups separated by 10,000 miles but participating in the same event.
>
> (1987: 214)

Media impacts

The displacement of objects in the USA–Australia gallery

As one of the first museums to engage at both a practical and conceptual level with the potential uses of electronic technologies for widening the audience for museums, the Canadian Museum of Civilization has had considerable influence. Echoes of this influence could be seen on the home page for the new National Museum of Australia before it opened its doors to the public. In discussing the role of electronic technologies in the new museum, staff had this to say:

> As 'a museum for the 21st century' extensive use will be made of communication technologies. Key features of the Museum identified for further development include a digital theatre with one of the world's largest video screens and a broadcast studio which will enable the Museum to connect with national and international communities as a significant part of its public programs.
>
> (http://www.nma.gov.au/newmuseum/index.htm)

But perhaps the issues raised by MacDonald are broader than the question of the use of electronic communication technologies. One of the effects of redefining the museum around the notion of information and its association with a media-based culture is the loss of claims to objectivity and authenticity made possible by the idea of the 'material'. This is clearly evident in contemporary museum practices, even in museums whose directors are not explicit advocates for electronic technologies. One example is the Australian National Maritime Museum's USA–Australia Gallery.[8] There is little discrimination in this gallery between objects, different kinds of pictorial images and electronic media. All three are subsumed under an exhibition narrative, as the following account of the development of the exhibition demonstrates.

One of the most pressing problems in setting up the gallery was the difficulty in finding appropriate objects with which to tell the story of the maritime links between the USA and Australia. Many of the interesting objects were already in major collections in the USA and were not always available for long term loan. Furthermore, the desired narrative was not always compatible with the use of objects. A 'televisual' documentary approach could deal with the issues the curators wanted to explore more effectively. This was the case, for example, with the display on Australia's involvement in the Vietnam War for which a database with a computer touch screen was developed. This database used material broadcast on television during the Vietnam War – a comment on the mediatized experience of the war in Australia – as well as interviews with navy personnel and their experiences.

These display techniques highlight the way in which objects have lost their central position. Collecting was 'display driven' and was not focused exclusively on objects. Photography became extremely important to the gallery's activities as did film. For example, if objects were not available for loan a photograph was requested instead. These eventually became graphics with accompanying labels, having a similar status to objects in their narrative role. The value of both was defined in terms of information implying that messages previously communicated by the object alone could now be communicated as effectively by a photographic image. Graphics became important not only as background material, providing context for the objects, but as artefacts in their own right. A reproduction was as valuable as the original for this purpose, despite a residual sense of loss amongst the curators that the original was unavailable for display. The mystique of authenticity had all but disappeared.

This disappearance or displacement of the object was taken one step further in the creation of an exhibition in video and in computer databases, accessed by touch screens. There was in fact a curatorial position assigned entirely to the research and development of these electronic exhibitions. In the USA–Australia gallery, videos were used to expand the interpretation of objects and to cover stories that could not be told through objects. Videos became an exhibition in themselves achieved through the visual reproduction of the real event or object. So, for example, the themes of the gallery are introduced by a video wall which uses a pastiche of images, superimposed on one another and constantly changing to communicate the subject of the gallery. The only interpretative aid is a musical/special effects sound track. There is no label and no spoken narrative.

The rise of 'constructed' narratives

As the above examples demonstrate, the displacement of the object is accompanied by the increasing importance of narrative. One of the most positive outcomes of these changes is the realization that museum exhibitions no longer have to make absolute claims. Indeed, they can even shift their focus to the construction of narratives and the development of various mythologies. A good example is The Autry Museum of Western Heritage in Los Angeles where exhibitions are explicitly aimed at showing how the idea of 'The West' developed both through actual historical experience and through popular culture, particularly film.

This museum's ease with notions of narrative is made clear from the first introductory label which reads:

> The West has been 'discovered' many times by different peoples. For
> thousands of years nomadic hunters followed game in search of food.
> Long before Europeans explored the region native peoples were farming,
> hunting, making pottery, weaving fabric, building towns, and following
> their own beliefs.
>
> Beginning in the mid 1500s Spanish explorers entered the West. They were
> followed later by Russian, French, English, and American adventurers.
> They came with varying motivations and discovered the West anew. Here
> were wildlife, plants, and people who were new and different to them.
> During a period of just over 300 years, they dominated the first discov-
> erers, redefined the region in their own terms, and left a history which is
> the basis of our Western Heritage.

For this museum, there is no such as thing as 'the' West. The American
West only makes sense as a cultural narrative which emerged over time and
through various historical experiences and attempts to represent those experiences.

This emphasis is so strong that the museum even goes so far as to make its point
through its marketing material. Thus, on its shopping bag, the Autry contrasts
historical experience and what it calls the 'mythological'. This is not in order
to ridicule the mythological by claiming it as a false representation. Rather, it
is to place the mythological as an equally powerful force in producing the
American West. The galleries at The Autry

> present the story of the West by contrasting the historical with the
> mythological. Art, film, and advertising have shaped perceptions of the
> region, and The Autry explores contemporary culture, as well as histor-
> ical realities. Whether it is the art of Albert Bierstadt, Frederic Remington,
> or N.C. Wyeth; the tools, clothing, and firearms of people who inhabited
> the West or the costumes, scripts, and props of Western film and televi-
> sion, The Autry offers an enjoyable and engaging opportunity to discover
> the legacy of the West.

This approach allows The Autry to use a variety of media in order to tell a
story. This further enables it to draw together a number of audiences in the one
space, from those interested in artistic representations of the West, to popular
culture buffs, historians and folklorists, quite apart from the general public. But
perhaps more importantly, it allows recognition of the variety of cultures which
have contributed to the making of the West.

In this way the museum is making a series of connections. These are not
only between traditional curatorial cultures and contemporary media; they are
also between groups which have historically been antagonistic towards one
another. This opens up possibilities of reconciliation through historical explanation. The museum is able to touch upon difficult historical experiences,

such as the Spanish conquest and its impact on indigenous culture, the history of the westward expansion of the United States and even the more contemporary effects of these histories on present day Californian society. In so doing, it mediates between various communities who are often in conflict. In one of its most touching exhibitions, for example, the museum explains that

> The Autry Museum of Western Heritage wishes to publicly recognise the contributions of all communities in the American West. It is our hope that the museum can serve as a center for dialogue and deliberation about community. We encourage you to leave your thoughts about community to share with other visitors and our museum staff.

The virtual museum

This notion of dialogue, based on an understanding of museums as essentially democratic institutions, is also reflected in the idea of the virtual museum. At their most simple level, virtual museums can be simply defined as an electronic media space in which images of museums, collections and displays precede or become superimposed on actual museums, objects and displays. For example, at the Tate Gallery in London it is possible to visit the Micro Gallery (sponsored by Microsoft) and get a full printout of the location of the pictures you want to see together with information about them. The effect is an individually customized tour of the museum. The parallel with the representation of the Assyrian collection in nineteenth-century magazines is striking. Both use images to construct access to a virtual museum in which the exclusivity of the museum is undermined.

The rhetorical deployment of electronic technologies against the image of exclusivity is demonstrated by Elizabeth Broun, Director of the Smithsonian Institute's National Museum of American Art:

> The new electronic media give us at last the tools needed to reach people everywhere, so art can fit into all kinds of experience, beyond the straightforward museum visit. The National Museum of Art is as committed to sharing what we have and what we know with people who may never come to our front door as we are to enhancing the experience of visitors in our galleries. Only a small percentage of our extensive collections can be displayed in our galleries; electronically, we can open a window into our storage spaces and research files, providing an invigorating context for visitors on-site and distant.
>
> (Broun in Noack 1995: 87)

The actual quality of these virtual museums varies of course as does the quality of access. As a number of commentators are increasingly suggesting (for examples see Besser 1997, Donovan 1997, Walsh 1997), most museum web sites have a very limited notion of 'access'. The majority amount to little more than a tourist brochure, while others assume that it is sufficient to enable access to museum databases without other responses either to the medium of the Web or to the new virtual visitors.

There are signs, however, that emerging technological possibilities are creating a space in which some museums are beginning to think about the nature of the Web as a new communication medium. This involves thinking through both the possible impact of the Web on the image of museums and on the way they might do things in the future. One of the more exploratory articles in this vein is Peter Walsh's (1997) piece 'The Web and the unassailable voice', which argues that the Web represents an important opportunity for museums to overcome the 'unassailable voice'. For Walsh the unassailable voice is the traditional voice of the museum which attempts to suppress differences in interpretation by speaking with one authoritative voice, giving the institution a monolithic character. It is a voice which hides the very complex processes which occur in museums in the act of collecting, cataloguing and developing exhibitions. The Web, by contrast, is a medium which represents the exact opposite; it makes it difficult to distinguish between different voices, making the establishment of any one voice above another very difficult. While the museum represents reason and order, the Web is chaotic in its organizational structure. The museum is an organization with clearly established hierarchies, especially over access to information. The Web is available to anyone who has access to a computer and internet connection. The authority of the museum is also emphasized by its rather static nature while the Web is constantly changing.

While Walsh recognizes that there are dangers in emulating the Web, most importantly, the potential loss of cultural authority, he argues that museums must adapt to the culture of the Web. This does not mean they must lose their distinctiveness. They need to lose the unassailable voice, but maintain cultural integrity. Walsh suggests that museums can achieve this by ensuring that their web sites follow a number of principles. The first is that museum web sites must be constantly updated. They cannot afford to remain static like permanent museum exhibitions. This will enable exhibitions created for the Web to reflect the actual process of knowledge formation, distancing themselves from the notion that what a museum says remains true for all time. In the process, museums will also begin to lose their image as distant and unfriendly places which do not relate well to contemporary issues. Museum web sites, Walsh argues, should also provide a facility for dialogue between visitors to the site and museum staff. He suggests discussion pages as one way to achieve this. And finally, he suggests that the provision of deeper layers of information, what could also be called interpretation, will distinguish the museum from other web sites and enable it to retain some authority.

Walsh's discussion has a number of points which can be connected to the work of other commentators and which serve as a useful framework from which to assess the value of museum web sites. One of the most important points is the idea that the Web enables museums to bring different points of information together on the one site where normally they would be held apart. This is possible because of the hypertextual qualities of the Web. Visitors can make links between different kinds of information held by the museum as well as to other related sites. Some commentators refer to this practice as the 'embeddedness' (McLaughlin 1996) of museums within the Web, while others call it 'connectedness'. Both concepts attempt to capture new practices of information management which break down disciplinary boundaries and hierarchical systems of cataloguing opening up the resources of museums to a wider audience. In this sense, museum web sites are promoting a more democratic notion of the museum by letting go of the traditional authoritative voice. In its most advanced form, they are using the possibilities created by the development of Dynamic Hypertext (Hitzeman *et al.* 1997), which makes it possible for information to be created in response to visitor queries rather than answers being limited by the formatting of existing databases.

The best sites are those which go beyond simply making their collection management databases available to the general public, thinking of the Web instead as an opportunity to manage information content. A basic step in this shift is the recognition that it is not enough to simply provide information. Rather, the museum must interpret the information or, in the words of Kevin Donovan (1997), add value to the information it possesses. The most straightforward way of achieving this is to become involved in storytelling rather than simply providing lists. Thus on-line exhibitions, for example, can be extended by linking in to collection databases but in ways which are framed by the act of interpretation. Another way of putting this would be to argue for the need for curatorial staff to be involved in web site design and content as well as collection managers.

So, what do museum web sites which move beyond a simple notion of access, beyond simply making information accessible, look like? How do they promote dialogue between visitors and museums and establish connections between information located both within the museum and outside of it? How do such sites promote a less 'unassailable voice' and move the museum away from its traditional elitist image?

There are a few examples which indicate the potential of the Web for museums as the technology develops and access to the internet becomes more widespread. Some of the more adventurous of these sites are those of university museums which have established partnerships with university computer support systems, computer science departments and sometimes outside firms interested in developing software systems. One of the more exciting web sites in this category is that of the Peabody Museum of Archaeology and Ethnology at Harvard University (http://www.peabody.harvard.edu).

As well as the standard pages giving information about the museum, such as its location, hours, admission prices, current exhibitions and so on, this site is unusual in that it explains the site to its virtual visitors, making the distinction between general information about the site and its special On-Line Features. This makes it very clear how the web site differs from the 'material' museum. In many other web sites it becomes quite difficult to tell the status of various so called exhibitions. Are they teasers to invite the virtual visitor to see the real exhibition at the museum itself or are they truly on-line exhibitions? The distinction is not always clear, even at the web site of museums such as the Canadian Museum of Civilization (http://www.civilization.ca). At the Peabody

Museum then, it is the On-Line Features section of the web site which provides the more innovative developments. These On-Line Features, according to the museum, 'provide the virtual visitor with a broader sense of the museum's object, photographic and archival collections, and research of the faculty and staff'. The aim, then, is to provide a greater level of depth which perhaps is not available within the galleries of the museum itself, including giving a name to the authors of the information presented. And indeed, the site does attempt to move in that direction, although there is further potential.

The on-line exhibition *The Ethnography of Lewis and Clark: Native American Objects and the American Quest for Commerce and Science*, for example, has a number of interesting features which differ from those normally found in a 'real' exhibition. There is far more extensive 'labelling text' than would usually be found on the museum's walls. This is taking advantage of the fact that it is much easier to sit at a computer and read a piece of text on the screen that it is to stand in front of a label on the museum wall. It also says something about who the museum thinks might use their web site – while the language is not difficult, the level of detail is considerable and is thus suitable for high school students doing their assignments, as well as providing greater depth for the well educated lay reader. It also provides some sort of compensation for the absence of the objects themselves.

The exhibition is not static as the site is upgraded as new knowledge comes to light. As Walsh argues, this is one of the advantages of a web-based exhibition over the traditional permanent installation. The exhibition is used to communicate to a broader public about an ongoing research project on the expedition of Lewis and Clark. The project involves locating a now dispersed collection of objects and gathering them together. Thus, while the number of objects currently on display is relatively small, there is the possibility of expanding it as more objects are located and researched. For the moment, those objects which are represented on the web site use the hypertext qualities of the Web to enable more detailed exploration of the objects themselves as well as access to information about the object. This ranges from limited catalogue descriptions to a curatorial essay on the history of the object, including such issues as how it was collected, an interpretation of the meaning of its physical attributes as well as a physical analysis of its fabric. These discussions are linked to specific images of the object so that the detail under discussion can be viewed by the virtual visitor.

Such object-based detail is further enhanced by the provision of links to scholarly articles by the curators around the subject of the exhibition. The university student is also catered for with references to further resources for study. There is even thought given to the issue of equity by making some of the pages on the site also available in Spanish, which is rapidly taking over from English as the main language in some parts of the USA. The disadvantage is that the site begins to look more like a well illustrated book than an exhibition, but then the computer screen cannot simulate the three dimensional environment of the museum itself.

Another exhibition which highlights the evolving nature of knowledge production within museums, as well as the processes involved in developing an exhibition, is the exhibition *Against the Winds: American Indian Running Traditions*, also at the Peabody Museum web site. This exhibition is very much in its early stages of development and represents the way in which audiences can be brought into the process of exhibition development. The introductory page to the site explains the background to the exhibition, the personnel involved and the advisory processes put into place. It also explains to the visitor that the exhibition is still under development, that only the first stage is actually up on the Web and that there are opportunities for the public to contribute their knowledge of American Indian Runners. The exhibition itself is very well structured, following a clear chronological framework within which there are a number of sub-themes. The actual presentation of the material available so far varies in quality. The earlier period, for which there are few documented images, consists mainly of extracts from a book on early Indian runners and is very disappointing. The contemporary period is more interestingly presented, with text especially written for the exhibition, images of contemporary runners and an indication of where further information can be gained.

Other features of the Peabody Museum site cater for the academic researcher such as Finding Aides On-Line. This feature provides lists of several archival collections in the museum, both photographic and paper. The facility is an excellent tool as the site provides a history of the archive itself, a biography of the people concerned and a detailed catalogue of the contents of the archive. While the documents themselves are not available on the site, it is possible to identify what part of the archive you are interested in and to contact the museum in order to arrange physical access to it. This would save hours of research in the museum itself.

The work of the museum staff is highlighted in a Special Projects section. For example, one feature of the site highlights the collaboration of museum staff with the Mexican government in developing a new museum at AltarQ and Copán, an ancient Mayan site. As well as providing an article on the history of the site and the project itself, the site also offers images of the buildings and objects discussed as well as of the new museum itself. An opportunity was also taken to develop the technology of quick time virtual reality a step further, to enable virtual visitors to focus on an object as well as to view a film of the gallery space itself. As well as providing as near as possible the feeling of actually being in the space itself – an experience not possible with the standard use of QTVR such as at the Canadian Museum of Civilization (http://www.civilization.ca) or the Uffizi Gallery (http://www.uffizi.firenze. it/QTVR/sala2M.mov) – the facility fully explains the technical aspects for those who are interested. In this way, the museum is sharing the knowledge developed by its own technical staff with other museums.

Another museum web site which attempts to present the research of its staff as an evolving, authored process, as well as making its archival material available to the general public, is that of the Berkeley Art Museum & Pacific Film Archive

123

(http://www/bampfa.berkeley.edu/main.html). While the exhibitions on this site are not standalone, but refer back to permanent and temporary exhibitions within the museum itself, they are nevertheless an attempt to provide a reasonable level of detail, both in terms of the images and in terms of interpretative material.

The film archive side of the web site is more extensive and includes an on-line database of film notes written by curatorial staff as well as copies of clippings on numerous films dealing with the Pacific. There is also an on-line collection database which enables access to object records as well as essays written by both curators and other scholars. The information has been adapted for the virtual visitor and is not simply a replica of the museum's own internal collection management system. Nevertheless it does require that the visitor have a prior knowledge of what they are searching for. It is not so friendly to browsers, indicating perhaps that this museum/archive perceives the Web as a resource to help them target research-based market niches as well as members of a more general public.

This becomes obvious if one looks at its other educational target audience – children. For this audience, the museum has developed an interactive guide to the museum to be used as a teaching aid. By following the guide and carrying out the various activities suggested within it, children are introduced not only to this museum but to the culture of museums in general, learning how to use them. For example, the guide introduces the museum label to children, explaining what kind of information a label presents and how it is laid out.

This use of the Web to reach multiple users is also a feature of the Carlos Museum at Emory University and Memorial Art Gallery of the University of Rochester web site (http://www.emory.edu/CARLOS/ODYSSEY/). While the web site has a lot of features aimed at students and scholars of archaeology, because of its university location, the site also fosters an interest in archaeology in children. An attempt has been made to use the characteristics of the Web as an aid in an educational programme called Odyssey. For example, technical words such as cuneiform are defined by placing them next to images. Children are encouraged, via the use of simple rhetorical questions and games, to learn to read images of objects for what they might tell them about the people who made and used them. In this way, the site manages to be interactive, getting children to use their imagination. In many ways they are taught to think the way an archaeologist does and in the process they learn to appreciate the value of material culture. Teachers using the site are given further material through a specialist bibliography aimed at them, while special bibliographies are also presented to the children and to a non-specialist adult audience.

An example of a site which caters for a general audience but which attempts to 'add value' to information is the web site for Monticello, Thomas Jefferson's home (http://www.monticello.org/index.html). As well as presenting the usual information aimed at intending visitors, the site offers a rich interpretation of the house, grounds, the life of Jefferson himself and the times in which he lived, for those who are not in a position to visit Monticello itself. The creators of the site used extensive excerpts from primary sources such as diaries and letters, as well as photographic images of the site itself, to provide a number of narratives which help to interpret the significance of Jefferson for American history as well as the history of Monticello. Each narrative stands on its own but the visitor is offered more in-depth knowledge through hyperlinks to further information. It is possible to build an understanding of important aspects of Jefferson's life, his habits, his house or of important objects.

An innovative exhibition on this site is one which is based on an oral history project which involved interviewing the descendants of slaves who had once lived on the site. Called *Getting Word: Oral History at Monticello*, the exhibition deals with difficult issues such as Jefferson's attitudes towards slavery, the actual experience of slaves living and working at Monticello and the lives of their descendants. Extensive use is made of visual images, primary sources from the time and family stories passed down through the generations. Researchers are also catered for through the provision of a database on Jefferson, links to the University of Virginia's archives on Jefferson, and a special feature which presents the work of curators on daily life at Monticello with links to primary sources as well as secondary articles.

All of these sites maintain a clear distinction between the museum itself and the representation of its work and collections on the Web. While the examples I have discussed are exploring ways in which the Web can add to their other activities and increase their audience reach, they do not claim to be either a replica of the real museum or a substitute for it. There are, however, some examples of cyber-museums which only exist through the technology of virtual reality and which attempt to replicate or reproduce actual sites. While mostly experimental and not yet widely accessible to the general public, these attempt to recreate in three-dimensional virtual experiences, 'real' temples, ancient cities and museums. In these museological creations it is possible to experience walking through the buildings and displays, communicate with guides and other real visitors who may be passing through the space at the same time as you but in reality be physically located in another country. For example, Carl Leffler at the Studio for Creative Inquiry at Carnegie-Mellon University is directing a project called the Networked Virtual Art Museum. The idea is that virtual visitors from a number of different points around the world will be able to visit virtual galleries at the same time, see each other, have independent motions and move objects at will. In one of the galleries, visitors will be able to wander about a virtual full scale replica of an ancient Egyptian temple of Horus while receiving lectures about it from costumed agents of that time period (Brill 1992 and Burd 1994).

Such extreme examples of virtual museums are interesting in that they also point to the use within cyberculture of the metaphor of the traditional museum. This is an interesting phenomenon, for if museums have been traditionally associated with centralized power, cyberspace is taken as the very opposite – as a radically deterritorialized space. Why then should representations of cyberspace involve images of the traditional nineteenth-century museum? Why is it that, as the museum moves away from a referent in a reality constructed through objects, as they change their architectural design towards more open and less imposing architectural forms, virtual reality takes up on the museum, in its nineteenth-century form, as a symbol for itself?

For example, in the film *Disclosure*, cyberspace holds the information which will provide the evidence needed by the protagonist, played by Michael Douglas, to prove his innocence of the charge of sexual harassment. Entry into this space of information is through a museum-like atrium, entered through a classical doorway. In this space are many doors which lead to different files just as from the traditional museum atrium, one can walk through a number of possible galleries. The space is a maze.

The symbol of the museum used in *Disclosure* is not the postmodern virtual museum but the nineteenth-century museum – the museum as both temple and universal archive. Why? One possible answer is indicated by the tone of the literature on virtual technology and the internet. Both emphasize access and democracy. Irrespective of the argument surrounding the issue of whether the information highway is indeed more democratic than other media, taking up the museum as a symbol and a virtual space makes such a claim more concrete.

As I have argued, museums have been associated with privileged access to knowledge. They have been 'sacred spaces' open to those who know how to read its rituals and texts (Duncan 1995). They were socially and culturally exclusive. Putting museums on the Net or into virtual reality immediately undermines such claims to exclusiveness – anyone can visit the Louvre or the Tate without physically having to go there. They can behave and comment as they want while doing so. They can even download or print copies of the art works they see.

Making 'forbidden' spaces open is a recurring theme of virtual reality tech-nologies – in video games where military activities such as flying fighter jets are available to children in simulation, and of course through simulated pornog-raphy. The availability of museums alongside these forms of entertainment only adds to the ways in which the museum, as a cultural icon, is increasingly impli-cated in contemporary media flows. Virtual reality is one of the ways in which traditional discourses of museums are being re-troped so that new asso-ciations for old institutions can emerge.[9] As we have seen, however, the associ-ation between museums and the media is not as new as these rhetorical claims would have it.

At the same time, however, it is the popular association of the museum with materiality and presence which also distinguishes the museum from the world of simulation. The museum, despite claims to the contrary, continues to share in the characteristics of the material world. As Andreas Huyssen (1995) argues, the suggestion that the mass media, especially television, have created an unquenchable desire for experiences and events, for authenticity and identity which television is unable to satisfy, puts the museum in a unique situation. This is because the increasing virtuality of the world seems to demand its own counterpoint in the materiality of the object that has withstood time. Existence in time creates its own aura, as Walter Benjamin (1973) pointed out, but this only becomes significant if it can be counterpointed by its opposite. As Huyssen argues,

> the need for auratic objects, for permanent embodiments, for the experience of the out of the ordinary, seems indisputably a key factor of our museumphilia. Objects that have lasted through the ages are by that very virtue located outside of the destructive circulation of commodities destined for the garbage heap. . . . The materiality of the objects themselves seems to function like a guarantee against simulations.
>
> (1995: 33)

The idea is particularly suggestive if one notes that the current museum boom emerged at precisely the point at which electronic technologies became the basis for discussions about the 'information society'. This parallels the way in which, in the nineteenth century, museum collections gained in popular status through their representation in the popular media of the day. What perhaps now needs discussion is the quality of the relationship between the material and the virtual. Rather than assuming that museums must choose between becoming virtual or remaining in the material world, between remaining conservative or becoming democratic, it is perhaps important to recognize that museums have always been implicated in questions of communication – questions which have always revolved around the relationship between objects, media and social relations.

6

Interactivity in museums: the politics of narrative style

> How can today's museums compete with television? Viewers are captivated
> by the action and excitement on the TV screen while museum visitors face
> only static exhibits in glass cases.
>
> (Stickler 1995: 36)

In this introduction to his short article on museum interactives John Stickler
replays some common motifs in the way museums are defined in relation to
contemporary media culture. Museum exhibits are perceived as static, unexciting and only requiring a passive form of appreciation; film, television, video
and multimedia presentations are, by contrast, 'interactive'.

One of the contexts for this criticism is the way many museums have traditionally organized their exhibits, with a strong linear narrative which allows
space for only one point of view – that of the curator/institution. Museum
critics point to the ways in which this single, linear narrative is expressed in
gallery designs which have a one way flow based on a clear sequence of
exhibits. These spatial arrangements are supported by strong ideologies which
determine the arrangement of the objects in ways which fix their meanings. The
most obvious of these are evolutionary narratives whether in the natural or
the social world (Bal 1992, Bennett 1995, Haraway 1985, Jordanova 1989).
The effect of these narratives is that the visitor is unambiguously placed as a
receiver of knowledge, as the end point of the production process rather than
in an interactive relationship to the objects being displayed.

These critiques have developed from two angles, each motivated by quite
different perspectives. The first has been an ideological critique, mainly from
within the academy, which has pointed out that strong linear narratives make
it almost impossible to achieve an equitable social representation. They bind
museums to their historical role in the processes of imperialism, colonialism and
nation-building. The second line of critique has been from within museums, and
is usually motivated by a simple recognition that the traditional authority of
museums alienates a significant number of potential visitors. This alienation has
become a problem in a context in which a growing number of curators are
arguing for an increased public and political role for the museum and governments are increasing the pressure for museums to become more self-funding.

The first line of critique is most effectively represented by the 'New Museology'. Like the broader field of cultural studies from which it takes its bearings, New Museology is interested in questions about the ways in which power is socially deployed. The line of criticism taken by new museologists has a long history within cultural studies, and its arguments have been well rehearsed. Strong narratives, which gain their strength from a linear, sequential perspective are associated with a politically conservative ideology, while weaker narrative forms are associated with ideologically progressive political positions.

For Tony Bennett, for example, strong evolutionary narratives are associated with nineteenth-century classification systems and a design philosophy which encourages linear displays. This linearity encourages a mode of walking which is organized and pedagogically orientated. As Bennett says, 'locomotion – and sequential locomotion – is required as the visitor is faced with an itinerary in the form of an order of things which reveals itself only to those who, step by step, retrace its evolutionary development' (Bennett 1995: 43). According to Bennett, the pedagogy developed by this technology of 'organised walking' is not just about how people are represented. It is also a technology which 'saturates the routines of the visitor as the lesson of art's progress takes the form of an itinerary that the visitor is obliged to perform. The museum converts rooms into paths, into spaces leading from and to somewhere' (44).

The second line of critique is embedded in the call for a greater use of media technologies in the museum environment. As Chapter 5 made clear, such a call is aligned with attempts to make museums more democratic and accessible. Media technologies are seen as an important strategy in making museums culturally relevant to an increasingly media-literate society. Thus, in the literature on museum interactives, the point is frequently made that their presence enlivens the museum, turning it from a static into an interactive space, making it more entertaining for a younger audience, introducing a 'fun' way to learn. As Stickler puts it,

> [t]wo key words, 'immersion' and 'interaction', combine with newly developed technologies to allow today's museums to hold their own with television, films and video games. If the diorama is the stereotypic example of traditional museum presentation, the 'immersion' concept takes away the viewing window and allows the public to walk right into the exhibit.
>
> (Stickler 1995: 36)

Modern interactives are seen as effective counters to Bennett's 'sequential locomotion' with its didactic objectives.

Like Stickler, I am interested in developing ways in which visitors can 'walk right into the exhibit' and thus play a part in producing its meaning, challenging the authority of the museum to produce and regulate their subjectivity. However, I do not see this development as being dependent on the use of multimedia interactives within exhibition spaces. As I will argue, most of the literature on museum interactives frames these as didactic tools based on some form of mechanistic activity. Visitors push a button, touch a screen or manipulate an object in order to elicit information. Adding a multimedia station to an exhibit will not, therefore, necessarily challenge a one-way flow of communication which the exhibition as a whole may be premised upon. Nor does multimedia in itself necessarily represent a more democratic, open medium of communication.

If the arguments of the 'New Museology' are right and the problem lies with the use of strong linear narratives, multimedia interactives will not, in themselves, challenge the linear narrative structure behind exhibition design. Instead, exhibition spaces need to be reconceptualized as having to be interactive in themselves. This requires museums to move away from a didactic, hierarchical model of communication towards an understanding of exhibition narratives as polysemic and open ended. The first step is to redefine, in the museum context, what might be meant by interactivity. As I hope to show, this will also have the effect of pointing out that the discursive production of an opposition between a museum experience and an interactive one is unhelpful as well as a misleading description of many contemporary museum exhibitions.

The chapter considers three museums as examples of different approaches to interactivity. I will attempt to show how each approach to interactivity determines the narrative tone of the museum and affects the way history is represented. The first example is concerned with 'technical' interactivity and the ways in which this approach limits historical understanding in the case of the exhibitions at the Museum of Tolerance in Los Angeles. Discussion here will be related to the specific American context of the Museum, focusing on the links between faith in the democratic possibilities of technology and the American ideology of individualism. I argue that a technological understanding of interactivity is used to support a strong linear narrative which prevents any negotiation of meanings.

My second example is the Australian National Maritime Museum which makes an explicit attempt to provide an interactive space within the narrative structure of the exhibitions. Using the findings of a visitor study report, I discuss both the problems and the possibilities of an exhibition design philosophy which moves away from strong narratives in museums. I call this approach 'spatial' interactivity.

Finally, I will discuss the Museum of Sydney as offering a possible middle ground: attempting to use the concept of interactivity to suggest a new space in which meanings can be negotiated, while maintaining an explicit political commitment. This I term 'dialogic' interactivity. Before I discuss these museums, however, it is worth reviewing how interactivity has been understood in museums.

Interactivity and museums

While the discourse on interactivity in museums is new, the idea is not. As a number of commentators have pointed out, the idea of interactive displays has a long history. Kathleen McLean (1993), for example, traces it back to as early as 1889, when the Urania in Berlin contained visitor activated models and a scientific theatre as well as to the Deutsches Museum in Munich which was experimenting with film and a variety of working models in 1907. McLean's choice of examples illustrate three of the main assumptions in contemporary discussions of interactivity – first that it involves the presence of some techno-logical medium, second that an interactive exhibit is a physical object which is added to the main display, and third that interactive displays are something which the visitor can operate, that it involves physical activity.

Such assumptions can be understood as a narrowing of the concept, a narrowing which has occurred largely as a result of contemporary media. Writing in 1981, Bonnie Pitman-Gelles (1981: 35) had a much wider view of interactivity when she explained that interactive exhibits

> provide a sense of discovery or direct experiences with objects. They appeal to a variety of senses and generally require the adult or child to handle materials, play roles, day dream, operate equipment and partici-pate in play or work. An interactive exhibit can be a single station involving push buttons or computer terminals, more complex visitor-activated units, or entire environments such as those at Colonial Williams-burg and the Florida State Museum's caves.
>
> (Pitman-Gelles 1981: 35)

While there is some overlap with McLean's definition, there is also space for an understanding of interactivity which sees it as an imaginative and conceptual activity rather than a physical one – it could be as simple as daydreaming, or an empathetic response to objects.

This breadth of definition has largely been lost from more contemporary discus-sions. Stephanie Koester (1993), in her discussion of interactive multimedia, can be taken as a representative of recent approaches, approaches which have a heavy investment on the part of multimedia companies. In her report for Archives and Museum Informatics, a company with interests in computer multimedia applications, Koester explicitly suppresses an older understanding of interactivity in favour of a more narrow, technologically oriented definition. She points out that the older definition saw many levels of interactivity, including the ability of free movement throughout the museum and the use of various media (objects, labels, pamphlets, audio tape, guide) to experience the exhibitions. However, she makes a distinction between this type of multimedia experience and interactive multimedia which she defines as

> computer-generation technologies that incorporate multiple media, such as text, sound, video, or graphics, into an integrated computer system, which then serves as an exhibit that can inform the visitor on a relevant museum topic using the most appropriate communications media.
>
> (Koester 1993: 9)

In indicating that she will only deal with the latter form of interactive multi-media, Koester limits discussion about interactivity to 'technical' interactivity. This prevents an understanding of more general ways in which museum exhibitions can be understood as interactive and thus as part of a media-oriented contemporary culture.

As a consequence of this perspective, interactivity seems to be generally understood as something which can be added to an already existing display and which most often involves some form of electronic technology. This has major implications, as the notion of interactivity becomes limited to the use of 'interactives', something which is designed by educators and designers in association with computer experts rather than something which is integral to the curation and design of an exhibition. Such a view is reflected in policy documents, such as the corporate plan from the British Science Museum during its redevelopment in the early 1990s. The plan proposed that as part of the redevelopment of the site, the museum would 'devote 15 per cent of the floorspace in the existing building to interactives' and that it would 'increase this proportion to 25 per cent when the new building extension, the West End Development, is complete' (Thomas 1994: 33).

Much of the literature on interactives sustains this approach with its emphasis on the dos and don'ts of museum interactives. For example, an article in the February issue of *Museums Journal* (1993) accepts the common equation of interactivity with computer technology. Given this, the task is to 'set out the options and give guidelines for successful multimedia installations' (Lewis 1993: 33). For Peter Lewis, those involved with the design of interactives have to ask the following basic questions:

> Is it a stand-alone educational tool?
> Is it part of the overall interpretation of the story being told in the gallery?
> Is it merely for entertainment?
> Is it being targeted at a specific age group?
> Will it consist of a single workstation or multiple positions?
> Who is the audience?
>
> (Lewis 1993: 33)

The next decision, according to Lewis, is to decide 'whether the display will be mechanical or audio-visual'. A list of technical advice then follows for each choice.

It is not surprising, given this approach, that interactivity is a topic of discussion for museum educators, children's museums, science centres and multimedia producers rather than history or art curators. This division is further deepened by suspicion on the part of curators that interactives are merely a form of entertainment rather than a philosophy which could improve museum communication. As John Stevenson admits, 'interactive centres are popular with visitors but their popularity makes some of us uneasy; we wonder how effective they may be and whether they have been established just to attract visitors rather than for educational reasons' (Stevenson 1994: 30). The opposition between education and entertainment is never far from the surface in these discussions, as is the assumption that interactives are mainly for children. As David Phillips argues, 'the interactive business has been mainly about making kids feel at home in museums, explaining, say, how aerofoils work in an annexe to a flight gallery' (Phillips 1994: 28). While no doubt this is tied to an older model of education in a museum context, it is also one of the factors preventing the concept of interactivity from gaining more widespread acceptance. It is something which is seen as appropriate in children's museums but not in adult ones. Hence, interactivity is most often discussed in the context of museum education with children as the main learners.

One consequence of this is that much of the discussion around interactivity, while it professes to be more open than traditional museum displays, is in fact concerned with models of learning which involve a simple communicative process – from the museum to the visitor. Thus, for example, McLean (1993: 95) states that designing an interactive exhibit 'requires an ability to integrate communication goals (what you want the visitor to *learn*) with behavioural goals (what you want the visitor to *do*), and even emotional goals (what you want the visitor to *feel*)' (italics in original text). Clearly, the assumption is that the museum defines what is being communicated and that the task of an interactive exhibit is to communicate that information effectively and fully. There is no space in this conception of interaction for visitors to make their own meanings or affect the display in some way – that is for a two-way model of communication. More than an educational tool, interactives are also management tools which are useful not only in communicating information but also in regulating behaviour and psychological states.

Even critical approaches to the effects of interactivity continue to maintain an understanding of interactivity as essentially technologically driven. For example, Andrew Barry's (1998) piece on interactivity in science museums is based on a definition of interactivity that assumes the presence of a technological interface. His main criticism is that interactives avoid the role of cultural and historical explanation. in the case of science museums this avoidance ultimately means that the new interactives fail to make links between the scientific principles they represent and the range of debates going on in society about science. They thus fail to communicate the value of science to society as well as its limitations. Reread from my perspective, however, Barry's criticisms could be made stronger if he engaged with the way in which interactivity is defined. While I entirely agree with him that contemporary interactives are not used for the role of cultural and historical explanation, I locate the reasons for this absence to the way in which interactivity is conceptualized. If we change the ways in which we think about it, it might also be possible to change the ways museums think about the function of interactivity. This is a suggestion that underlies my analysis of the Museum of Tolerance in Los Angeles.

Technological interactivity and its limitations: the Museum of Tolerance

A very clear example of the limitations of a technical focus in designing interactive displays is the Beit Hashoah Museum of Tolerance in Los Angeles. This is a museum with a serious message – to explain how intolerance is alive in contemporary society and to combat its spread, using the Holocaust as the ultimate example. While the aims of the museum are a fine example of the way museums can be used to stimulate discussion about serious issues, I will argue that the Museum ultimately fails these aims as open-ended communication is eclipsed by high tech interactives. At the Museum of Tolerance, a technical definition of interactivity is used to support a strong linear exhibition text which is firmly embedded within a metanarrative of individualism. Intolerance is framed as an individual problem which can only be overcome at the personal level. Such a narrative framework and the way in which it is textually and technologically produced severely limits the possibilities for a more complex understanding of the social bases of intolerance.

Of course, there are a number of reasons why this museum may have chosen an interpretative strategy which focused on the individual. Perhaps the most obvious is the location of the Museum in Los Angeles. In presenting its purpose as combating intolerance everywhere, the Museum was able to secure public funding from the Californian State Legislature in a city where violence between and within different racial groups is endemic. As a number of critics have pointed out (Norden 1993, Rosenfeld 1995, Wiener, 1995), this led to one of the museum's central problems – negotiating the need to discuss intolerance in general while keeping faithful to an established historical tradition which depicts the Holocaust as a unique event which cannot be compared with any other.

This tension between an exclusive understanding of the Holocaust and the need to counteract acts of racial violence all over the world is reflected in the initial stages of the Museum's development. As Edward Norden (1993) points out, the initial plan was simply to have a 'Beit Hashoah' – or 'House of the Holocaust'. Such 'houses' memorialize the Holocaust, claiming a special place for it, apart from other instances of racial violence. However, this view of the Holocaust has been diluted in recent years as the term began to be used more generally to describe genocide and other acts of intolerance. As Rosenfeld (1995) has pointed out, the language of the Holocaust is now 'regularly invoked by people who want to draw public attention to human-rights abuses, social inequalities suffered by racial and ethnic minorities and women, environmental disasters, AIDS, and a whole host of other things'.[1] The idea of victimhood is used to link such disparate experiences of acts of social intolerance. As Rosenfeld (1995) explains,

> the rhetoric of 'oppression' has become a commonplace of contemporary American political, academic, and artistic discourse, and its exponents frequently take recourse to the signs and symbols of the Nazi Holocaust to describe what they see as their own 'victimisation' within American society.

In drawing a comparison between being a victim of the Holocaust and other instances of victimization, the moral imperative to stand up to instances of intolerance is strengthened.

This latter understanding of the importance of the Holocaust as a universal reminder of the results of intolerance underpins the work of the Simon Wiesenthal Foundation. As well as developing the museum, this Jewish human rights agency is renowned for its fight against racism all over the world. Such an association, appealing to a worldwide constituency, would quite naturally locate its fight within a universalist rhetoric with recourse to abstract rather than socially specific discourses. The Holocaust is thus produced at a rhetorical level as the greatest expression of evil the world has ever seen – 'the ultimate example of man's inhumanity to man' (Museum of Tolerance pamphlet). At the same time the Holocaust is also a source of individual symbols of resistance which represent the redemption of mankind. The idea that individuals can and should resist expressions and acts of intolerance is thus an important feature of American approaches to the Holocaust.

This approach clearly has a basis in powerful American ideologies of individualism in which the social good is seen to rest in the hands of individuals rather than in social structures. As the basis for American democracy, the ideology of individualism is produced in the museum as the main counter to intolerance. For in the twentieth century, it has been democracy, and more specifically American democracy, which is seen in America as having provided the main bulwark in the fight against Fascism and more recently Communism – political ideologies which are routinely identified with totalitarianism. However, the museum's approach to interactivity, based on a technological interpretation, has more in common with totalitarian than democratic approaches to cultural production. This is because their approach closes off the negotiation of meaning at the same time as producing high levels of crowd control. The ideological narrative might be one of individualism but the means used to express it are those of mass communication.

How, then, does the Museum of Tolerance combine a technically oriented definition of interactivity with an ideology of individualism while at the same time using mass communication techniques? Or, to put the question another way, what is the relation between the museum's use of interactives and the way the exhibition's narrative is textually produced?

The Museum of Tolerance advertises itself as a high tech, interactive museum. As its brochure explains, 'this high-tech, hands-on experiential Museum focuses on two themes through unique interactive exhibits: the dynamics of racism and prejudice in America, and the history of the Holocaust'. These interactive exhibits 'engage visitors in real-life situations that help to identify their own existing and potential prejudices' (Museum of Tolerance pamphlet). They range from computerized maps which at the press of a button show the existence and location of various hate groups throughout America to exhibits that set up a confrontation between the visitor's values and the effects of stereotyping, prejudice and intolerance. For example, an exhibit called *Matching Pairs* asks the visitor to select sets of images representing people. The aim is to reveal racial, gendered and class values which affect our choices. Such a display is reinforced by a cacophony of images and sounds that reproduce racist and gendered values amongst many other prejudices. The framework for an individualist under-standing of intolerance is thus set up. In going through each interactive, visitors are led as individuals on a path of greater self-awareness in which their own role in the production of intolerance can be recognized. In this, museum tech-nology has a double function – to make the message of the museum accessible to each individual and to emphasize that the solution to the problem of intolerance lies with the individual.

The interactive capability of many of the exhibits is used to help the visitor monitor their own levels of intolerance and compare it with those of others. In an interactive on the Los Angeles riots of 1992, for example, it is possible to compare your reactions to the events with those of others. In this interactive, visitors are asked their opinion on a number of questions relating to the events of 1992. Their answers are tabulated and given back to them as a percentile of all answers. Technology thus becomes an extension of individual people, a cybernetic self-monitoring system which can be used to reinforce the message that social ills are a result of individual dispositions.

This technological monitoring of each person's level of intolerance is replicated in a number of interactive exhibits which point out the mind set of each person. Interactive exhibits are designed to test each visitor's assumptions about age, gender, colour and class. These measures thus become examples of intolerance rather than ever being used as explanatory categories. There is no class analysis of the Los Angeles riots, for example – only a statistical monitoring of where violence erupted and which groups engaged in it. Issues of class, race, economics, gender are not explicitly discussed as the basis for intolerance. They are merely presented as examples of it.

The use of high tech interactives to suggest that the basis of intolerance is personal rather than social is emphasized textually in the way the exhibition space is organized. What I find disturbing about this phenomenon is the way in which a message of individual responsibility is produced by a highly organized system of visitor control. A system which not only controls where the visitor walks, the order in which they can see exhibits and the amount of time they can spend in front of them, but also then fixes this experience within an indi-vidualist ideology. The narrative thus produced is strongly linear – in a chrono-logical and ideological sense – and it has the authority of American culture itself. The result is an absence of space within which critical questions might be asked and a historical understanding of the events and processes gained.

The entire visit to the Museum of Tolerance is a highly managed affair. Visitors gather in the entrance lobby and are called together as a group, where they are required to show their entry ticket before they are allowed to pass a guard who stands at the entrance to the spiral ramp which forms the backbone of the museum. Visitors are then asked to follow the guide down the ramp into the bowels of the building. The experience of walking down the ramp is fore-boding. One senses that difficult things lie ahead. On reaching the bottom the guide stops the group and explains that this is a museum about intolerance and the evil which it produces. The guide explains that everyone is intolerant and that the displays are designed to prove this. Each one has a message which we, the visitor must learn if we are to join the fight against racism. We are then asked to make sure we go through each interactive exhibit before we view either the films or the Holocaust section.

The language used is both moralistic and didactic – we are told how to think and what to do. This is reinforced by a right of passage experience in which visitors have to choose between two doors to gain access to the 'Tolerancenter'. The one on the left is under the sign 'intolerant' while the one on the right is signposted 'tolerant'. In case someone has not received the message, the guide then informs us that should we choose the door which says 'tolerant' we would find our way barred. The visitor is thus channelled into the exhibition space with their subjectivity already defined for them. The strategy is confrontational, even to those who are sympathetic to the messages the museum is interested in communicating. While this confrontation is useful in forcing self-awareness it prevents a deeper understanding of the social basis of intolerance. This is because many of the responses to the material presented are encouraged at an emotional level rather than from a process of historical enquiry. The effect is compounded by a sense of self-censorship in the presence of so much suffering which prevents the development of a critical, open attitude to the exhibition.

The Tolerancenter is a large enclosed room entirely dominated by the multi-media interactives discussed above. These are the stations which we must engage with in order to learn both how we are intolerant and the mechanisms which those in power use to produce us as such. The didactic aim is clearly to make us aware of these processes so that we can resist them. The multimedia interactives in this space have been designed within a model of communication which assumes a one way flow of information. They have a 'message' which it is our task to grasp. In McLean's (1993) terms they are successful exhibits in so far as they are clear in their educational, behavioural, and emotional goals.

At one level, the lessons these interactives have to offer are useful – they point to the way in which language has been used to denigrate people who are different from oneself on the basis of gender, age, ethnicity, colour, even weight. They show how constant repetitions of simple messages through a public forum such as the media produces ideologies which place one group in power and another as subordinate. They also show how these ideologies become embedded in the very structures and institutions of society. The point is made that alternative ways of looking at the world are erased, partly by achieving total saturation.

Yet, it is precisely this same strategy which is used by the museum itself to manage the rest of the visit, especially through the Holocaust Section which is the centrepiece of the experience. The techniques used are those of total immersion. The exhibits recreate the feel and atmosphere of living in Nazi Germany as a Jew, through a series of technically brilliant dioramas which are 'brought alive' through film and audio, replicating the experience of being trapped. In order to get out, the visitor has to go through each exhibit in the order in which it is displayed. The visitor is enclosed in a one way tunnel with the guide constantly monitoring the pace. Even if the guide were not there, the dioramas would control the pace of the visitor as they light up as the visitor comes through, activating their film reels and the audio recordings. Once these are finished, the lights go off and the next diorama lights up. There are no labels, no possibility to backtrack or to read again.

This linearity is further emphasized by the chronological presentation which starts in 1920s Berlin, a time of false optimism, through the rise of Hitler, his control of all systems of public communication, the development of the Second World War and its impact on the Jewish population, ending with the 'Final Solution' – the attempted genocide of European Jewry, described in graphic detail in a simulation of the Auschwitz gas chambers in the Hall of Testimony. At the very end, there is some effort to document the efforts of those who tried to save Jews, but this is framed as an exception which each individual needs to build upon. The design philosophy of the museum is thus a linear one, based on a chronological approach, while its curatorial intent is to achieve total emotional control of the visitor. This control is aided by the attempt to identify each visitor with an actual Jewish person who lived and more often than not died during the Holocaust. After the historical introduction to Germany, each visitor gets a computer generated identity card which they carry with them as they walk/experience the display. At the end, they are asked to return their identity card to the computer and receive a biography of the person they carried with them. Personal identification with the victims is completed.

What are the strengths and limitations of such an approach? On the positive side the museum encourages personal empowerment – a belief that the actions of an individual can make a difference. For Americans this empowerment is also the re-affirmation of their own cultural values. These values, which are seen as universal, can then be used to construct a space which promotes identification with other cultures. There is also the important work of remembering the Holocaust. On the negative side, however, this remembering is achieved by emotive identification with the victims rather than through a nuanced historical understanding. This makes it difficult to make historical comparisons with the present, despite the stated aims of the Tolerancenter. Nothing can be as evil as the Holocaust, no specific example of intolerance can be compared with it. An emotive understanding also preempts the possibility of looking for social reasons as to why the Holocaust and, indeed other instances of large scale racism, occur.

The problem is perhaps captured by Shane Maloney (1994) in his account of his family's visit to the Museum. Maloney describes how the emotional impact of the displays made it impossible for him to experience them with a spirit of critical enquiry. Silence was the only possible response. Remembering the replica of the gas chambers at Auschwitz, Maloney writes:

> In this setting, however contrived and grotesque, my pen and notebook seem out of place, a profanity. I put them away.

> We sit in wincing, self-conscious silence and listen.

> The story we hear is poignant and horrible and concerns the means of selection for murder of a group of young boys. . . . The tape ends, but the silence does not.
>
> (Maloney 1994: 17)

The problem of silence as the only possible response is one which critics have also identified in relation to other museums which also memorialize the Holocaust. As Mireille Jucheau (1996) argues in her study of the Sydney Jewish Museum,

> it is perhaps not enough, now that certain forms of historical technique are being questioned, merely to present a set of stories about the past without reference to the processes that formed those stories and the context within which they come to be represented.
>
> (70)

This is particularly so with a historical event which most describe as unrepresentable. There is a need to capture this inability to represent by allowing for narrative ruptures. For Jucheau, these ruptures could be as simple as a physical space which disrupts the linear narrative of exhibitions, maybe even a dead end. For her, the Jewish Museum in Berlin is more successful in providing these narrative disjunctures than the Sydney museum, because it provides architectural spaces which go nowhere and which cut across the exhibitionary spaces.

Jucheau's concern for open rather than closed narratives is supported by her use of Saul Friedlander and his suggestion that an important aspect of historical representations of the Holocaust is the necessity to balance between emotive appeals and those which seek to envelop the experience of the victims in a protective distance. As he says, achieving this balance entails

> the imperative of rendering as truthful an account as documents and testimonials will allow, without giving in to the temptation of closure. A resolved account of the disaster avoids confronting some of the most troubling aspects of that event – its inexplicable quality, its multiple and disparate effects; the lingering symptom, the invisible emotional freight carried by its witnesses.
>
> (Friedlander in Jucheau 1996: 74)

A number of critics of the Museum of Tolerance have suggested a relation between ideological closure and the use of 'television formats'. A good example is perhaps Nicola Lisus' and Richard Ericson's (1995) work on the museum which attempts to deal with the contradictions I have noted above between an appeal to interactivity and a highly controlled environment. Pointing to the importance of televisual culture in informing the museum's use of multimedia, Lisus and Ericson argue that 'while the visitor is provided with the sensation of being in a "free-flicker" environment, the individual is not as free as she seems' (7). The museum, they argue,

> has managed to tap into and mimic the emotive power of the television format but at the same time has managed to transmodify it. The Museum

139

determines what images will be seen, and in what sequence, all the while making visitors feel that they are passing through a free-flow environment.

(7–8)

They further suggest that this tension, while carefully controlled in the Tolerancenter through the use of multimedia interactives, is completely displaced in the Beit Hashoah section where the visitor is propelled completely into the narrative with no space for critical distance at all. The result is emotional empathy without historical understanding.

While I agree with Lisus and Ericson that this is indeed what happens at the Museum, I am not sure that the problem is entirely due to the 'televisual format'. For them the problem is with the medium being used – television, they suggest, can only produce spectacle. While recognizing that spectacle can have positive political outcomes in encouraging people to act from an emotional basis, they agree with critics of the 'society of the spectacle' (Baudrillard 1983, Debord 1988, Eco 1986) that rational understandings have no place in the medium. The problem with spectacle is that

> the visitor's ability to define and maintain control over the experiences that are imposed upon her is incrementally lost. The real – or rather those things that define the real, namely memory and history – collapses, in degrees, into the fantastic, the fictional, the unreal.
>
> (Lisus and Ericson 1995: 13)

While this is indeed a problem in presentations such as those at the Museum of Tolerance, where there is no relief or change in the mode of presentation, I would argue that the problem stems more broadly from American culture itself. It may not be so much in media images but their use in a society which believes in the democratizing effects of technology and in individual action as the basis for political change. The loss of historical understanding, and indeed the very way in which the Holocaust is understood and represented, has more to do with an ideology of individual free will than it has to do with television culture.

This analysis also throws light on those who like the museum's use of high tech to support a narrative of individual responsibility. For example, Wiener (1995) suggests that the museum presents its audience with a potentially radical interpretation of the Holocaust because the Tolerancenter depicts all visitors as perpetrators rather than asking them to identify with the victims. For Wiener, the political potential of such a move is enormous:

> It's a startling message, since our coming to the museum ought to demonstrate that we are among the virtuous. It's especially startling for Jewish visitors: How could we, the victims, be perpetrators? To suggest that victims can become perpetrators offers an extraordinary truth.
>
> (Wiener 1995)

Unable to see how this strategy springs from American culture itself, Wiener argues that the museum, despite a brave start, is unable to sustain the argument because of the need to depict the Holocaust as a unique experience. Thus, he argues, visitors move from being perpetrators to witnesses, losing their ability to act. Unlike Wiener, I would argue that the Museum is not radical but conservative, using a central American ideology to negotiate the tension between an exclusivist understanding of the Holocaust, which seeks to specify its unique circumstances, and the local American need to sustain a rhetoric of individual free will. It is this tension which results in a lack of historical awareness not televisual culture. Unlike Lisus and Ericson, I want to suggest that a judicious use of the medium and the ways in which it works can offer insights into history. It is in this context which I would like to turn to two Australian examples.

'Spatial' interactivity at the Australian National Maritime Museum

The Australian National Maritime Museum's approach to exhibition design presents an almost diametrically opposed strategy to that of the Museum of Tolerance, despite the use by both museums of film, television and photographic media. At the Maritime Museum, every attempt was made to avoid linear narratives. In the context of the above discussion, the differences in narrative style suggest that contemporary media culture can operate beyond spectacle and engage with critical perspectives. However, the move from a linear, chronological understanding of historical representation has its own problems, not least of which is visitor confusion and a sense that a public, group understanding of historical narratives might no longer be possible. I want to explore these questions by a close analysis of a visitor study conducted for the museum in late 1991, which tried to grapple with the Maritime Museum's approach to storytelling. As I will show, the study reflects the author's own inability to accept nonlinear narratives.

Towards the end of 1991, the museum commissioned a study of visitors' perceptions. Environmetrics Pty Ltd were chosen to conduct this study and produce a report. From the museum's point of view the report was to provide a series of recommendations which would guide it in making future decisions about the type of exhibits it would have, inform its marketing strategy and provide it with basic information as to who its visitors were, what they expected and how they reacted to the museum.

The Environmetrics' report criticized the museum for failing to offer strong narratives and routes which would guide visitors in their reading of the displays. In its introduction to the report, Environmetrics stated that 'many visitors had difficulty finding a logical and efficient route through the museum. Their experience of the museum is often of a "piecemeal" collection which does not hang together to build a strong story of Australia's maritime history' (Environmetrics 1992: 7). As a preface to its recommendations, the report goes on to state:

141

> Many visitors expected from the name of the museum that they would come away with a global understanding of Australia's maritime history. They expected the museum to convey this in a linear fashion from the beginning to the present, and to bring it alive.
>
> (7)

Many of the recommendations are therefore aimed at instructing the museum on how to construct a linear narrative out of its displays.

Within the Museum itself, there was a lively debate between policy makers, curators and designers over whether museums should have strong narratives to direct visitors. For curators, the question of which form of narrative to choose is closely linked to a shift away from taxonomic collection policies towards exhibitions based on thematic collection policies. This is a move which reflects an ideological shift in the way the curators' position is imagined – a shift away from the curator as a source of knowledge to the curator as a producer (discussed in Chapter 4). From a policy perspective there is a tension between the museum as a 'national' institution and the need to service a number of different communities. While the national status of the museum finds expression in a rhetoric of national identity, political and economic imperatives partially deconstruct this nationalist rhetoric (discussed in Chapter 2). The policy of access, in particular, pluralizes the notion of a single national community. This is a policy which dovetails very well with the new orientation to market niches (discussed in Chapter 2).

These debates indicate that questions of narrative, and by extension of representation, cannot be understood as separate from the institutional, economic, technological and policy contexts that inform them. The debate over narrative is firmly linked to larger issues such as the shifting status of the state, changing forms of the economy and the shifting geopolitical position of Australia. Thus, for example, the choice for many curators is not defined only by their ideological position but also by the recognition that federal government funding is essential to the survival of the museum, a recognition which necessarily requires them to embrace to some extent a strong narrative of nationhood.

While all of these contexts have an impact on how narratives are spatialized at the Australian National Maritime Museum I want to concentrate on the impact of the media and bring the discussion back to interactivity. The museum's use of the notion of interactivity relies on a particular use of narrative which owes little to an understanding of media as spectacle. An analysis of this use makes it possible to develop not only an alternative understanding of interactivity as non-technological; it also allows for a more complex reading of the impact of televisual culture on museums than that normally articulated by critics of 'infotainment'. Discussion will centre first on issues of design through a number of design policy documents produced by or for the National Maritime Museum which will be contrasted with the views of Environmetrics. This will then become the basis for a broader exploration of the issues which are raised in these reports.

Narrative as a design issue

In one of its earliest design policy statements, the newly formed National Maritime Museum signalled its interest in breaking down large narrative structures to a level which enabled the viewer to establish a personal connection with the display. The *Exhibition Master Plan* of 1986 stated that 'Large ideas and large artifacts will be reduced to a personal scale so that the visitor will more readily be able to relate to the exhibition' (Exhibition Design Services Pty Ltd 1986: 5). The importance of allowing the visitor to make connections with the exhibits was understood to work at a variety of different levels:

> The visitor's involvement with the exhibition is dependent on his/her knowledge at the time. There must therefore be many levels and ways in which a visitor can make contact with the exhibition and develop an interest in it: emotional, physical, intellectual, associational etc.
>
> (1986: 7)

This desire to involve visitors at various levels reflects an approach to interactivity which demands input from both the viewer and display. The approach is one which sees communication as a two way process without a predetermined hierarchy in which the museum's mission is to educate an uneducated visitor. The visitors themselves are to have an active role in the process, becoming co-authors in the production of meanings. Significantly, this activity is not defined by the use of technology in the first instance. The museum papers do not discuss the use of interactives but identify a need to make the museum space an interactive one.

By 1987, the museum design team, working with consultants, had come to the realization that in order to establish smaller displays and themes which made such interactive processes possible, it was important to establish a separate identity for each thematic display. This meant that each theme had to be physically separate and have its own design philosophy. However, at the same time, there was a need for some sort of unifying structure or principle which linked the exhibits and helped the visitors in orienting themselves:

> A visitor will be confronted with a vast array of ideas, concepts, objects, and elements. A confused and fatiguing experience can result unless these confrontations can be structured, by design, into a hierarchy. This hierarchy will assist the visitors in finding their way around the Museum, focusing on those elements of interest to them, and extracting the level of information their interest demands.
>
> (Australian National Maritime Museum 1987b: 19)

Thus, though each display was to stand on its own, it was recognized that some ordering principle was still required, a principle which both linked and recognized the separate identity of each display.

The problem was solved by a circulation structure which would guide the flow of people around the museum but which would, at the same time, help to establish the separate identity of each exhibit. As the 'Design strategy and implementation study' put it,

> these semi-permanent elements form the link between the scale of the building enclosure and the exhibits. Termed 'Transitional Structures', these elements will create a rational framework within which the individuality of each exhibition can be developed.
>
> (Australian National Maritime Museum 1987b: 19)

This meant that the traditional linear connection between displays, which was achieved either thematically, chronologically or by object type was consciously rejected at the very early design stages. It also meant that there was no expectation on the part of designers and curators that visitors had to see every exhibit in order to fully understand the 'message'. There *was* no single message. Not only was each theme its own entity, but sub-themes themselves could stand on their own. Furthermore, in many cases, there was no necessary order to either the themes or the sub-themes. Everything was organized around individual 'vignettes' – displays which could stand on their own with no necessary connection to the displays on either side. While these vignettes were not part of a linear narrative, there was also the opportunity to make connections or contrasts between displays: 'The design of each individual exhibit must evolve from a knowledge of how visitors will move through it. The design should exploit thematic links, contrasts and relationships perceived by "serial viewing"' (ANMM 1987b: 20). The difference from the Beit Hashoah section of the Museum of Tolerance could not be more marked.

Understanding serial narratives: a media approach

This 'serial viewing' can perhaps be understood as the same type of process that occurs in watching certain genres of television and video clips which do not have a tight narrative structure – for example, soap operas and music video clips. The lack of a narrative structure with a clear linear development makes it almost impossible to fix meanings. Meanings are only made through the activity of the viewer. This is a process which Eric Michaels defines as a process of 'self-inscription' (1987: 91) and which I take to be the same in principle as the concept of interactivity. It involves the insertion of the reader/viewer into the text momentarily as the subject of the narrative. In facilitating this, Michaels argues, the electronic media has developed a format which offers the audience 'a vehicle for densely packed narrative information outside of any narrative line' (86). Genres like the music video clip offer a series of vignettes which are creatively juxtaposed in order to 'invite narrative interest without providing specific narrative content' (86). Video clips and other forms of electronic texts are

> a new form of expression which invite the audience into a space in the text created by distancing signifier from signified. In this new kind of room within the text, the reader/viewer is required to locate himself [*sic*] in order to search for meaning.
>
> (91)

Michaels' contribution to debate on television formats is important. Rather than understanding this culture as one of spectacle, in which by definition the viewer can play no active part other than to be totally subsumed by the text, Michaels offers a view of media texts which highlights the activity of the viewer in producing the final meaning of that text.

This is an understanding which can also be taken to the museum. The viewing of displays in a museum can also be understood as a process of self-inscription, particularly when the sequence of the displays is not linear but works through individual display vignettes which, if serialized through the activity of viewing, 'invite narrative interest without actually possessing specific narrative content'. That is, the displays are not embedded within a strong narrative outside of the

Figure 6.1 This photograph shows the entry to the circulation structure which looks rather like a gangway. From this 'gangway' it is possible to choose which display areas to move into, go up a level and have a bird's eye view of the Museum, or go down a level into the lower gallery where the Navy and Leisure exhibitions are located. The possible choices offered by this circulation structure can be likened to a hypertext program which has multiple entry paths and therefore the possibility of the construction of multiple narratives.

Photographer: Jenni Carter, 1991. Australian National Maritime Museum collection. Reproduced courtesy of the Museum.

145

text. Self-inscription makes the process of viewing a series of images – whether in electronic form or in museums – highly interactive.[2] There is a space for activity on the part of the viewer which cannot be controlled by the producers of the video or exhibition but which nevertheless becomes part of its production. In a way, the interactive space allowed by this new form of narrative collapses the very distinction between a producer and a consumer. Both are involved in the process of making meanings which are never fixed. Predetermined routes or narratives are not part of the structure of this new form of text, for, within the new form, there is always the possibility of an accidental connection. The sequence of images can never fix narrative meaning.

The positive effect of self-inscription is that it allows for a pluralizing of narratives and therefore of perspectives and subjectivities. There cannot be a single narrative viewpoint and meaning is not fixed. However, this also means that the ideological valence of the text in question is not fixed either. This presents certain problems for theories of representation which rely on an idea of meaning as being fixed within the text. In semiotic analysis, textual representations are understood to mark a specific ideological position. If these representations are open not only to different interpretations but resist narrative within their structure, discussions about the ideological nature of the text are problematized. Texts can no longer be understood as operating hierarchically, from the top down. This does not mean that the activity of the audience should be understood as a 'bottom up' activity. It is not just a question of resistance to dominant forms of representation and narratives, resistance to narratives produced from the 'centre'. It is more that something has changed in the very structure within which representations take place.

Tom O'Regan exemplifies this shift in his discussion of Hollywood film which he bases on Eric Michaels' work with the Warlpiri community in Yuendumu (Central Australia). For Michaels, the success of Hollywood films in this remote Aboriginal community was an example of how Hollywood had developed genres which were open to multiple interpretations. These genres, Michaels argues, are less threatening to the maintenance of the local Aboriginal culture, than Australian-produced dramas and documentaries which involved direct representations of Aboriginal society – even where these attempt to be 'sympathetic'. This is because the latter are far more likely to break tribal laws. As O'Regan (1990: 72) comments,

> from a standpoint of cultural maintenance, Eric can consider it 'promising' that . . . 'the most popular genres appear to be action/adventure, soapies, musicals and slapstick, and forms such as game shows, entertainment variety, gossip and other types which invite the audience to construct multiple texts out of their fragmented semiotic resources. . . . As the least character motivated, most formulaic fictions, they may encourage active interpretation and cross-culturally varied readings.'

In other words, the further away a genre is from linear narratives, the more chance it has of crossing cultural boundaries. This also means that, for the film and television industries, questions of narrative have an economic as well as an

146

ideological base. As O'Regan comments in one of his articles, 'for popular film, as with aesthetic texts generally, ranges of interpretations are actively solicited and even invited. . . . Indeed such pluralising of meaning is an important component of the "demand management" of Hollywood' (1994: 352). As he says,

> the 'conversation' between producers and audiences is designed to minimise obstacles to participation on the part of potential audiences, but this strategy of incorporation is achieved through a communicative inefficiency (which is exploited *most efficiently*) as propositional contents are bent further, opportunities for partial misunderstanding are increased and even encouraged. *And this is not a problem.*
>
> (1994: 339–340, emphasis in original)

The politics of serial narratives in museums

How, then, can we understand the negative reaction to serialization in the museum by the Environmetrics report? Why is it that the report authors portray the lack of linear narrative structures as a problem which the museum must fix? What type of exhibitions are valorized by the report? Are those exhibitions which are attacked for their lack of linear narratives in any way different from those which are not criticized? These questions will inform the remaining analysis of the Australian National Maritime Museum.

The valorization of linear narratives by Environmetrics appears to be based on the assumption that history museums should be organized chronologically. The chronological representation of the Holocaust in the Museum of Tolerance's Beit Hashoah conforms to this expectation. As such it is consistent with an image of the museum inherited from the nineteenth century. The Maritime Museum, however, did not fulfil these expectations. As the report writers noted, most visitors whom they accompanied through the museum had difficulty in finding a natural route through the museum:

> [T]here was a general expectation that the museum as a whole would have an 'efficient' route which would cover all the main sections . . . many visitors follow very convoluted paths which double back, crossover and miss whole sections.
>
> (Environmetrics 1992: 48)

The expectation of an 'efficient' route is also an expectation of Environmetrics who seem to imply that the visitors got it wrong and 'miss whole sections' (see Figures 6.2 to 6.4 for an illustration of this point).

For Environmetrics, it is not normal that exhibitions should require viewers to circulate and criss-cross a space. Exhibitions should be designed so that a one way flow is the 'natural' path. While, as Eric Michaels argues, some television and video clips have established a structure which exploits the lack of narrative continuity through serialization and the use of vignettes, museums are still expected to have continuous or sequential narratives. The lack of an obvious starting point was disconcerting for both the visitors and Environmentrics – visitors can walk down and begin with the USA–Australia gallery or walk up the ramp through a series of individual displays with no narrative connection and begin with the *Discovery* exhibition. Serendipity or chance encounters are part of the design plan of the museum, but one which is disconcerting to some visitors.[3]

The consistent characterization of this serendipity as a problem by Environmentrics is particularly evident in their comments on the requirement for visitors to make a choice about which display area they will see first. According to the report, the museum contained a number of points where alternative routes were possible. However, these decision points 'offered several alternatives without providing clear enough clues about what the consequences of each choice might be' (Environmetrics 1992: 51). One example picked out by the report is on the upper level of the museum, in the *Discovery* exhibition (see floor plan of the area). Here, the report explains, people are confused by three possible pathways: 'one leads further into the *Discovery* gallery and the other two (on each side of Fish on Poles) lead out of the gallery to the unknown, to "somewhere else"' (52). That 'somewhere else' is a display on Aboriginal and Torres Strait Islander uses of the sea. Although it is never made explicit, it becomes evident that for the report writers, a more 'natural' path would be to include the Aboriginal and Torres Strait Islands display within the main body of the *Discovery* exhibition.

While Environmetrics had no quarrels with the *Discovery* exhibition itself which is given high marks for visitor satisfaction, the placement of this exhibit to the side affronted their sense of chronology, for the absence of linearity prevents an easy temporal narrative in which the Aboriginal maritime experience is relegated to antiquity, with no links to history since European settlement. Thus they make no reference to the fact that many of the artefacts and practices referred to in the display were still in use. Instead, they chose to highlight the success of the display as due to the popularity of 'primitive art' (73). However, most of the objects were not art but maritime technology – boats, fishing nets and spears, as well as evidence of trade patterns with Pacific Islands.

The inability to differentiate between the two classes of objects is not an issue in the main area of the exhibition which deals with the 'white' discovery of the Pacific. It would seem that Environmetrics' disconcerted reaction to the placement of the Aboriginal display is based on a Western narrative about Aboriginal peoples which places them in the past, without considering that the disruption of this narrative may be deliberate. The assumed need for linearity thus makes them blind to the possibilities of critique which are part of the exhibition's layout. Thus the layout of the gallery is criticized for the fact that the most obvious entry point does not conform to the expectation that 'history is linear' (73). Had there been a linear pattern between the two, the Aboriginal display would not have offered the possibility, however dim, of being read as another experience of the sea which is contemporaneous with white Australia rather than prior to it.

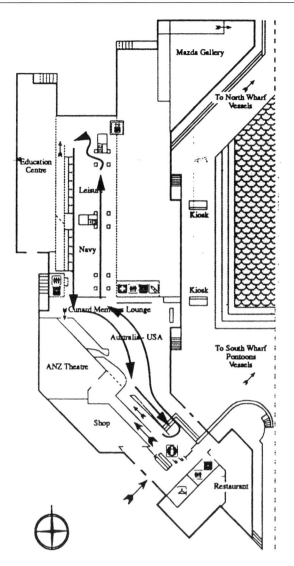

Figure 6.2 Diagram A: floor plan of lower level, Australian National Maritime Museum – first preferred route.

The route indicated here begins in the nineteenth-century side of the USA–Australia gallery. It then follows the right-hand side of the Navy and Leisure galleries and returns through the left-hand side of Leisure, Navy and the USA–Australia gallery. This effectively means that the serialized narratives within each theme are further broken down by the routes the visitors take.

Diagram in Environmetrics Pty Ltd, May 1992, Australian National Maritime Museum – Visitor Study, Sydney, p. 48. Australian National Maritime Museum collection. Reproduced courtesy of the Museum.

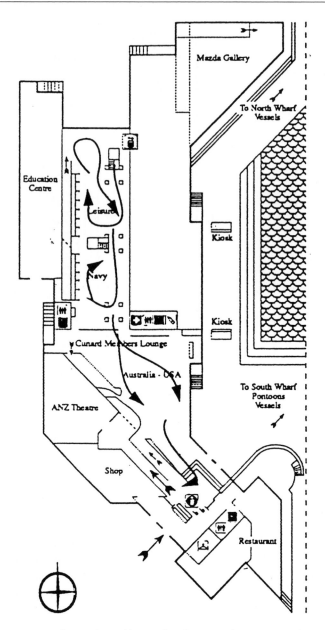

Figure 6.3 Diagram B: floor plan of lower level, Australian National Maritime Museum – second preferred route.

The routes followed by visitors in this diagram show how their experience of the museum does not follow the traditional linear, sequential narrative structure. Instead, visitors double back and criss-cross over their own tracks. This may mean that they do not follow a chronology or theme in the 'correct' way. However, the serialized nature of the displays encourage this type of 'meandering'.

Diagram in Environmetrics Pty Ltd, May 1992, Australian National Maritime Museum – Visitor Study, Sydney, p. 49. Australian National Maritime Museum collection. Reproduced courtesy of the Museum.

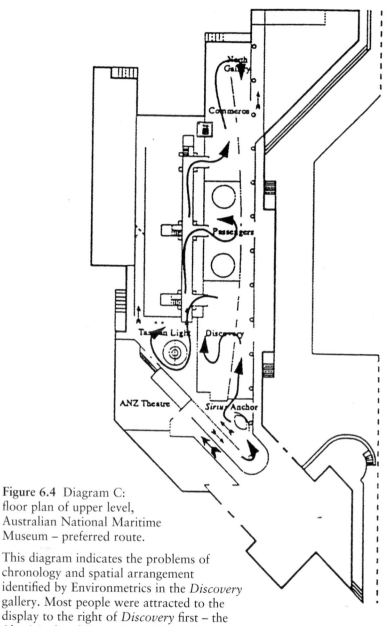

Figure 6.4 Diagram C:
floor plan of upper level,
Australian National Maritime
Museum – preferred route.

This diagram indicates the problems of
chronology and spatial arrangement
identified by Environmetrics in the *Discovery*
gallery. Most people were attracted to the
display to the right of *Discovery* first – the
Aboriginal and Torres Strait Island display. For Environmetrics it would have been
more 'natural' to place this display at the entrance to the *Discovery* exhibition from
the circulation structure (see Figure 6.5). In this plan, that entry is the exit from the
gallery. Chronology could then assert itself and the indigenous uses of the sea could
be safely relegated to a past prior to the the white 'discovery'. As it is, the two areas
co-existed in tension as they do in the subsequent reconfiguration.

Diagram in Environmetrics Pty Ltd, May 1992, Australian National Maritime Museum – Visitor
Study, Sydney, p. 49. Australian National Maritime Museum collection. Reproduced courtesy of the
Museum.

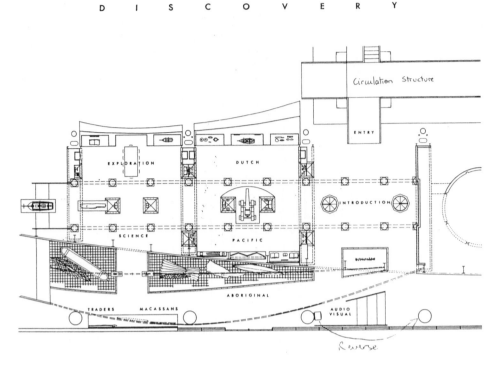

Figure 6.5 Floor plan of *Discovery* gallery.

This diagram shows the original design plan for the *Discovery* and Aboriginal section of the Museum. The main entry was envisioned from the circulation structure. The introduction area with the two globes and the 'fish pole' sculpture as a background provided a choice for museum visitors – right into the 'European' discovery or straight through to the Aboriginal and Torres Strait Island display. The two galleries have since been redesigned as part of an ongoing process of research and evaluation.

Floor plan in Australian National Maritime Museum, Design Review, 28 June 1989. Australian National Maritime Museum collection. Reproduced courtesy of the Museum.

Serial narratives and history genres

The report's treatment of displays which do not deal with 'public' histories – histories such as those of the discovery of Australia – adds a further layer to the problem of narrative. For displays which do not involve public or national narratives, but are nevertheless organized according to the principles of serial narratives, are not positioned as problematic in the Environmentrics report. When a 'vignette' or 'serial' approach is used in more 'social history' types of display where 'ordinary' people and experiences are the subject of the display, the possibilities for establishing personal connections are highly valued. Here the possibility of interactive displays is viewed more positively by the report writers. Linearity and chronology are not constructed as significant issues in 'experiential' displays.

Figure 6.6 This photograph of the original introductory area to the *Discovery* gallery shows the space under discussion, in which visitors made a choice between turning right or going straight ahead to the Aboriginal section of the gallery.

Note: This exhibition area has since been reconfigured. The introductory area now contains an explicitly contemporary exhibition focusing on the lives of living Aboriginal and Torres Strait Island people. It is also framed in a post-Mabo context, a context which did not exist at the time of the first exhibition's opening. The contemporary nature of the new exhibition prevents visitors from equating the spatial organization of the display with a conservative narrative which relegates Aboriginal culture to the past. Photographer: Jenni Carter, 1991. Australian National Maritime Museum collection. Reproduced courtesy of the Museum.

For example, in *Passengers*, an exhibition about the experience of travelling by sea, loosely framed within the history of migration to Australia, individual displays are praised for the opportunities they present for individual and group recollection and personal identification. *Setting the table*, for example,

> was able to evoke a lot of memories for the people who had actually been on passenger liners – they could remember the crockery, the cutlery and it was one of the displays that helps people connect to the museum.
>
> (Environmetrics 1992: 77)

One of the more popular displays dealt with the wave of immigration following the Second World War. In *Refugees* and *Displaced Persons* the displays 'allow visitors to stand and watch and get into the memories of other people, which was particularly valued by older respondents in this research' (1992: 78).

The vignette approach was also considered successful if it worked by creating general impressions or images, a mood or feeling. This is interesting in terms of Michaels' description of vignettes as 'inviting narrative interest without providing specific narrative content'. Thus *Hazards Under Sail*

> does not overrate the objects, the objects themselves are actually fairly slight, being little pieces of china, a bit of a doll and a glass jar, so it is just pleasant. People look at these objects not to understand the object but to remember about shipwreck and the danger of the sea which is part of its romance and mystery. This display succeeds in conveying this very appropriately.
>
> (Environmetrics 1992: 75–76)

The social history displays allowed for emotional involvement or interaction on the part of the viewer which came close to Michaels' understanding of self-inscription as the insertion of the viewer into the text as subject. Environmetrics put it this way:

> The key emotional experience offered by the ANMM to adult visitors is the opportunity for them to make connections with their own experience, history, or family history. These connections were exciting, thrilling moments of discovery. The shock of recognition often placed the visitor right in the museum.
>
> (Environmetrics 1992: 46)

In these cases it would seem that Michaels' claim that the postmodernist space is about 'self-inscription' and that this process is particularly associated with the electronic media, is having some impact on the way in which some museum exhibitions are designed.

Environmetrics' approval of 'mood' exhibitions and of exhibitions which establish a personal connection appear to contradict the recommendation for increased use of linear narratives, a contradiction which is never recognized. As the report recognizes, visitors get a thrill out of discovering themselves as the subject of the exhibition. This thrill is amplified if the discovery happens by chance:

people like to look around by themselves, and discover new things, rather than being shown around. People do not like their museum experience to be rigidly planned and organised. It is apparent that, overall, people like to have their own discovery experience.

(21)

The report then never resolves an internal contradiction. There is a perceived need for more linear narratives and a spatial structure which guides the visitor in a one-way flow. This is especially so if the visitors are to understand the 'global' story of the Australian maritime experience and if their sense of chronology is to be rewarded. That the museum might have consciously moved away from global narrative frameworks and a strong nationalist history which defined Australian society as a single community is never recognized. However, the need for personal space, for 'self-inscription', *is* recognized in the more overt social history-based displays. The report seems unable to recognize that a global theme, thematic routes and a chronological arrangement of the displays may well destroy the visitor's experience of discovery encouraged by 'designed serendipity'.

This tension is symptomatic of a wider problem in 'imagining' the museum. The use of linear narratives and their association with cultural master-narratives such as that of the nation has underpinned the definition of the museum as a public space. In their singularity, linear narratives were universal. Thus it was possible to talk about museum visitors as 'the public' or as 'the people' as if they were undifferentiated. The narratives in history museums were likewise universal, subsuming the experiences and histories of different communities into the one historical experience of the nation as a single community (Duclos 1994). The introduction of social history, however, was one of the catalysts for breaking down this singular narrative. As individualized communities, people and places became a site for study and a subject for display, the notion of a single public began to disintegrate. This may have affected the museum to the extent that it too can no longer be understood as a public space in which the territory of the nation is imagined and represented as a fixed, linear, all-encompassing narrative.

The notion of the museum as a rational public space is further problematized by the effect of electronic technologies which encourage serial rather than linear narratives. As I have shown, the evolving nature of museum displays as a medium which invites narrative through the play of intertexts places the museum firmly within the logic of the electronic media. This is a logic which encourages self-inscription, that is the collapse of a distinction between viewer and viewed. For notions of a public space to be maintained there needs to be a distance between the representations of the public sphere and those who view them, a distance which linear narratives are designed to produce. Only then is it possible for the viewer to be integrated within the public being produced. Without this distance, however, the distance between the personal and the public cannot be maintained. The potentially limitless possibility for the museum to create more and more spaces for self-inscription make it almost impossible to maintain a distinction or a separation between the public and private spheres.

It is perhaps the disappearance of these certitudes which makes both the public and museum critics wary of exhibitions which refuse a strong referent. And yet, it is this refusal which may make it possible for museums to engage with history in more complex ways, allowing different perspectives to be represented. The danger, of course, is the lack of a curatorial perspective. The difficulty for those museums who wish to be less didactic and more interactive is to achieve a balance between multiple points of view while maintaining an editorial line which is not reductive. In some ways, the problem at the National Maritime Museum was a lack of a curatorial line. The Museum lacks a strong conceptual focus. It does not attempt, for example, to deal with the theme of the sea as an organizing idea. This means that its six themes – Discovery, Leisure, Passengers, Commerce, Navy and the USA–Australia gallery – do not coalesce around any discussion point. There is a need then, to develop an approach to interactivity which remains open ended but which nevertheless engages in a dialogue from a position. It is to this end that I now turn to my final case study, the Museum of Sydney. While it also has a spatial understanding of interactivity, this museum does organize its exhibitions around a concept – in this case cross-cultural communication. In so doing, it moves beyond 'spatial interactivity' and begins to develop 'dialogic interactivity'.

Dialogic interactivity at the Museum of Sydney

Like the Maritime Museum, the Museum of Sydney on the site of first Government House (MoS) also approaches the question of interactivity from a conceptual basis which is not premised on a technological definition. And like the Maritime Museum, the Museum of Sydney also has a strong sense of the importance of spatial experiences. To this sense, however, it also adds a notion of dialogue. This is perhaps best expressed by its first Senior Curator, Peter Emmett, who defines the museum's space as 'a spatial composition, a sensory and sensual experience; a place to enter, senses and body alive. Its meanings are revealed through the physical experience of moving through it' (Emmett 1995: 115). In stressing the experiential dimension of the museum space, Emmett is also stressing the notion of shared communication, of dialogue.

The subject matter of the museum is helpful in this regard, for it deals with cross-cultural exchange during the early years of white settlement in and around Sydney Cove. In an unusual move, the museum decided to go beyond the original brief of interpreting the historical site, which contains the foundations of first Government House, to interpreting the city of Sydney. This enabled it to set up a series of cross-cultural dialogues – between past and present, between indigenous and settler voices, between the museum and its visitors, between traditional historical knowledge and contemporary critiques of that knowledge.

A little history

Since its rediscovery by archaeologists, the site of the first Government House has become associated with the clash of different cultures. As Sharon Sullivan pointed out, the site represents the clash of cultures, of different histories – indigenous Australia, penal settlement and outpost of empire (Sullivan 1995). Such a history is going to mean very different things to different groups in the present.

The site became the focus of public attention in 1982, when the New South Wales (NSW) government decided to lease the site for commercial development. The Department of Environment and Planning requested an archaeological dig before any building commenced. Begun in 1983, the dig revealed the footings of first Government House as well as a lot of debris dating back to the period between 1788 and 1845, when the house was knocked down. In the lead up to the Bicentenary of European settlement in 1988, these discoveries fed a growing interest in the origins of the Australian nation. A spirited public campaign to save the site was begun and an association called the Friends of First Government House was established. It included historians, archaeologists, heritage administrators, National Trust Members, the Fellowship of First Fleeters, the Women's Pioneer Society, the Bloodworth Association, opposition politicians and members of the media. In 1985, the NSW government finally decided to preserve the site. Over the next six years, archaeologists continued to explore the site and to recover material from it. When it was eventually handed over to the Historic Houses Trust of NSW in 1991, it was almost inevitable that different opinions should develop about the site's significance and the most appropriate ways to deal with them.

Unlike the Friends of First Government House, the Trust did not interpret the site's significance in terms of a narrative about the birth of the nation. Instead, it viewed the site as significant for its potential to articulate the relations between the process of colonization and contemporary political issues. Rather than being a museum to the House, focused on the site itself, it became a museum to the ideas and the historical processes the House represented. Thus, in its policy statement for the Museum, released in 1992, the Trust said:

> The most potent and provocative significance of first Government House site is as a symbol of British colonisation of Australia in 1788 and its subsequent role as the seat of British authority in the colony. To Australians in the 1990s this symbolism will mean different things to different people. Hence first Government House site becomes a symbol of different perspectives on how we see ourselves as Australians today.
>
> (Historic Houses Trust in Ireland 1995: 100)

Such a statement angered the Friends of First Government House whose aim had been to preserve the site for its significance as the birth of the nation. They wanted the House to be its focus. In their reply to the Trust, the Friends focused on the primacy of the site as a way of anchoring historical interpretation:

> The foundations of Government House were laid in the same year as the foundation of the nation now known as the Commonwealth of Australia. They are the only known remains from 1788. The life of this building and its additions thus coexists with the Convict Era of Australian history. As such it represents a tangible record of continuous occupation and development not only of the formation years of Australia but also of the broader concerns of colonialism and imperialism in the nineteenth century. These tangible links, the very foundation of a nation, are unique.
>
> (Friends of First Government House site in Ireland 1995: 100)

While the Friends accepted that the site could be interpreted as a symbol of 'colonialism' and 'imperialism', they wanted such a history to be framed as the beginnings of the Australian nation-state. But the debate is not only about whether the site should be interpreted as the birth of the nation. It is also about the claims that can be made from the historical record. While the Friends of First Government House had no qualms about anchoring the interpretation of the site in a narrative of nationhood, the museum was working with a notion of history which saw it as a set of fragments which stood as metaphors for the present. For the museum, history is always an act of interpretation and as such it is an intervention in the present for the future. For Emmett, this intervention had to be located in contemporary politics: 'at a time when native title, British inheritance, republicanism – are front page news' it is impossible to 'sustain a museum dedicated to a chronology of events that affirm a nationalist mythology' (Emmett 1995: 112). This meant that the museum went on a mission to set up correspondences between the past and the present and by extension, between different cultures. To do this, the museum engaged both with New Historiography and with the New Museology. It became self-reflexive, developing displays which commented on past historical and museological practices. By questioning received ideas, the museum hoped to provide a space for dialogue, for public discussion.

This approach was also made possible by the fact that the museum had almost no objects to work with. The main focus of the site, the house, no longer existed. Only its foundations remained and the conservation plan stipulated that these remain covered. The archaeological dig had produced very few complete objects and these spoke mostly of the lifestyle of the inhabitants. There was little material from the site itself which could be used to explore its impact on the indigenous population, on convicts or any other groups. To explore these themes, the museum had to locate other material and work from the written historical record. These practical problems were also part of the context in which the museum decided to move beyond the confines of the site when shaping its approach to exhibition design. This was an approach which required extending the ways in which museums normally provide interactive experiences.

Creating dialogue

How is the notion of experience and interactivity produced at this museum and how does it relate to the museum's view of history? At first sight, the claim that the museum is interactive might appear too strong. Push button computer inter-actives do not dominate. But multimedia experiences do, in the sense that sound, objects, visual images, text and video walls are combined in provocative ways. To some extent, this is what all museums do. However, this museum uses these media to some unusual effects. The sound of the human voice, for example, is used to create imagined and reconstructed dialogues, rather than access to oral histories. Text is used not in the conventional series of interpre-tative labels, moving from the general to the specific, but as literary and histor-ical quotations engraved on to the wall surfaces. Graphics tend not to be photographs but especially created digital video installations which are an exhi-bition in themselves. The effect of this treatment is constantly to pose questions, suggestions, rather than finished statements which tend to fix the narrative in the authoritative voice of the museum. The result are some rather unusual exhi-bitions, both inside and outside the museum building.

Unlike the National Maritime Museum or the Museum of Tolerance, the Museum of Sydney does not have an imposing building. In fact, as Kay Schaffer (1996) points out, you could almost miss it. While this has a practical reason – in that part of the conservation management of the site was to cover it up and prevent any further building from taking place – the effect is to create an open public space which almost becomes part of the street. The museum is, to some extent, an extension of the street life rather than an imposition on it. This is reflected in the decision to have one of the galleries as a glass box, jutting out, away from the building and above the plaza. The effect is a double one – passers by can be viewers as well as viewed and the contents of the exhibitions inside the museum are visually linked with the urban space to which they refer. This lack of a boundary between the museum and the street is further rein-forced by using this open space as an exhibition space with the aim of setting up a dialogue between passers by and the museum.

To this end, the plaza has two structures on it. One is an opening on to the ground beneath the plaza, exposing the foundations of first Government House. To anyone who stops and looks, it is immediately evident that there is something significant below the ground. The second structure is a public sculpture with a difference. As one walks through the plaza towards the museum building at the back, one is invited to meander through a stand of sculptured timbers resem-bling tree trunks which call for your attention with strange murmurings. On coming up close, one is able to hear human voices speaking in a now unknown tongue – that of the original inhabitants of the area, the Eora people. The trunks themselves house a core sample of ancient Aboriginal middens, attesting to the existence of another culture. This is further emphasized by the names of many of the Aboriginal inhabitants of the area at the time of white settlement which are burnt on to the wood. The signatures of many of the First Fleet Officers are also displayed on these trunks, etched on to metal plates.

This introduction to the museum already contains many of its interpretative strategies. There is a constant juxtaposition of material remains from both Aborigines and newcomers. The relationship between the two is by no means a settled one. Second, there is the use of sound to suggest the possibility of communication, of dialogue, however brief it might have been. And third, the visitor is required to move in this space, taking in both visual and auditory experiences. It is these characteristics that perhaps best represent the combination of a spatial interactivity with a dialogic one and its potential for historical interpretation. The approach is captured in Emmett's comment that the museum's 'medium and methodology is about the poetics of space, the choreography of people, the relation of things and senses, spatial and sensory composition, to exploit the sensuality and materiality of the museum medium' (1995: 115).

This approach is continued as one enters the museum. Before visitors can get to the welcome counter to purchase an entry ticket, they have to come through a glass door/enclosure. As well as being a liminal space between the inside and the outside of the museum, this space is also an auditory experience. Paul Carter (1996), a historian with an interest in the possibilities of sound in capturing moments of instability, was commissioned by the Museum of Sydney to create a sound exhibition for the entry space. Carter developed *The Calling to Come*, an auditory experience based on the Diaries of William Dawes. Dawes was an Officer of the First Fleet, an astronomer and a linguist. One of the few people to have an interest in understanding and recording the local Eora language, Dawes' diary reveals his attempts to communicate with Patyegarang, an Aboriginal woman with whom he had a relationship. The diary is the only record we have of one man's attempt to translate between the two cultures. In the exhibition Carter tries to capture this attempt at translation between two cultures through a sound recreation of Dawes' and Patyegarang's attempts to understand one another's culture through language. The exhibit is difficult to understand – perhaps too difficult – but the attempt reveals in itself the difficulties of cross-cultural encounters.

Once inside the museum proper, the visitor is greeted by a three-storey high multimedia wall. The wall provides a constantly moving set of images of Sydney and its environs at the time of first contact and in the present. The Aboriginal presence is loud and clear. It is impossible to come away from the museum and still believe in the concept of *terra nullius* – that Australia was an empty land at the time of settlement. The landscape is full of human presences – both people and their material culture. It also moves from past to present, making it clear that there is a continuity of Aboriginal presence in the Sydney area. Addressing a younger audience familiar with multimedia presentations, this exhibit is not a touch screen interactive. Nor does it provide a static image. The constantly moving wall of images demands interaction, but on the viewers' own terms. There is no spoken narrative or label, only a musical sound track.

For the museum, the use of digital technology to produce these moving walls represents a shift away from a technical understanding of interactivity which relies on mechanical models of interaction. This shift is also seen by the museum as symptomatic of a new understanding of the role of museums. In an interview with George Alexander and Kurt Brereton, Gary Warner, the Audio Visual and Computer Projects Coordinator at the Museum, pointed out that multimedia was used to provide one more layer of interpretation, one more visual and auditory experience. The contemporary nature of this experience, he argued, enables the museum to move beyond the popular understanding of museums as mausoleums to the preservation of dead cultures. As Alexander and Brereton indicate, this attempt also has an impact on the status of the museum's interpretation of the past. For Alexander and Brereton, this museum 'hopes to be less a mausoleum of dead cultural artefacts than a kind of electronic layer-cake of interpretations capable of being revoked or transformed' (1995: 7).

It is part of the museum's intention that its interpretations should be unstable and capable of constant renegotiation. This involves a recognition that history can only ever be a set of fragments about the past. The result is a multitude of small narratives, which do not come together to make one large metanarrative. To use Jucheau's expression, 'the seams are allowed to show'. As Alexander and Brereton point out,

> [h]istory is always a cobbled collection of fragments masquerading as a seamless picture of the way it really was. The question is whether you try to spak-fill the cracks and gaps or show the ruins and fragments as testaments to our desire to remake the whole with all the political, cultural and social implications attached.
>
> (8)

The Museum of Sydney makes a very clear choice for the latter.

This belief that digital technologies can transform the status of museum narratives is different in character from Stickler's attempt to argue that interactives make the museum modern and contemporary. At the Museum of Sydney, multimedia is not simply a technology which will turn a static space into an interactive one. Rather, it is a medium which is uniquely suited to a notion of history as a set of fragments. As Ross Gibson (1994/95) argues, the relationship is even closer; multimedia, and its basis in electronic reproduction techniques make it impossible not to question a notion of history which makes claims on the basis of authenticity and truth. Even visual evidence, Gibson argues, can no longer be understood as an unmediated attempt to represent 'reality'. Interpretation appears to be all that remains: 'suggestion and persuasion rather than unequivocal proof are now probably the best you can hope for when using imagistic and sonic "documentation" to present "truths" about the world' (Gibson 1994/95: 64). But, as Gibson realizes, interpretation provides an opportunity for dialogue, for an exchange of views. Translated to the museum, this means that historical interpretation can only be tentative and open-ended. This is an attitude which makes the museum open to the cultural negotiation of meanings.

This insight provides the basis for the *Bond Store Tales*, an exhibition curated by Gibson. In this exhibition, Gibson uses 'digitized image and sound systems to deliver ever-reconfiguring "micro-narratives" or "testimonials" about everyday life in the Sydney environs' (1994/95: 63). Interactivity is intrinsic to this exhibition because the order of the 'virtual exhibits' is not predetermined by the museum but by the activity of the visitors and the choices they make about which exhibits to linger on. As Gibson explains it, the Bond Store exhibits are activated by the movement of the visitors:

> as viewers move throughout the meaning-full space of the Museum, looking at objects and at images of objects, dozens of little histories combine and recombine, over time, in a virtually limitless 'metanarrative' pattern. The Museum visitors follow their curiosity and the etherial culture 'responds' by 'telling' some of the stories derived from research into the material culture. Depending on the chancy contiguity of story to story as the visitors wander and scrutinise, unstable histories get knitted together out of the micro-histories that 'arise' in any stint of vigilance. During a 30 minute period, therefore, a visitor can gather up a kind of demountable, questionable-yet-persuasive history, which is patently provisional and fleeting.
>
> (Gibson 1994/95: 65)

Recalling the practice of putting all goods in a bond store as they arrived on trading ships and releasing them only once a tax had been paid, the Bond Store exhibit uses the metaphor of a holding space to entice visitors into hearing stories from the past. While based on careful historical research, the characters represented through the medium of holograms are fictional. The stories they have to tell represent the clash of cultures which are part and parcel of a busy maritime port where settlers came into conflict with local indigenous populations, traders from all over the Pacific visited and attempts to develop a town continued despite Aboriginal resistance. The holograms which emerge out of black space as visitors move around the room represent convicts, Aboriginals, servant girls, officers and their ladies, visiting traders. They all have a story to tell which undermines received ideas of the period. They are like ghosts from the past, returning to haunt modern understandings.

Beyond the Museum of Sydney

The museum's interpretation of history and its attempt to reflect it through a 'dialogic' approach to interactivity is not without its problems. Some of these relate to the contested nature of the site while others have to do with the style of interpretation. The notion of dialogue necessitates the acceptance of multiple voices. This stance, however, angers those who wish the museum to interpret the site of first Government House as the birth of the nation (Friends of First Government House 1994 in Ireland 1995) as well as those who take the site as representing the moment of invasion and colonization (Hansen 1996, Marcus 1996). The former accuse it of being 'politically correct' while the latter accuse it of being apolitical or not coming down strongly enough on the history of dispossession.

Representing the latter view, Guy Hansen (1996), for example, sees a 'Fear of the Masternarrative' as leading to a lack of political commitment. Uncomfortable with the notion that history can only ever be interpretation, Hansen accuses the museum of sitting on the fence in regard to the history of Aboriginal dispossession. Julie Marcus (1996) also accuses the museum of not paying enough attention to indigenous history. She sees this as an act of conscious marginalization. When put side by side with the reactions of the Friends of First Government House, it is hard not to conclude that the museum is caught between an interpretation of Australian history in terms of nation-building and another which sees it in terms of invasion and dispossession. The very fact that the museum can be attacked for either having too strong a narrative of historical revisionism or no narrative at all seems to indicate that lack of a curatorial perspective is not the main problem at the museum.

Debate about the nature of the museum's representation of history is also made more difficult by the methodologies the museum uses as part of its interpretation strategies. Many of its exhibits are like art installations. In fact, many of them were produced by artists rather than curators. However, they use historical material. This hybrid character – neither a social history museum nor an art gallery – is part of this museum's approach to creating a dialogic interactive space. However, it leads to complaints from both art and social history curators unused to the blending of such different traditions. It also leads to charges of elitism.

A major problem with the Museum of Sydney is its demand for high levels of knowledge on the part of the visitor – both about history and about knowledge production in museums. This is a museum for museum lovers and for those with an interest in contemporary media installations. It is not a museum for the general public. Its treatment of objects is highly aestheticized. What once was rubbish is displayed in pleasing arrangements, even if the message is still one of bric-a-brac. There is little attempt to contextualize the objects according to their history of use. Despite being a social history museum, it treats everyday objects as art. While this may be an interesting play on the nature of museum knowledge, it leaves those without the necessary knowledge unable to play the game. The dialogue has a limited audience.

The question, then, is whether a dialogic approach to interactivity can be developed in ways which speak to broader audiences, using their own cultural languages, while still dealing with important political issues. Further work is needed on the part of museums to locate ways in which dialogue can occur over contemporary social concerns using the language of popular culture. But a more complex notion of interactivity should go some way at least towards making this possible. I have tried to indicate a space for museums and contemporary media forms to be thought through together rather than as necessarily opposed. As I have shown, this also requires a recognition that interactive museum environments are not simply a result of the application of multimedia technologies to the museum space. Both need to be thought of as communication media. Questions as to how to make them less didactic or hierarchical apply to both mediums.

The Museum of Sydney represents a first step in this direction. In conceptualizing museums as a space for dialogue, its staff took the first steps by relativizing its truth claims. Interestingly, the Museum did this by thinking through multimedia technologies alongside historical interpretation. The next step might be, as Anne Curthoys (1996) perceptively points out, to represent this relativization not only from the perspective of the converted. The Museum also needs to represent some of the 'old-fashioned' historical narratives which it implicitly sets itself against. Dialogue would then take place inside the museum as well as outside in ways which might be less antagonistic. As the National Maritime Museum understood, narrative interest can be created by juxtaposition. Museums need to have the courage to use multiple interpretations of history side by side.

Conclusion

> What needs to be captured and theorised today is . . . the ways in which the museum and exhibition culture in the broadest sense provides a terrain that can offer multiple narratives of meaning at a time when the metanarratives of modernity, including those inscribed into the universal survey museum itself, have lost their persuasiveness, when more people are eager to hear and see other stories, to hear and see the stories of others, when identities are shaped in multiply layered and never-ceasing negotiations between self and other, rather than being fixed and taken for granted in the framework of family and faith, race and nation.
>
> (Huyssen 1995: 34)

This book has attempted to do three things. First, it has liberated the idea of the museum from the iron bars imposed on it by its association with modernity. Second, it has enabled a fresh encounter between cultural studies and the historiography of museums enabling a more positive relationship between academic theory and museological praxis. And third, it has strongly suggested that contemporary museum trends have historical precedents rather than being a radical break with past practices.

While not wanting to argue that museums did not play an important role in the development of modernity I have suggested that this role has been a more complex one than that described in the majority of discussions on museums. Following Andreas Huyssen I have distinguished between two different visions of modernity. The first vision defines the museum as the antithesis of all that is 'modern' by describing it as a 'mausoleum'. The second is one that associates it almost exclusively with the operation of power and thereby associates the museum with institutional forms of oppression. Both of these I have sought to resist. I have suggested that modernity needs to be understood not only in terms of increased forms of rationality (the Foucaldian approach) but also in terms of *irrationality*. Rather than conduct this argument at the level of theory I have drawn attention to the ways in which the continued implication of museums within popular culture can offer a source of alternative meanings. Popular culture is one of the ways in which governmental rationalities are softened even if they are not completely erased. It is also an important area for museums to establish connections with their contemporary audiences. It is for this reason that Chapters 1 and 2 took some time to tease out the complexities of new museum developments within tourist and leisure precincts while also attempting to draw some connections with nineteenth-century exhibitionary complexes.

The aim, then, was also to suggest connections between the emergence of new economic contexts and attempts by museums to find new relationships with their audiences. It is no accident that the placement of a new museum within a tourist complex such as Darling Harbour is associated with challenges to the traditional authority of museums. As I have documented throughout the book, such challenges are posed by the inclusion of electronic technologies within the museum space, the concern with everyday life and popular culture and by the development of new subject spaces as a result of the development of non-linear display narratives.

Such trends are often seen as solely a response to the new commercial imperatives. However, I have also wanted to refuse this reduction. In my interpretation of the Western Australian Maritime Museum, the pressures to change proceed from a much wider questioning of the public role of museums, a questioning which interrogates traditional understandings of museums as research institutions. Such questioning, I suggest, is the outcome of a particular experience of modernity in which the relationship between public institutions, particularly those with an educational role, has increasingly moved towards greater contact with audiences through the use of populist discourses. The danger of such discourses, however, is of course the production of bland celebratory narratives.

In breaking the association between museums and mausoleums and museums and theories of ideology, I have also attempted to open up the ways in which museums can be thought about – to re-imagine the museum. This has involved a questioning of a common assumption within cultural studies – that the expression of power is always stable and fixed. Such a move allows us to consider museums as dynamic rather than static, concerned only with the past. Sites like museums, which are losing their traditional cultural authority in the face of an increasing demand to engage with a variety of contexts, offer interesting possibilities for cultural critics. Where authority is unstable, political possibilities are opened up. The task for cultural studies, as well as for museums, is to recognize the instabilities and failures of power and encourage the possibilities this allows for a more open form of museum practice.

In this context, a tradition of a priori negativity towards museums is not very helpful. While I would not want to claim that museums are faultless, I do want to argue that a more positive approach to museums may have more political effect. In *We Gotta Get out of this Place*, Lawrence Grossberg (1992) recounts an incident at the Canadian Museum of Civilization in Ottawa in which an attempt to establish lines of communication between a group of academics and museum staff was unsuccessful. For Grossberg, the lack of communication was in part a result of the failure of the academics to recognize and respond to the rapidly changing contexts and practices of museums. The papers presented to museum staff by the academics at this conference were all predictably critical of the capitalist, imperialistic, Eurocentric, ethnocentric, racist, sexist biases, not only of particular displays, but of the design philosophy of the museum as well. They demanded that, in one way or another, the entire project be dismantled or turned over to 'the people' on behalf of whom the various critics were all sure they could speak.

(Grossberg 1992: 89)

As Grossberg comments, the criticisms did have a grain of truth. 'It is easy enough for those who are trained to find evidence of the structured inequalities of our society – classism, nationalism, imperialism, racism, sexism, homophobia, Eurocentrism – coded into the practice of the museum' (90). However, in being so single-minded in their criticisms, conference delegates lost an opportunity 'to think about strategic changes, and to negotiate for tactical (and therefore limited and imperfect) compromises which might have offered other political possibilities to the public as they moved through the museum' (90). The curators, of course, only became more entrenched in their view that 'these intellectuals would never understand the beneficent possibilities offered by (their) pedagogical and cultural institution' (90).

Like Grossberg, I do not believe that an aggressive critical position on the part of intellectuals is the best strategy for achieving real political change. Grossberg is only one of a number of intellectuals in the field of cultural studies who is beginning to question the appropriateness of what Stuart Cunningham calls cultural studies' 'command metaphors of resistance' (Cunningham 1992: 9). Others, particularly in the museum field, include James Clifford (1997), Andreas Huyssen (1995), Sharon Macdonald and Gordon Fyfe (1996) and Tony Bennett (1995, 1998a). In its theoretical breadth and focus on museums, Bennett's work is particularly useful in this regard. Like Grossberg, Bennett is concerned to broaden the debate to the way in which cultural critics do cultural analysis challenging the assumptions of cultural critique itself. One of the reasons why this book focuses so much on his work is that he attempts to move away from those 'command metaphors of resistance' with specific reference to museums. That the book is also a critique of his particular approach to achieving this end is not to deny the value of the attempt itself.

Given the range of changes that this book has documented, the importance of the attempt should be clear. Certainly, it should not be surprising if the continued attack on museums by academic critics is met with distrust and in some cases anger in museums themselves. No professional likes to be continually criticized along the same lines if change is actually occurring. The effect is that cultural critics are widely perceived as having little to offer the museum community and as being out of touch. These perceptions are reinforced because of the tone these critiques often take. In the introduction to their book *Museum Culture*, Daniel Sherman and Irit Rogoff (1994) explain that 'all of the essays in the book share the conviction not only that museums have a history, but also that their enterprise entails an attempt to conceal it' (Sherman and Rogoff 1994: x). Setting up the critic as the detective who will discover and make

167

known this ugly truth may give the critic the higher moral ground. However, the result is an unbridgeable gulf between the values of critics and curators. Despite a desire to reform the museum, the distance that is constructed is so great that communication becomes impossible.

The problem I am attempting to identify is not one of intentions. I think both Sherman and Rogoff are interested in museums and would like the opportunity to engage with them. Unfortunately, though, the nature of their rhetoric only encourages the continued production of an equally polemical conservative defence of the museum on the part of some museum professionals – a defence which only serves to confirm established critiques of museums. As I have argued, this is a defence which claims for the museum an apolitical space based on a nineteenth-century distinction between the cultural and economic spheres (Chapters 1, 2 and 3). Culture, and more specifically the arts, are seen to represent universal values, values which are above class antagonisms, local politics and economic processes. The position is supported by a positivist epistemology in the study of material culture and art (Chapter 5).

Defensive arguments from museum professionals only provide ammunition for those who want further evidence of the political and class-based nature of the museum. Yet, ironically, polemical criticism and conservative defence agree on the issue of commercialism (Chapter 3). While the museum establishment is busy trying to preserve an understanding of the museum as separate from, and above, the economic sphere, cultural critics are criticizing the commercialization of museums and art galleries. Many of the attacks on the Heritage Industry come close to arguing that culture should be separate from the economy, a line of argument which directly contradicts the attack on museum display practices as denying the economic contexts of production. An increasing number of critics are wanting to have it both ways.

One of the effects of this development is that the history of museums is being rewritten from both left and right perspectives as a fall from a pre-commercial Garden of Eden. Once upon a time, museums had standards, ethics and sought to promote historical understanding. Under the impact of the tourist industry, however, commercial gain became the first objective and these values were lost. In the minds of some critics, museums and heritage sites are no longer interested in history itself (Walsh 1992).

This book has attempted to offer a tactical intervention in what I take to be an unhealthy and unproductive situation of mutual antagonism between museum professionals and intellectual critics. For example, in establishing museums as continuous with a number of contexts, from the media to urban regeneration programmes, from new patterns of financial investment to new geopolitical arrangements, I have increased the number of possible sites for dialogue to occur. This is a direct challenge to those who think museums only look towards the past and are either blind or unconcerned with contemporary political issues. Museums can provide a site from which to launch discussions of contemporary media cultures, tourism, cultural policy, changes in architectural design, the effects of new electronic communication systems, the role of urban regeneration programmes in post-industrial economies, and changes in geopolitics. This is quite apart from possible discussions arising from the content of the exhibitions they develop. These bridges are thus an invitation for cultural critics to walk across and view these changes from a new perspective.

In rewriting the historiography of museums I have also sought to dampen the emergence of defensive discourses from inside museums. Rather than seeing the range of changes that are currently occurring as the destruction of museums, it may be useful to pause for a moment and revisit the past. Cultural critics and museum historians have an important role to play here in dissociating museums from the aesthetic modernist discourse which has enveloped them for the greater part of the twentieth century. Some important work is already being done in this area. Thus, for example, Tony Bennett's and Eilean Hooper-Greenhill's efforts to provide a genealogy of museums which place them within discourses of civic reform and crowd control are important. But we also need to recover other histories – particularly those that associate museums with popular pleasures, new urban, cosmopolitan cultures and with consumerism.

The real importance of these histories is in questioning an understanding of current developments as a complete break from the past. The association of museums with commerce, the media, popular culture and tourism is not a new phenomenon. While Huyssen's account of contemporary museum culture, for example, is refreshing for its ability to recognize change, it is nevertheless tinged with selective amnesia. Huyssen's problem is, like many other critics, that he discusses museums in the abstract, continuing to produce them as a single, unified discursive object. The only difference from other critics is that he liberates museums from modernity and thus allows a freeing up of the possible meanings associated with them. In this book, however, I have suggested that some of these meanings may have always been present in museums. That this history has not been more visible is simply a sign of the stranglehold of a modernist aesthetic discourse.

In Chapter 1, for example, I recount a 'virtual' war between the British Museum and the popular press in the 1850s for the power to control the representation of the Assyrian collection. The press won the 'war' because of its ability to make accessible visual material about the collection to a broad popular readership. The result was a collapse in the distinction between the Museum's representation of the Assyrian collection and popular representations. The merging of the Museum and popular culture culminated in the authentication by the Museum of the stage set for the play *Sardanapalus* which was based on the Museum's collection.

As other examples throughout the book also illustrate, museums were associated with popular pleasures, with the emergence of an urban, popular culture. They were also deeply implicated in commercial culture, sharing the same techniques of display and playing a role in the economy of the nation through the teaching of 'materialism'. Despite the rhetoric of the recent Heritage Debate (Chapter 3), therefore, many of these concerns are not new.

169

The implication of all these arguments is that museums are not pre-given as a discursive object. While some museums do support the values of the hegemonic block, are associated with high culture and with the point of view of capital, this is not the case for all. Establishing the continuity of museums with other cultural formations is one way of recognizing other situations and involvements.

Notes

Introduction

1 For an account of the practice of collecting art as a military trophy during the Napoleonic period at the Louvre see Andrew McClellen's book (1999) *Inventing the Louvre: Art, Politics and the Origins of the Modern Museum in Eighteenth-Century Paris*, Berkeley, Los Angeles and London: University of California Press.

1 Unmasking a different museum: museums and cultural criticism

1 There are many different uses of Foucault's work. Some of them work in other directions from those of Bennett by stressing the museum's role as a disciplinary institution (Hooper-Greenhill 1992) or the museum's role as a bourgeois, conservative institution (Crimp 1995).

2 I am aware of the many discussions as to the dating of the beginning of modernity. In the context of this chapter I am concerned with the development of the modern metropolis in the nineteenth century.

3 A history of the way museums have been represented in film would, I think, reveal how museums are often thought of as spaces for illicit behaviour rather than the space of conformity normally accorded to them within academic analyses.

2 Floating the museum

1 It is not only maritime museums which are being developed in close proximity to waterways. Other kinds of museums, such as art museums and general national museums, are also being built along rivers or harbours. The Tate Modern, Te Papa, the National Museum of Australia, The Museum of Civilization in Ottawa and Bilbao Guggenheim are only some examples.

2 For de Certeau, 'space' is produced by the activities of walkers and cannot exist outside of those activities. 'Spaces' are produced by constant trajectories, while 'places' are produced by planners and builders.

3 For an account of the politics of this process see Shirley Fitzgerald and Hilary Golder (1994) *Pyrmont & Ultimo Under Siege*, Hale & Iremonger, Sydney.

4 See, for example, Valda Rigg (1994) 'Curators of the colonial idea: The museum and the exhibition as agents of bourgeois ideology in nineteenth-century New South Wales' *Public History Review*, vol. 3: 188–203.

5 A British example of this would be the revamped National Maritime Museum in Greenwich. In providing an interdisciplinary approach to maritime history this museum is also concerned to destabilize traditional narratives about the nation. The extent of its success in doing so can be appreciated through reading the heated media debate that followed the reopening of the Museum in 1999.

3 From *Batavia* to *Australia II*: negotiating changes in curatorial practices

1 *Australia II* was built in Fremantle, with funding provided by one of Western Australia's biggest entrepreneurs, Alan Bond. As a result of its win in America, the next Cup was unsuccessfully defended by Australia in Fremantle. The holding of the America's Cup in 1987 led to the economic recovery of Fremantle and its reinvention as a heritage town.

2 While the phrase was made famous by Marx, it has been taken up as the title of Marshall Berman's book dealing with the experience of modernity in the city. It is this latter context to which I am referring.

3 While Bennett uses Buss to make the point that earlier forms of visitor control were done through guided tours rather than architectural design, I am interested in this passage for what it reveals as the museum's attitude towards their visitors rather than how visitor control is achieved. In this passage visitors are produced as both ignorant and as in need of constant monitoring.

4 The reading I offer is, of course, my own and does not necessarily represent the views of staff at the Museum.

5 This is despite the fact that the museum also developed an interest in nineteenth-century shipwrecks off the Western Australian Coast, particularly iron steamships.

6 Government Review of Functions: Western Australian Museum. Historical Background 069.09941 (pamphlet box).

7 Minutes of the Historical Material Advisory Committee Meeting, 21 December 1964, Western Australian Museum, in McCarthy (1993).

8 Notes on an Informal Meeting of the Historical Material Advisory Committee, 20 October 1966, in McCarthy (1993).

9 Minutes of the Historical Material Advisory Committee, 25 June 1969, in McCarthy (1993).

10 Historical Materials Advisory Committee Minutes, 16 September 1969, in McCarthy (1993).

11 Minutes of the Historical Material Advisory Committee, 25 June 1969, in McCarthy (1993).

12 Geoffrey Bolton, a historian from the University of Western Australia, served on this committee from 1966 to 1973. Within Western Australian historiography Bolton is a towering figure, known as a defender of the conservative establishment and for writing within a 'consensus' model of history. Another very influential historian from the University of Western Australia was Frank Broeze. Originally from Holland, Broeze became involved in the Maritime Museum and established his reputation as a historian of the maritime history of Western Australia.

13 Joint Committee on Maritime History and Archaeology Revised Terms of Reference, 1970.

14 The split between research and display was further consolidated by a decision to split the two functions into separate departments. Under the Museum Act of 1969 the Museum was divided into five departments. The curatorial departments were the Divisions of Natural Sciences and Human Studies. They were responsible for carrying out the scientific work of the Museum and the care of the collections (Bailey 1979: 22). Then there were separate departments for display, education and administration. These divisions led to a curatorial culture within the Museum as a whole that did not understand the curatorial role as including the development of exhibitions.

15 When discussions first began, the new museum was referred to as the Maritime Industries Museum. Eventually, the word 'industries' was dropped from the title, causing even more confusion between the two sites.

4 'A place for all of us'? Museums and communities

1 While cultural policy studies has also taken place elsewhere, most notably in Canada and in the UK, there is a generally recognized tradition within Australia centred at the Key Centre in Brisbane. For a discussion of cultural policy studies more generally, including the place of the Australian version, see Jim McGuigan (1992) *Culture and the Public Sphere*, London and New York, Routledge.

2   Clifford's efforts here are somewhat similar to Hooper-Greenhill's (2000) application of the notion of interpretive communities to the different interpretations of the Hinemihi – a Maori house whose history implicates it in just the kind of cross-cultural context Clifford is interested in exploring. Hooper-Greenhill looks at the various meanings of the house according to who is speaking (Maori, original collector, National Trust). Of interest to her is how all of these interpretations can/should affect the present day interpretation of the house.

3   My account of Mitchell is based on conversations I had with members of the local Progress Association while I undertook a small consultancy for the local museum/tourist information bureau.

5   Beyond the mausoleum: museums and the media

1   While somewhat dated, the work of Harold Innis and Marshall McLuhan has enjoyed a renaissance, connecting with more recent debates about the nature of the so-called 'information society' (Castells 1989, 1996, Poster 1990). In Australia at least, their work has provided the focus for at least two different journal issues (see *Continuum*, 'Dependency/space/policy: A dialogue with Harold A. Innis', ed. I. Angus and B. Shoesmith, 1993; and *Media International Australia with Culture and Policy*, No. 94, February 2000).

2   This is of course alongside an equally important tradition of displaying copies of major artworks. In the case of copies, though, what was being taught was not so much the value of the original but a lesson in art historical traditions. It could be argued that this particular tradition of displaying copies is an early precursor of the notion, to be argued later in this chapter, that electronic technologies privilege notions of information above the material existence of the object itself. Nevertheless, our main inheritance from the nineteenth-century museum is a valuing of the material world.

3   While Goodman, like Bennett and other commentators, is correct in pointing out that the nineteenth-century museum stressed its alliance with science, this was not the only tradition of show and tell. There was also a strong tradition of more theatrical presentations which developed from the earlier displays at fairs and which continued both at the international exhibitions and in museums proper. This is the tradition of the diorama where objects are shown not in classificatory schemas but in a recreated setting – what Barbara Kirschenblatt-Gimblett (1998) calls the in situ display, as opposed to the in context display. As we have seen in Chapter 1 and will see in Chapter 6, this more theatrical tradition also has its parallels in contemporary museum practice, especially in the renewed emphasis on the notion of experiential displays.

4   While Bennett (1995, 1998a) violently disagrees with Adorno's argument that museums can be understood as mausoleums, arguing instead that rather than imprisoning objects, museums made them available to an ever widening audience, he nevertheless shares his view that museums represent the dominant power structures. They differ perhaps in the value they attribute to this. Adorno never wavers from interpreting the museum's role as repressive, while Bennett wavers between an equally negative interpretation (for example, in his essay 'Museums and "the People"' 1988a) and a more positive interpretation of the possibilities offered by a governmental understanding of culture (1998a). Bennett's blindness towards his commonalities with Adorno is, perhaps, a result of the fact that both critics universalize quite distinctive and separate models of what a museum is – Bennett universalizes the British model, based on the utilitarian tradition in English political thought, while Adorno universalizes the continental model derived from the development of the Louvre Museum during the Napoleonic period.

5   An English example is provided by Hooper-Greenhill (2000) in her analysis of the early history of the National Portrait Gallery in London. Here she makes the point that the idea of the National Portrait Gallery pre-dated its actual development through the publication of bound periodicals of prints representing famous people at both a local and a national level.

6   At the end of 1998 George MacDonald was appointed Director of the Museum of Victoria in Australia. This is a museum that is also exploring the possibilities offered by electronic technologies to engage a wider audience.

7   Interestingly, these are precisely the range of services offered by another model of the nineteenth-century museum in America – the dime museum. According to its historian, Andrea Stulman Dennett (1997), the American dime museum was based on the idea of providing a series of experiences, ranging from traditional object-based displays, to theatrical presentations, movies and restaurants. Like today, there was an attempt to educate through entertainment.

8   The following analysis is based on my experiences and observations while working as a curator in the USA–Australia Gallery at the Australian National Maritime Museum in 1991.

9   For an interesting article on virtual reality tropes see Chris Chesher (1994). He uses the notion of tropes to argue that new technologies such as virtual reality are popularized through the use of older narratives/tropes. This is an inversion of my argument in which new technologies give new meanings to old tropes such as the museum.

6   Interactivity in museums: the politics of narrative style

1   Direct quotations from Rosenfeld (1995) and Wiener (1995) do not have page numbers because they are in electronic format. There is no way of establishing a correct page number.

2   There is a possible critique here of the assumption by Stickler that dioramas offer only static presentations which are antithetical to the principles of television. In their similarity to vignettes, dioramas can also invite self-inscription as the viewer walks through them. What usually prevents this self-inscription from taking a positive value is the implication of traditional dioramas within a larger narrative frame of reference which is linear and authoritative and which does not offer a possibility for multiple meanings to emerge.

3   The difficulty of 'educating' audiences into new narrative styles is also commented on by Natalie Heinich (1988) who argues that visitors to the Pompidou Centre in Paris find its lack of linear displays disconcerting. As she says: 'the capacity to "drift" is not so easy to acquire as one might think' (Heinich 1988: 210).

Bibliography

Abjorensen, N. (1988) 'Museums blast from the past', *The Sydney Morning Herald*, Saturday 2 July: 8–9.

Adorno, T. (1967) 'Valéry Proust Museum in Memory of Hermann von Grab' in T. Adorno (ed.) *Prisms*, London: Garden City Press: 175–185.

Alexander, E. (1979) *Museums in Motion: An Introduction to the History and Functions of Museums*, Nashville: American Association for State and Local History.

Alexander, G. and Brereton, K. (1995) 'Museum of Sydney', *Photofile* 44: 7–10.

Altick, R.D. (1978) *The Shows of London*, Cambridge, MA and London: The Belknap Press of Harvard University Press.

Ames, M. (1986) *Museums, the Public, and Anthropology: A Study in the Anthropology of Anthropology*, Vancouver: University of British Columbia Press.

—— (1992) *Cannibal Tours and Glass Boxes: The Anthropology of Museums*, Vancouver: UBC Press.

Ames, P.J. (1988) 'A challenge to modern museum management: Meshing mission and market', *The International Journal of Museum Management and Curatorship* 7(2): 151–157.

Anderson, M. (1991) 'Selling the past: History in museums in the 1990s' in J. Rickard and P. Spearrit (eds) *Packaging the Past? Public Histories*, Melbourne: Melbourne University Press, 24(96): 130–141.

—— (1993) 'Roundtable – access: Commitment or containment?', *Museums National* 2(3): 4–7.

Angus, I. and Shoesmith, B. (eds) (1993) 'Dependency/space/policy: A dialogue with Harold A. Innis', themed edition of *Continuum: Journal of Media and Cultural Studies* 7(1), Murdoch University: Centre for Research in Culture & Communications.

Appadurai, A. (1990) 'Disjuncture and difference in the global economy', *Public Culture* 2(2): 1–24.

Appadurai, A. and Breckenridge, C.A. (1992) 'Museums are good to think: Heritage on view in India' in I. Karp, C. Mullen Kreamer and S.D. Lavine (eds) *Museums and Communities: The Politics of Public Culture*, Washington: Smithsonian Institution Press, 34–54.

Armstrong, M. (1992–3) ' "A jumble of foreignness": The sublime musayums of nineteenth-century fairs and expositions', *Cultural Critique* (Winter): 199–250.

Babich, B.E. (1994) 'On malls, museums and the art world, postmodernism and the vicissitudes of consumer culture', *Art Criticism* 9(1): 93–109.

Bailey, E. (1979) 'The Western Australian Museum', Unpublished paper, Perth: Western Australian Museum Library, 069.09941BAI.

Bal, M. (1992) 'Telling, showing, showing off', *Critical Inquiry*, 18(Spring): 556–594.

—— (1994) 'Telling objects: A narrative perspective on collecting' in J. Elsner and R. Cardinal (eds) *The Cultures of Collecting: From Elvis to Antiques – Why do We Collect Things?*, Melbourne: Melbourne University Press: 97–115.

Barringer, T. and Flynn, T. (eds) (1998) *Colonialism and the Object: Empire, Material Culture and the Museum*, Museum Meanings Series, London: Routledge.

Barry, A. (1998) 'On interactivity: Consumers, citizens and culture' in S. Macdonald (ed.) *The Politics of Display: Museums, Science, Culture*, The Heritage: Care–Preservation–Management Programme, London and New York: Routledge: 98–117.

Baudrillard, J. (1983) *Simulations*, New York: Semiotext.

Bearman, D. (1993) 'Interactivity in American museums', *Museum Management and Curatorship* 12: 183–193.

Benjamin, W. (1973) 'The work of art in the age of mechanical reproduction' in H. Arendt (ed.) *Illuminations*, New York: Schocken Books: 217–252.

Bennett, T. (1988a) 'Museums and "the people"' in R. Lumley (ed.) *The Museum Time Machine: Putting Cultures on Display*, London: Routledge: 63–86.

—— (1988b) *Out of Which Past? Critical Reflections on Australian Museum and Heritage Policy*, Griffith University, Brisbane, Institute for Cultural Policy Studies.

—— (1988c) 'The exhibitionary complex', *New Formations* 4: 73–102.

—— (1989a) 'Culture: Theory and policy', *Culture and Policy* 1(1): 5–8.

—— (1989b) 'Museums and the public good: Economic rationalism and cultural policy', *Culture and Policy* 1(1): 37–51.

—— (1990) 'The political rationality of the museum', *Continuum* 3(1): 35–55.

—— (1992a) 'Putting policy into cultural studies' in L. Grossberg, C. Nelson and P. Treichler (eds) *Cultural Studies*, New York: Routledge: 23–37.

—— (1992b) 'Museum, government, culture', *Sites* 25: 9–23.

—— (1993) 'Useful culture' in V. Blundell, J. Shepherd and I. Taylor (eds) *Relocating Cultural Studies – Developments in Theory and Research*, London: Routledge: 67–85.

—— (1994) 'The Multiplication of Culture's Utility: The Art Gallery Versus the Alehouse', Inaugural Professorial Lecture, Faculty of Humanities, Griffith University, Institute for Cultural Policy Studies.

—— (1995) *The Birth of the Museum: History, Theory, Politics*, London: Routledge.

—— (1998a) *Culture: A Reformer's Science*, London: Routledge.

—— (1998b) 'Speaking to the eyes: Museums, legibility and the social order' in Sharon Macdonald (ed.) *The Politics of Display: Museums, Science, Culture*, London and New York: Routledge: 25–35.

Bennett, T., Bulbeck, C. and Finnane, M. (1991) *Accessing the Past*, Brisbane: Institute for Cultural Policy Studies, Griffith University.

Benson, S.P. (1979) 'Palace of consumption and machine for selling: The American department store, 1880–1940', *Radical History Review* 21(Fall): 199–221.

Berck, B. (1992) 'Museums: Rethinking the boundaries', *Museum (Unesco, Paris)* XLIV(2): 69–72.

Berman, M. (1988) *All That Is Solid Melts Into Air: The Experience of Modernity*, New York: Penguin Books.

Besser, H. (1997) 'Integrating collections management information into online exhibits: The Web as facilitator for linking two separate processes' in D. Bearman and J. Trant (eds) *Museums and the Web 97: Selected Papers*, Pittsburgh: Archives & Museum Informatics: 201–206.

Bickford, A. (1995) 'The archaeological project 1983–1990', *Sites: Nailing the Debate: Archaeology and Interpretation in Museums*, Sydney: Museum of Sydney on the site of first Government House: 65–73.

Blaswick, I. and Wilson, S. (eds) (2000) *Tate Modern: The Handbook*, London: Tate Publishing.

Bohrer, F.N. (1994) 'The times and spaces of history: Representation, Assyria, and the British Museum' in D.J. Sherman and I. Rogoff (eds) *Museum Culture: Histories, Discourses, Spectacles*, Minneapolis: University of Minnesota Press: 197–222.

Bourdieu, P. and Darbel, A. (1991) *The Love of Art: European Art Museums and their Public*, Cambridge: Polity Press.

Boylan, P. (ed.) (1992) *Museums 2000: Politics, People, Professionals and Profit*, The Heritage–Care–Preservation–Management Programme, London: Museums Association in conjunction with Routledge.

Brill, L. (1992) 'Art meets cyberspace in a VR museum', *Computer Graphics World* 115(12): 14.

Buck-Morss, S. (1991) *The Dialectics of Seeing: Walter Benjamin and the Arcades Project*, Cambridge, MA: MIT Press.

Burd, S. (1994) 'Into a computer landscape', *The Chronicle of Higher Education* 41(3): A48.

Burton, A. (1999) *Vision & Accident: The Story of the Victoria and Albert Museum*, London: V&A Publications.

Carter, P. (1987) *On the Road to Botany Bay: An Essay in Spatial History*, London: Faber.

—— (1996) *The Calling to Come*, Sydney: Museum of Sydney on the site of first Government House.

Casey, D. (2001) 'Museums are still teachers: Style changes haven't eroded educational value', *The Australian*, Tuesday, 31 July: 15.

Castells, M. (1989) *The Informational City: Information Technology, Economic Restructuring, and the Urban–Regional Process*, Oxford: Blackwell.

—— (1996) *The Rise of the Network Society*, Cambridge, MA: Blackwell Publishers.

Certeau, M. de (1988) *The Practice of Everyday Life*, Berkeley: University of California Press.

Chesher, C. (1994) 'Colonizing virtual reality: Constructions of the discourse of virtual reality', *Cultronix* (Fall), http://eng.hss.cmu.edu/cultronix/chesher.

Clifford, J. (1985) 'Objects and selves: An afterword' in G.W. Stocking (ed.) *Objects and Others: Essays on Museums and Material Culture*, Madison: University of Wisconsin Press: 236–246.

—— (1992) 'Traveling Cultures' in L. Grossberg, C. Nelson and P. Treichler (eds) *Cultural Studies*, New York: Routledge: 96–116.

—— (1997) 'Museums as contact zones' in *Routes: Travel and Translation in the Late Twentieth Century*, Cambridge: Harvard University Press.

Cohen, H. (guest ed.) (2000) 'Revisiting McLuhan', special theme section of *Media International Australia/Culture and Policy* 94: 5–130, Griffith University: Australian Key Centre for Cultural & Media Policy.

Coombes, A.E. (1992) 'Inventing the "postcolonial": Hybridity and constituency in contemporary curating', *New Formations* 18: 39–52.

—— (1994) *Reinventing Africa: Museums, Material Culture and Popular Imagination*, New Haven and London: Yale University Press.

Crimp, D. (1985) 'On the museum's ruins' in H. Foster (ed.) *Postmodern Culture*, London: Pluto Press: 43–56.

—— (1995) *On the Museum's Ruins*, Cambridge, MA: MIT Press.

Cunningham, S. (1992) *Framing Culture: Criticism and Policy in Australia*, Sydney: Allen & Unwin.

Curthoys, A. (1996) 'The Museum and new ways of understanding Australian history' in *Sites: Nailing the Debate: Archaeology and Interpretation in Museums*, Sydney: Museum of Sydney on the site of first Government House: 217–223.

Debord, G. (1988) *Comments on the Society of the Spectacle*, trans. Malcolm Imrie, London: Verso.

Delroy, A. (1991) 'Pragmatics & "Progress": The Evolution of the Perth Museum at the Turn of the Century', Unpublished paper, Perth: Western Australian Museum.

Department of the Arts, Sports, the Environment, Tourism and Territories (DASSETT) (1990) *What Value Heritage? A Perspective on the Museums Review and the Performance of Museums*, Canberra: AGPS.

Dias, N. (1998) 'The visibility of difference: Nineteenth-century French anthropological collections' in Sharon Macdonald (ed.) *The Politics of Display: Museums, Science, Culture*, London and New York: Routledge: 36–52.

DiGirolamo, R. (2001), 'Research dying art in "super" museums' in *The Australian*, Wednesday, 25 July: 3.

Docker, J. (1994) *Postmodernism and Popular Culture: A Cultural History*, Cambridge: Cambridge University Press.

Donato, E. (1979) 'The museum's furnace: Notes towards a contextual reading of *Bouvard and Pécuchet*' in J.V. Harari (ed.) *Textual Strategies: Perspectives in Post-Structuralist Criticism*, Ithaca: Cornell University Press: 213–238.

Donovan, K. (1997) 'The best of intentions: Public access, the Web & the evolution of museum automation' in D. Bearman and J. Trant (eds) *Museums and the Web 97: Selected Papers*, Pittsburgh: Archives & Museum Informatics: 127–134.

Duclos, R. (1994) 'Creating the nation: Museums and the display of cultural identity', *Museums National* 3(2): 7–9.

Duncan, C. (1995) *Civilizing Rituals: Inside Public Art Museums*, London and New York: Routledge.

Duncan, C. and Wallach, A. (1980) 'The universal survey museum', *Art History* 3(4): 448–469.

Durrans, B. (1988) 'The future of the other: Changing cultures on display in ethnographic museums' in R. Lumley (ed.) *The Museum Time Machine: Putting Cultures on Display*, London: Routledge: 144–169.

Dyster, B. (2000) 'Sydney 1879: Colonial city, global city' in P. Proudfoot, R. Maguire and R. Freestone (eds) *Colonial City Global City: Sydney's International Exhibition 1879*, Sydney: Crossing Press.

Eco, U. (1986) *Travels in Hyper Reality*, trans. William Weaver, Toronto: Harcourt Brace Jovanovich.

Emmett, P. (1995) 'WYSIWYG on the site of first Government House', *Sites: Nailing the Debate: Archaeology and Interpretation in Museums*, Sydney: Museum of Sydney on the site of first Government House: 107–120.

Ettema, M.J. (1987) 'History museums and the culture of materialism' in J. Blatti (ed.) *Past Meets Present: Essays about Historic Interpretation and Public Audiences*, Washington DC: Smithsonian Institution Press: 62–85.

Fahy, A. (1995) 'New technologies for museum communication' in E. Hooper-Greenhill (ed.) *Museums, Media, Message*, Museums: New Visions, New Approaches Series, London: Routledge: 82–96.

Farrely, E.M. (1989) 'Amid the frivolity, a serious interloper', *Sydney Morning Herald*, 25 March 1989: 44.

Fenton, J. (1984) 'The Pitt-Rivers Museum, Oxford' in *Children in Exile: Poems 1968–1984*, New York: Random House: 81–84.

Fewster, K. (1991) 'Down to the sea in monorails: Urban renewal and recent maritime museum developments', *Great Circle* 13(2): 74–81.

—— (1993) 'From the Director', *Signals*, 25: 3.

Fitzgerald, S. and Golder, H. (1994) *Pyrmont & Ultimo Under Siege*, Sydney: Hale and Iremonger.

Foucault, M. (1977) *Discipline and Punish: The Birth of the Prison*, London: Allen Lane.

Fowler, P. (1989) 'Heritage: A post-modernist perspective' in D. Uzzell (ed.) *Heritage Interpretation*, Vol. 1, London: Frances Pinter: 57–63.

Georgel, C. (1994) 'The museum as metaphor in nineteenth-century France' in D.J. Sherman and I. Rogoff (eds) *Museum Culture: Histories, Discourses, Spectacles*, Minneapolis: University of Minnesota Press: 113–122.

Gibson, M. (1994) 'Information and the territorial imaginary: Is there a split in the critical humanities?' *CQU Working Papers in Communication and Cultural Studies* 2: 19–26.

Gibson, R. (1994/95) 'The ether of everyday life', *Metro Magazine* 100 (Summer): 63–65.

—— (1995) *The Bond Store Tales*, Sydney: Museum of Sydney on the site of first Government House.

Gilroy, P. (1993) *The Black Atlantic: Modernity and Double Consciousness*, London: Verso.

GLLAM (Group for Large Local Authority Museums) (2000) *Museums and Social Inclusion: The GLLAM Report*, Leicester: Research Centre for Museums and Galleries (RCMG).

Glazer, J.R. and Zenetou, A.A. (1994) *Gender Perspectives: Essays on Women in Museums*, Washington and London: Smithsonian Institution Press.

Goodman, D. (1990) 'Fear of circuses: Founding the National Museum of Victoria', *Continuum* 3(1): 18–34.

Goss, J. (1993) 'The magic of the mall: An analysis of form, function and meaning in the contemporary retail built environment', *Annals of the Association of American Geographers* 83(1): 18–47.

Green, M. (1989) 'Is it Armageddon?', *Museums Journal*, 89(4, July): 8.

Greenhalgh, P. (1988) *Ephemeral Vistas: The Expositions Universelles, Great Exhibitions and World's Fairs, 1851–1939*, Manchester: Manchester University Press.

—— (1989) 'Education, entertainment and politics: Lessons from the great international exhibitions' in P. Vergo (ed.) *The New Museology*, London: Reaktion Books: 74–98.

Grossberg, L. (1992) *We Gotta Get out of This Place: Popular Conservatism and Postmodern Culture*. New York: Routledge.

Hallen, H. (1988) 'Darling Harbour: Hans Hallen talks with Phillip Cox', *Architecture Bulletin* (September): 3–5.

Hansen, G. (1996) 'Fear of the "masternarrative": Reflections on site interpretation at the Museum of Sydney', *Museum National* 5(2): 18–19.

Haraway, D. (1985) 'Teddy bear patriarchy: Taxidermy in the Garden of Eden, New York City, 1908–1936', *Social Text* (Winter): 20–63.

Hartley, J. (1992) *The Politics of Pictures: The Creation of the Public in the Age of Popular Media*, London: Routledge.

—— (1995) 'Journalism and modernity', *Australian Journal of Communication* 22(2): 20–30.

Harvey, D. (1985) *The Urbanization of Capital*, Oxford: Basil Blackwell.

—— (1987) 'Flexible accumulation through urbanization: Reflections on post-modernism in the American city', *Antipode* 19(3): 260–286.

—— (1989) *The Condition of Postmodernity: An Enquiry into the Origins of Cultural Change*, Oxford: Basil Blackwell.

Heinich, N. (1988) 'The Pompidou Centre and its public: The limits of a utopian site' in R. Lumley (ed.) *The Museum Time Machine: Putting Cultures on Display*, London: Routledge: 199–212.

Henderson, G. (1998) 'The redevelopment of the Western Australian Maritime Museum' in G. Henderson (ed.) *Indian Ocean Week 1997 Proceedings*, Perth: Western Australian Museum, 42–48.

Hewison, R. (1987) *The Heritage Industry: Britain in a Climate of Decline*, London: Methuen.

—— (1991a) 'Commerce and culture' in J. Corner and S. Harvey (eds) *Enterprise and Heritage: Crosscurrents of National Culture*, London: Routledge: 162–177.

—— (1991b) 'The Heritage Industry revisited', *Museums Journal* (April): 23–26.

Hinsley, C.M. (1991) 'The world as marketplace: Commodification of the exotic at the World's Columbian Exposition, Chicago, 1893' in I. Karp and S.D. Lavine (eds) *Exhibiting Cultures: The Poetics and Politics of Museum Display*, Washington: Smithsonian Institution Press: 344–365.

Hitzeman, J., Mellish, C. and Oberlander, J. (1997) 'Dynamic generation of museum web pages: The intelligent labelling explorer' in D. Bearman and J. Trant (eds) *Museums and the Web 97: Selected Papers*, Pittsburgh: Archives & Museum Informatics: 253–260.

Hooper-Greenhill, E. (1992) *Museums and the Shaping of Knowledge*, The Heritage: Care–Preservation–Management Programme, London: Routledge.

—— (1994) 'Beyond the boundaries: Reaching out to audiences', *Traditional Boundaries, New Perspectives*, Sydney: Museums Australia Inc. NSW.

—— (ed.) (1995) *Museum, Media, Message*, Museums: New Visions, New Approaches Series, London and New York: Routledge.

—— (ed.) (1997) *Cultural Diversity: Developing Museum Audiences in Britain*, Contemporary Issues in Museum Culture Series, London: Leicester University Press.

—— (2000) *Museums and the Interpretation of Visual Culture*, Museum Meanings Series, London and New York: Routledge.

Horne, Donald (1984) *The Great Museum*, Sydney: Pluto Press.

Hunter, I. (1988) *Culture and Government: The Emergence of Literary Education*, Basingstoke: Macmillan Press.

—— (1994) *Rethinking the School: Subjectivity, Bureaucracy, Criticism*, St Leonards, NSW: Allen & Unwin.

Huntley, P. (1988) 'Darling Harbour: A critique', *Property Investor* (February): 8–12.

Huxley, M. and Kerkin, K. (1988) 'What price the Bicentennial? A political economy of Darling Harbour', *Transition* (Spring): 57–64.

Huyssen, A. (1995) *Twilight Memories: Marking Time in a Culture of Amnesia*, London: Routledge.

Innis, H.A. (1973) *The Bias of Communication*, Toronto: University of Toronto Press.

Ireland, T. (1995) 'Excavating national identity' in *Sites: Nailing the Debate: Archaeology and Interpretation in Museums*, Sydney: Museum of Sydney on the site of first Government House: 85–106.

Janes, Robert R. (1997) *Museums and the Paradox of Change: A Case Study in Urgent Adaptation*, 2nd edition, Glenbow Museum, Calgary: University of Calgary Press.

Johnson, W. (1998) 'Vic bitter' in *Fremantle Herald*, Saturday 1 August 1998: 8.

Jordanova, L. (1989) 'Objects of knowledge: A historical perspective on museums' in P. Vergo (ed.) *The New Museology*, London: Reaktion Books: 22–40.

Jucheau, M. (1996) 'Forgetful memory: The Holocaust, history and representation', *UTS Review* 2(2): 68–89.

Karp, I. and Lavine, S.D. (eds) (1991) *Exhibiting Cultures: The Poetics and Politics of Museum Display*, Washington: Smithsonian Institution Press.

Karp, I., Mullen Kreamer, C. and Lavine, S.D. (eds) (1992) *Museums and Communities: The Politics of Public Culture*, Washington: Smithsonian Institution Press.

Kassay, M. (1994) 'Interactive multimedia: Computers, public access and museums', *Museum National* 3(2): 10–12.

King, A. (1990) 'Architecture and the globalization of culture' in M. Featherstone (ed.) *Global Culture, Nationalism, Globalisation and Modernity*, London: Sage: 397–411.

Kirschenblatt-Gimblett, B. (1991) 'Objects of ethnography' in I. Karp and S.D. Lavine (eds) *Exhibiting Cultures: The Poetics and Politics of Museum Display*, Washington: Smithsonian Institution Press: 386–443.

—— (1998) *Destination Culture: Tourism, Museums, and Heritage*, Berkeley: University of California Press.

Koester, S.E. (1993) *Interactive Multimedia in American Museums*, Archives and Museum Informatics Technical Report, 16.

Kohlstedt, S.G. (1983) 'Australian museums of natural history: Public priorities and scientific initiatives in the 19th century', *Historical Records of Australian Science* 5(4): 1–29.

Koven, S. (1994) 'The Whitechapel Picture Exhibitions and the politics of seeing' in D.J. Sherman and I. Rogoff (eds) *Museum Culture: Histories, Discourses, Spectacles*, Minneapolis: University of Minnesota Press: 22–48.

Krauss, R. (1990) 'The cultural logic of the late capitalist museum', *October* 54: 3–17.

Lash, S. and Urry, J. (1991) *The End of Organised Capitalism*, Cambridge: Polity.

Lash, S. and Urry, J. (1994) *Economies of Signs and Space*, London: Sage.

Lennon, J. (1995) *Hidden Heritage: A Development Plan for Museums in Queensland 1995–2001*, Brisbane: Arts Queensland.

Lewis, P.N. (1993) 'Touch and Go', *Museums Journal* (February): 33–34.

Lisus, N.A. and Ericson, R.V. (1995) 'Misplacing memory: The effects of television format on Holocaust remembrance', *British Journal of Sociology* 46(1): 1–19.

Lowenthal, D. (1998) *The Heritage Crusade and the Spoils of History*, Cambridge: Cambridge University Press.

Luke, T. (1996) 'Memorialising mass murder: Entertainmentality and the United States Holocaust Museum', *Arena Journal*, New Series (6): 123–143.

Lumley, R. (ed.) (1988) *The Museum Time Machine*, London: Routledge.

Lumley, R. (1994) 'The debate on heritage reviewed' in R. Miles and L. Zavala (eds) *Towards the Museum of the Future: New European Perspectives*, Museums: New Visions, New Approaches Series, London: Routledge: 57–69.

MacDonald, G.F. (1987) 'The future of museums in the global village', *Museum* 155: 212–213.

—— (1988) 'Epcot Centre in museological perspective', *Muse* 6(1): 27–31.

—— (1991) 'The museum as information utility', *Museum Management and Curatorship* 10: 305–311.

—— (1992) 'Change and challenge: Museums in the information society' in I. Karp, C. Mullen Kreamer and S.D. Lavine (eds) *Museums and Communities: The Politics of Public Culture*, Washington: Smithsonian Institution Press: 158–181.

MacDonald, G.F. and Alsford, S. (1989) *A Museum for the Global Village*, Hull: Canadian Museum of Civilization.

Macdonald, S. (1996) 'Theorizing museums: An introduction' in S. Macdonald and G. Fyfe (eds) *Theorizing Museums*, London: Blackwell Publishers/The Sociological Review: 1–18.

Macdonald, S. and Fyfe, G. (1996) *Theorizing Museums*, London: Blackwell Publishers/The Sociological Review.

Macdonald, S. and Silverstone, R. (1990) 'Rewriting the museums' fictions: Taxonomies, stories and readers', *Cultural Studies* 4(2): 176–191.

Maloney, S. (1994) 'The Holocaust on fast-forward', *Eureka Street*, 4(4): 16–17.

Malraux, A. (1967) *Museum Without Walls*, London: Secker and Warburg.

Marcus, J. (1996) 'Erotics and the Museum of Sydney', *Olive Pink Society Bulletin* 8(2): 4–8.

Marinetti, F.T. (1909) *Fondazione e manifesto del futurismo*. Pubblicato dal *figaro* di Parigi il 20 Febbraio 1909. Milano: Direzione del Movimento Futurista.

Maslen, G. (1988) 'Australia: Economic pragmatism, self-reliance sustain expansion', *Museum News* (September/October): 33–34.

McClellen, A. (1999) *Inventing the Louvre: Art, Politics, and the Origins of the Modern Museum in Eighteenth-century Paris*, Berkeley, Los Angeles and London: University of California Press.

McGuigan, J. (1992) *Culture and the Public Sphere*, London and New York: Routledge.

McLaughlin, M.L. (1996) 'The Art Site on the World Wide Web', http://www-ref.usc.edu/~mmclaugh/mclaugh.html.

McLean, K. (1993) *Planning for People in Museum Exhibitions*, Washington: Association of Science-Technology Centers.

McLuhan, M. (1967) *Understanding Media: The Extensions of Man*, London: Sphere Books Limited.

Mellor, A. (1991) 'Enterprise and heritage in the Dock' in J. Corner and S. Harvey (eds) *Enterprise and Heritage: Crosscurrents of National Culture*, London: Routledge: 93–115.

Merriman, N. (1989) 'Museum visiting as a cultural phenomenon' in P. Vergo (ed.) *The New Museology*, London: Reaktion Books: 149–171.

—— (1991) *Beyond the Glass Case: The Past, the Heritage and the Public in Britain*, Leicester: Leicester University Press.

Michaels, E. (1987) 'My essay on postmodernity', *Art and Text* 25: 86–91.

—— (1990) 'A model of teleported texts (with reference to Aboriginal television)', *Continuum* 3(2): 8–31.

Miles, R. (1993) 'Exhibiting Learning', *Museums Journal* 93(5): 27–28.

Miles, R. and Zavala, L. (eds) (1994) *Towards the Museum of the Future: New European Perspectives*, The Heritage: Care–Preservation–Management Programme, Museums: New Visions, New Approaches Series, London: Routledge.

Montaner, J.M. (1995) *Museums for the New Century*, Barcelona: Editorial Gustavo Gili, S.A.

Morris, M. (1988a) 'Panorama: The live, the dead and the living' in P. Foss (ed.) *Island in the Stream*, Sydney: Pluto Press: 160–227.

Murray, D. (1904) *Museums, Their History and Their Use*, Glasgow: J. Maclehose & Sons.

Museum Management and Curatorship (1993) 'Tourism and the museum industry: Paymaster, pollutant and worse? Editorial', *Museum Management and Curatorship* 12: 123–126.

Nava, M. (1995) 'Modernity tamed? Women shoppers and the rationalisation of consumption in the interwar period', *Australian Journal of Communication* 22(2): 1–19.

Negrin, L. (1993) 'On the museums's ruins: A critical appraisal', *Theory, Culture and Society* 10: 97–125.

New South Wales Ministry for the Arts, Museums Advisory Council (1994) *Future Directions for Regional and Community Museums in NSW,* Sydney.

Newhouse, V. (1998) *Towards a New Museum,* New York: The Monacelli Press.

Noack, D.R. (1995) 'Visiting museums virtually', *Internet World* (October): 86–91.

Norden, E. (1993) 'Yes and no to the Holocaust museums', *Commentary,* [Electronic], 96(2): 23(10). Available: Expanded Academic ASAP/A14156042 [1997, August].

O'Regan, T. (1990) 'TV as cultural technology: The work of Eric Michaels', *Continuum* 3(2): 53–98.

—— (1992a) '(Mis)Taking policy: Notes on the cultural policy debate', *Cultural Studies* 6(3): 409–423.

—— (1992b) 'Some reflections on the "Policy Moment"', *Meanjin* 51(3): 517–532.

—— (1994) 'Two or three things I know about meaning', *Continuum* 7(2): 327–374.

Phillips, D. (1994) 'Heureka! It's hands on', *Museums Journal* 94(5): 28–29.

Pigott, P.H. (Chairman) (1975) *Museums in Australia in 1975: Report of the Committee of Inquiry on Museums and National Collections including the Report of the Planning Committee on the Gallery of Aboriginal Australia,* Canberra: Committee of Inquiry on Museums and National Collections.

Pitman-Gelles, B. (1981) *Museums, Magic & Children: Youth Education in Museums,* Washington: Association of Science-Technology Centers.

Plummer, C. and Young, B. (1988) 'Darling Harbour public spaces', *Landscape Australia* 1: 12–22.

Pointon, M. (ed.) (1994) *Art Apart: Art Institutions and Ideology Across England and North America,* Manchester and New York: Manchester University Press.

Porter, G. (1988) 'Putting your house in order: Representations of domestic life' in R. Lumley (ed.) *The Museum Time Machine: Putting Cultures on Display,* London: Routledge: 102–127.

—— (1990) 'Gender bias: Representations of work in history museums', *Continuum* 3(1): 70–83.

—— (1996) 'Seeing through solidity: A feminist perspective on museums' in S. Macdonald and G. Fyfe (eds) *Theorizing Museums,* Oxford: Blackwell Publishers/The Sociological Review: 83–104.

Poster, M. (1990) *The Mode of Information: Poststructuralism and social context,* Cambridge: Polity Press in association with Basil Blackwell.

Powell, S. (2000) 'The People's Museum', *The Weekend Australian* 21–22 (October): 16–18.

Resnicow, D. (1994) 'What is Watkins really asking?', *Curator: The Museum Journal* 37(3): 150–151.

Riegel, H. (1996) 'Into the heart of irony: Ethnographic exhibitions and the politics of difference' in S. Macdonald and G. Fyfe (eds) *Theorizing Museums,* Oxford: Blackwell Publishers/The Sociological Review: 83–104.

Rigg, V. (1994) 'Curators of the colonial idea: The museum and the exhibition as agents of bourgeois ideology in nineteenth-century New South Wales', *Public History Review* 3: 188–203.

Roberts, L. (1994) 'Rebuttal to "Are museums still necessary?"', *Curator: The Museum Journal* 37(3): 152–154.

Rosenfeld, A.H. (1995) 'The Americanisation of the Holocaust', *Commentary,* [Electronic], 99(6): 35(6). Available: Expanded Academic ASAP/A16965521 [1997, July].

Rydell, R.W. (1984) *All the World's a Fair: Visions of Empire at American International Expositions, 1876–1916,* Chicago: University of Chicago Press.

Samuels, R. (1994) *Theaters of Memory, Volume 1: Past and Present in Contemporary Culture,* London: Verso.

Saumarez Smith, C. (1989) 'Museums, artefacts, and meanings' in P. Vergo (ed.) *The New Museology,* London: Reaktion Books: 6–21.

Schaffer, K. (1996) 'Reconstructing "our" past: The Museum of Sydney', *Olive Pink Society Bulletin* 8(2): 22–25.

Sheets-Pyenson, S. (1988) *Cathedrals of Science: The Development of Colonial History Museums During the Late Nineteenth Century*, Kingston, Ontario: McGill-Queen's University Press.

Sherman, D. and Rogoff, I. (eds) (1994) *Museum Culture: Histories, Discourses, Spectacles*, Media & Society 6, Minneapolis: University of Minnesota Press.

Sherman, D.J. (1994) 'Quatremere/Benjamin/Marx: Art museums, aura, and commodity fetishism' in D.J. Sherman and I. Rogoff (eds) *Museum Culture: Histories, Discourses, Spectacles*, Minneapolis: University of Minnesota Press: 123–143.

Simon Wiensenthal Center (1993) *Beit Hashoah: Museum of Tolerance*, Santa Barbara: Albion Publishing Group.

—— (1997) *Museum of Tolerance* (pamphlet).

Stanbury, M. (1987) 'Maritime archaeological material: A catalyst in the development of the Western Australian Maritime Museum', *6th International Congress of Maritime Museums Proceedings*, Amsterdam and Rotterdam: 104–115.

Stannage, T. (1993) 'New Norcia in history' in Tom Stannage (ed.) *New Norcia Studies*, No. 1, New Norcia: The Archives, Research and Publications Committee of the Benedictine Community of New Norcia: 1–8.

Stannard, B. (1986) 'Phillip Cox and the new Venice', *The Bulletin* 28 January: 36–39.

Stevenson, J. (1994) 'Getting to grips', *Museums Journal* 94(5): 30–32.

Stickler, J.C. (1995) 'Total immersion: New technology creates new experiences', *Museum International* (*Unesco, Paris*) 47(1): 36–40.

Stulman Dennett, A. (1997) *Weird and Wonderful: The Dime Museum in America*, New York: New York University Press.

Sullivan, S. (1995) 'Archaeology, sites and museums' in *Sites: Nailing the Debate: Archaeology and Interpretation in Museums*, Sydney: Museum of Sydney on the site of first Government House: 45–62.

Szekeres, V. (1995) 'A place for all of us', *Public History Review* 4: 59–64.

Taylor, B. (1994) 'From penitentiary to "Temple of Art": Early metaphors of improvement at the Millbank Tate' in M. Pointon (ed.) *Art Apart: Art Institutions and Ideology Across England and North America*, Manchester: Manchester University Press: 9–32.

Teslow, T.L. (1998) 'Reifying race: Science and art in *Races of Mankind* at the Field Museum of Natural History' in Sharon Macdonald (ed.) *The Politics of Display: Museums, Science, Culture*, London and New York: Routledge: 25–35.

Thomas, G. (1994) 'The age of interaction', *Museums Journal* 94(5): 33–34.

Trodd, C. (1994) 'Culture, class, city: The National Gallery, London and the space of education, 1822–57' in M. Pointon (ed.) *Art Apart: Art Institutions and Ideology Across England and North America*, Manchester: Manchester University Press: 33–49.

Urry, J. (1991) *The Tourist Gaze: Leisure and Travel in Contemporary Societies*, London: Sage.

Vergo, P. (ed.) (1989) *The New Museology*, London: Reaktion Books.

Virilio, P. (1986) *Speed and Politics: An Essay on Dromology*, New York: Semiotext(e).

—— (1991) *The Lost Dimension*, New York: Semiotext(e).

Wallace, M. (1995) 'Changing media, changing messages' in E. Hooper-Greenhill (ed.) *Museum, Media, Message*, London and New York: Routledge: 107–123.

Walsh, K. (1992) *The Representation of the Past: Museums and Heritage in the Postmodern World*, The Heritage: Care–Preservation–Management Programme, London: Routledge.

Walsh, P. (1997) 'The Web and the unassailable voice' in D. Bearman and J. Trant (eds) *Museums and the Web 97: Selected Papers*, Pittsburgh: Archives & Museum Informatics: 69–76.

Wark, McK. (1988) 'On technological time: Virilio's overexposed city', *Arena* 83(Winter): 82–100.

—— (1992) 'Speaking trajectories: Meaghan Morris, antipodean theory and Australian cultural studies', *Cultural Studies* 6(3): 433–448.

—— (1993) 'Lost in space: Into the digital image labyrinth', *Continuum* 7(1): 140–160.

—— (1994) *Virtual Geography*, Bloomington and Indianapolis: Indiana University Press.

Watkins, C.A. (1994) 'Are museums still necessary?', *Curator: The Museum Journal* 37(1): 25–35.

Weil, S.E. (1990) 'The proper business of the museums: Ideas or things?' in *Rethinking the Museum and Other Meditations*, Washington: Smithsonian Institution Press.

Weil, S. (1995) *A Cabinet of Curiosities: Inquiries into Museums and their Prospects,* Washington: Smithsonian Institution Press.

West, B. (1988) 'The making of the English working past: A critical view of the Ironbridge Gorge Museum' in R. Lumley (ed.) *The Museum Time Machine: Putting Cultures on Display*, London: Routledge: 36–62.

Wiener, J. (1995) 'The other Holocaust museum (Simon Wiesenthal Center Museum of Tolerance)', *Tikkun*, [Electronic], 10(3): 22(5). Available: Expanded Academic ASAP/A16936689 [1997, July].

Williams, C. (1992) 'The museum of the future', *21 Century* (Winter): 84–86.

Williams, R.H. (1982) *Dream Worlds: Mass Consumption in Late Nineteenth-century France*, Berkeley: University of California Press.

Witcomb, A. (1993) 'From treasure house to touch screens: Museums in the age of electronic reproduction', *Public History Review* 7(1): 75–84.

—— (1994) 'Postmodern space and the museum – the displacement of "public" narratives', *Social Semiotics* 4(1/2): 239–620.

—— (1995) 'From stasis to flows: Museums in the information society' in *Information Flows, CQU Working Papers in Cultural Studies*, Central Queensland University: 35–44.

—— (1996) 'Floating the Museum: A Cultural Analysis of the Australian National Maritime Museum', Doctoral dissertation, Central Queensland University.

—— (1997a) 'On the side of the object: An alternative approach to debates about ideas, objects and museums', *Museum Management and Curatorship* 16(4): 383–399.

—— (1997b) 'From citizens to tourists: The new political rationality of the museum' in L. Quinn and L. Seear (eds) *Proceedings of the Museums Australia 1995 National Conference: Communicating Cultures*, Brisbane: Museums Australia: 124–128.

—— (1997c) 'The end of the mausoleum: Museums in the age of electronic communication' in D. Bearman and J. Trant (eds) *Museums and the Web 97: Selected Papers*, Pittsburgh: Archives & Museum Informatics: 143–150.

—— (1998a) 'Beyond the mausoleum: Museums and the media', *Media Information Australia* incorporating *Culture and Policy* 89 (November): 21–33.

—— (1998b) 'Maritime rhetorics, tourism and the Australia National Maritime Museum' in G. Henderson (ed.) *Indian Ocean Week 1997 Proceedings*, Fremantle: Western Australian Maritime Museum.

Witcomb, A. and Mauldon, V. (1996) 'Local museums and cultural policy: Reforming local museums?', *Culture and Policy* 7(1): 75–84.

Wittlin, A.S. (1949) *The Museum: Its History and its Tasks in Education*, London: Routledge & Kegan Paul.

—— (1970) *Museums: In Search of a Usable Future*, Cambridge, MA: MIT Press.

Primary sources

Arts Queensland (1996) Museum Development Program Brochure.

Australian National Maritime Museum (1987a) 'Analysis of the commercial opportunities available to the Australian National Maritime Museum', Interim Council Agenda Papers, Sydney: Australian National Maritime Museum: 12–32.

Australian National Maritime Museum (1987b) 'Design strategy and implementation study', Interim Council Agenda Papers, Sydney: Australian National Maritime Museum.

Australian National Maritime Museum (1989) 'Design review: discovery', Unpublished manuscript, Sydney: Australian National Maritime Museum.

Cox Howlett & Bailey Woodland (1998) *Fremantle Waterfront: Draft Masterplan for the Redevelopment of the Western End of Victoria Quay*, Draft Report for the Government Property Office, Perth: Cox Architecture Planning Design.

Darling Harbour Authority (1986) *Darling Harbour: The New Dimension*, J. Hallows, Sydney: Macquarie Publications, File 91/001 Part 1.

Environmetrics Pty Ltd (May 1992) *Australian National Maritime Museum – Visitor Study*, Sydney: Australian National Maritime Museum.

Exhibition Design Services Pty Ltd (1986) *National Maritime Museum of Australia Exhibition Master Plan*, Sydney: Australian National Maritime Museum.

Fry, G. (1987) 'Starting from scratch: The fast track museum', Australian National Maritime Museum R 01.0049 Pt. 2.

Green, J. (1991) 'Submission to the State Task Force for Museums Policy with regards to the operation of the Western Australian Museum at Fremantle', Western Australian Maritime Museum.

Hawke, R. (1987) in *Muse News* clipping, Spring 1987, File 91/001.

McCarthy, M. (1993) 'From the Inside: Shipwrecks and the Western Australian Museum, 1957–1972', Unpublished, Western Australian Maritime Museum.

—— (1996) 'The potential Xantho/Broadhurst Exhibition: A vision statement (for information and discussion)', August, Unpublished, Western Australian Maritime Museum.

—— (1997a) 'The new maritime museum and the proposals to relocate maritime archaeology considered', Internal Discussion Paper put forward for discussion at the Department of Maritime Archaeology meeting, 5 August, Western Australian Maritime Museum.

—— (1997b) 'A comment on the Director's statement "What do I want" from the proposed maritime museum redevelopment', Internal Discussion Paper, Western Australian Maritime Museum.

McLauchlan, R. (1993) *Memorandum Regarding Marketing Strategy Progress Report*, Sydney: Australian National Maritime Museum.

New South Wales Government (n.d.) 'Memo to Minister Cohen' in File No. 88/761 Pt. 1.

New South Wales Treasury (1986) *Darling Harbour Development: Cost Benefit Analysis*, Sydney: New South Wales Treasury.

Stanbury, M. (1997) 'The maritime museum redevelopment: What do I want from it, as Director of the WA Maritime Museum? A response', Internal Discussion Paper, Western Australian Maritime Museum.

Western Australian Museum (1995) *Community Access Gallery: Policy and Guidelines*, Fremantle: Fremantle History Museum.

Web sites

Berkeley Art Museum and Pacific Film Archive, [Online], Available: http://www/bampfa.berkeley.edu/main.html [2001, November 21].

Canadian Museum of Civilization, [Online], Available: http://www.civilization.ca [2001, November 21].

Carlos Museum at Emory University and Memorial Art Gallery of the University of Rochester, [Online], Available: http://www.emory.edu/CARLOS/ODYSSEY/ [2001, November 21].

Monticello, Thomas Jefferson's home, [Online], Available: http://www.monticello.org/index.html [2001, November 21].

National Museum of Australia, [Online], Available: http://www.nma.gov.au/newmuseum/index.htm [1999, February].

Peabody Museum of Archaeology and Ethnology at Harvard University, [Online], Available: http://www.peabody.harvard.edu [2001, November 21].

Uffizi Gallery, [Online], Available: http://www.uffizi.firenze.it/QTVR/sala2M.mov [2001, November 21].

Index